MUSEUM METAMORPHOSIS

AMERICAN ALLIANCE OF MUSEUMS

The American Alliance of Museums has been bringing museums together since 1906, helping to develop standards and best practices, gathering and sharing knowledge, and providing advocacy on issues of concern to the entire museum community. Representing more than 35,000 individual museum professionals and volunteers, institutions, and corporate partners serving the museum field, the Alliance stands for the broad scope of the museum community.

The AAM's mission is to champion museums and nurture excellence in partnership with its members and allies.

Books published by AAM further the Alliance's mission to make standards and best practices for the broad museum community widely available.

 American Alliance of Museums

MUSEUM METAMORPHOSIS

CULTIVATING CHANGE THROUGH CULTURAL CITIZENSHIP

nico wheadon

ROWMAN & LITTLEFIELD
Lanham • Boulder • New York • London

Published by Rowman & Littlefield
An imprint of The Rowman & Littlefield Publishing Group, Inc.
4501 Forbes Boulevard, Suite 200, Lanham, Maryland 20706
www.rowman.com

86-90 Paul Street, London EC2A 4NE

British Library Cataloguing in Publication Information Available

Library of Congress Cataloging-in-Publication Data

Names: wheadon, nico, 1984- author. | American Alliance of Museums.
Title: Museum metamorphosis : cultivating change through cultural
  citizenship / nico wheadon.
Description: Lanham : Rowman & Littlefield Publishers, [2022] | Includes
  bibliographical references and index.
Identifiers: LCCN 2021046780 (print) | LCCN 2021046781 (ebook) | ISBN
  9781538130421 (cloth) | ISBN 9781538130438 (paperback) | ISBN
  9781538130445 (ebook)
Subjects: LCSH: Museums and community—United States. | Museums—Social
  aspects—United States—Case studies. | Museums and minorities—United
  States—Case studies. | Museums—Management—Social aspects—Case
  studies. | Organizational change—United States—Case studies.
Classification: LCC AM7 .W44 2022 (print) | LCC AM7 (ebook) | DDC
  069—dc23
LC record available at https://lccn.loc.gov/2021046780
LC ebook record available at https://lccn.loc.gov/2021046781

∞™ The paper used in this publication meets the minimum requirements of American National Standard for Information Sciences—Permanence of Paper for Printed Library Materials, ANSI/NISO Z39.48-1992.

For *We the People. For Us, By Us*
who know ourselves as such.

There are times when personal experience keeps us from reaching the mountain top and so we let it go because the weight of it is too heavy. And sometimes the mountain top is difficult to reach with all our resources, factual and confessional, so we are just there, collectively grasping, feeling the limitations of knowledge, longing together, yearning for a way to reach that highest point. Even this yearning is a way to know.[1]

—bell hooks

NOTE

1. hooks, bell. *Teaching to Transgress: Education as the Practice of Freedom.* New York: Routledge, 1994.

CONTENTS

CONTENTS

FIGURES

KEY TERMS

The key terms are listed in order of appearance in the book.

Museum
   An institution devoted to the procurement, care, study, and display of
   objects of lasting interest or value.[1]
Metamorphosis
   Change of physical form, structure, or substance, especially by super-
   natural means.[2]
Cultivate
   To improve by labor, care, or study.[3]
Change
   Transformation.[4]
Cultural Citizenship
   The right to be different (in terms of race, ethnicity, or native language)
   with respect to the norms of the dominant national community without
   compromising one's right to belong, in the sense of participating in the
   nation-state's democratic processes.[5]
   Cultural practices and beliefs produced out of negotiating the often ambiv-
   alent and contested relations with the state and its hegemonic forms that
   establish criteria of belonging, within a national population or territory.[6]

NOTES

1. "Museum." Merriam-Webster, accessed September 1, 2021, https://www.merriam -webster.com/dictionary/museum.

2. "Metamorphosis." Merriam-Webster, accessed September 1, 2021, https://www .merriam-webster.com/dictionary/metamorphosis.

3. "Cultivate." Merriam-Webster, accessed September 1, 2021, https://www .merriam-webster.com/dictionary/cultivate.

4. "Change." Merriam-Webster, accessed September 1, 2021, https://www.merriam-webster.com/dictionary/change.

5. Rosaldo, Renato. "Cultural Citizenship in San Jose, California." *Political and Legal Anthropology Review* 17, no. 2 (1994): 57–63, accessed September 1, 2021, http://www .jstor.org/stable/24497930.

6. Ong, Aihwa et al. "Cultural Citizenship as Subject-Making: Immigrants Negotiate Racial and Cultural Boundaries in the United States." *Current Anthropology* (1996): 737–62.

ACKNOWLEDGMENTS

To my people. To Malik D. Lewis, my beloved and partner in all things. Thank you for emboldening me to embrace risk and dream out loud, during this book's creation and always. Your mind is magnificent, Boo, and the immediacy of your insights impacted this project in myriad ways. To my mother, Lin, for your commitment to building beauty in the world and your refusal to accept the ugly parts as they are. Thank you for modeling radical creativity and a tenacity of spirit to resist the status quo, from which I draw courage every day. To my father, John, for seeding a relentless, intellectual curiosity in me and for nourishing it over the years. Some call it *intensity*, but I've learned to consider it my most defining attribute, and I'm grateful for it. To David, Paul, Randy, and Nooshin: Thank you for your unyielding support over the years, which has taken many forms and buoyed me along this nontraditional path. And to my matriarchs, Edwyna, Harriet, and Josephine: Thank you for teaching me to lead with instincts and integrity above all else.

To my colleagues. To the former Public Programs & Community Engagement team at the Studio Museum in Harlem: Thank you for the many strengths you lent to the colossal task of building a museum department from the ground up. Adeze Wilford, Alexis Gonzalez, Rachel Morillo, Chayanne Marcano, Henry Murphy, Anaïs Duplan, Devin Malone, and Terence Washington: your hopes for and critiques of museum practice continue to serve as beacons in this work. To my former colleagues from the inHarlem working group at the Studio Museum in Harlem, Shanta Lawson, Lauren Haynes, Liz Gwinn, Shannon Ali, Evans Richardson, Naima J. Keith, Amanda Hunt, Connie H. Choi, Legacy Russell, Hallie Ringle, Eric Guy Booker, Hallie Hobson, and Sheila McDaniel:

I'm grateful for the opportunity to have learned from and worked alongside each of you during such a transformative moment in the museum's history. And to the members of the Studio Museum's Community Advisory Network: Thank you for the many wisdoms you so faithfully shared and for the energy and excitement you brought to the collective work of reimagining the museum's local citizenship.

To my mentors. To Thelma Golden: My witnessing your fierce care for artists so early in my career and growing to understand its nuances and institutional applications over the past 15 years has been a gift. Thank you for your steady mentorship and support. My circuitous journey through the Studio Museum was the most formative of my professional life, and your openness to my nonlinear path emboldened me to build a praxis all my own. To Derrick Adams: Thank you for your early faith in me as a leader and for holding space for me to hone my professional voice at Rush Arts Gallery. So many lasting relationships have roots in those three wild years we spent coloring outside the lines in Chelsea. And most importantly, thank you for encouraging me to remain open in my perception of myself and resist labels in an art world eager to confine through categorization. It's fitting that your artwork graces the cover of this book—so thanks for that too.

To Tina M. Campt: Thank you for daring me to teach through my lived experience of museums and for your unparalleled vision for bridging art history, theory, and practice. The Harlem Semester's prompt to site learning beyond traditional frameworks continues to inform my pedagogical approach today. Similarly, the cross-sector collaborations it engendered also serve as inspiration for this volume. You more than anyone else have driven me to mobilize cultural citizenship by moving institutions beyond the static infrastructures they've inherited. To Courtney J. Martin: You are someone I have known, through some odd magic of the soul, my entire life. Thank you for embodying the rigor and candor I continue to scaffold my leadership around every day. Your care for the nuances and minutiae of cultural work inspires me greatly, and I draw both patience and clarity from your long view of time. And to Thyrza Goodeve: During the time that I had almost lost the practice of writing altogether, you were the beacon home. Thank you for reminding me of the power of art to start a conversation and for encouraging me to rediscover my voice at the precise moment I needed it most. I'm eternally grateful to you for daring me to take up space in disruptive ways that are authentic to who I am becoming every day.

And to this community of practice. To the American Alliance of Museums Press, Rowman & Littlefield Publishing Group, and my editor, Charles Harmon: Thank you for your work building scholarship and dialogue around museum practice. I'm honored to publish my first book with you, and by the opportunity to wield this platform to help usher new perspectives into the canon. To this book's research consortium—Malik D. Lewis, Chayanne Marcano, Imani Butler, and Min Jie Teh: Your insights on how to decenter institutional authority and dismantle hierarchy through this book's very construction were so on time. And to the 43 collaborators on and contributors to this volume: I have no words—because they are all already here, raw and on the page.

Thank you, Jordan Casteel, Shaun Leonardo, Miguel Luciano, Lina Puerta, Deborah Berke, Mario Gooden, Maitland Jones, Eric Guy Booker, Maren Hassinger, Kendal Henry, Diya Vij, Jamaica Gilmer, Kemi Ilesanmi, Shani Peters, Chayanne Marcano, David Rue, Lauren Argentina Zelaya, Ryan N. Dennis, Vashti DuBois, Lauren Kelley, Jasmine Wahi, Shawnda Chapman, Ruby Lerner, Melissa Cowley Wolf, Elia Alba, Tina M. Campt, Connie H. Choi, Leslie Hewitt, Shanta Lawson, Dr. Dawn Brooks DeCosta, Kyle Williams, Nisa Mackie, Alexandra Nicome, Victoria Sung, Juliana Rowen Barton, Michelle Millar Fisher, Zoë Greggs, Gabriella Nelson, Amber Winick, Nicole Ivy, Dr. Ariana A. Curtis, DéLana R. A. Dameron, and Sandra Jackson-Dumont. I am grateful to be in your orbit and for the opportunity to think and dream out loud alongside each of you. Our riffs produce noise like I've never heard it before. Thank you for this jazz and for your willingness to freestyle, together.

PREFACE

Take me into the museum and show me myself, show me my people, show me soul America. If you cannot show me myself, if you cannot teach my people what they need to know—and they need to know the truth, and they need to know that nothing is more important than human life—then why shouldn't I attack the temples of America and blow them up?[1]

—June Jordan

Over the past few decades, museums have staged some of the most powerful conversations I've had. They've served as platforms through which I've built community, engaged heroes, and found love. It wouldn't be an overstatement to claim my most important personal and professional relationships have roots in the museum space. It would, however, be disingenuous to end my portrait of museums here, as this is only the underpainting to a more layered scene. Despite the haze of retrospection, I recall with tragic clarity how museums have *also* staged some of the worst acts of racism, cultural erasure, and subjection I've witnessed: days where museum actions or inactions led to divisive rifts among communities, heroes falling from altars, and love losing its way. The persistence of this paradoxical tension, alongside my commitment to working cooperatively to bridge it, serve as the genesis for this volume.

A brief chronology of my movements through museums and museum-like spaces is important here, as it is around these seminal experiences—and the enduring relationships they've produced—that the framework for this book is scaffolded. As a young person, I associated museums with a fraught choreography of push and pull, where guardians dictated my relationship to and interpretation of objects that, for me, held only prescribed value. As a Black, queer woman, I—like poet and activist June Jordan—saw neither myself nor the souls of my people holistically represented in these encyclopedic museums. So, from a young age, I rejected the premise that museums are expert stewards of culture, and I fashioned an arts education all my own. I learned the language of visual art as a practicing artist in high school and college; engaged in nonacademic communities of practice, mentorship, and critique as a postgraduate in New York City; and later reentered the museum as a worker eager to learn from—and subvert where necessary—its inner mechanisms.

From 2006 to 2007, I served as a curatorial intern, and later curatorial assistant, at the Studio Museum in Harlem, where I supported the production of numerous exhibitions and publications. It was during this moment of discovery that I articulated a distinction between contemporary art museums (sites of production, engagement, and belonging) and encyclopedic museums (sites of my early childhood trauma), as our work helped me draw meaningful connections between art history and its contemporary relevance. I also identified my preference for museums that serve living artists and was seduced by the unrivaled magnetism of the Studio Museum's mission, which drew me, for the first time, into community with other Black cultural workers.

In 2007, I left the Studio Museum to serve as gallery manager and later curatorial director at Rush Arts Gallery & Resource Center, an artist-founded and artist-led nonprofit in New York's Chelsea arts district. Rush supported many of those same early-career artists of color I'd been building community with 100 blocks north, at the Studio Museum. I worked alongside artist, mentor, and gallery director Derrick Adams, and we mounted offbeat exhibitions and programs that mobilized a community of practice unlike any I'd ever known.

In 2010, I—the only full-time staff at the gallery—was laid off as collateral damage in the recession that threatened to wipe other small, culturally specific nonprofits off the map while numerous, majority-white cultural institutions coasted along, endowments in tow. It was then that I began to question the living legacies of institutional racism in the cultural sector and the inequity of the nonprofit industrial complex as it's been designed.

I began researching alternative institutional frameworks that center people over profit and sustain through community buy-in over philanthropic buyout. In my research, I encountered anthropologist Renato Rosaldo's concept of *cultural citizenship*, which asserts that "even in contexts of inequality people have a right to their distinctive heritage."[2] His call for the democratization of existing institutions—coupled with my want to acquire the necessary tools to build sustainable "for us, by us" alternatives—drastically shifted my course.

Later that year, I moved to London in pursuit of a master's degree in creative and cultural entrepreneurship from Goldsmiths, University of London. The program, designed for and by creatives, empowers students to develop business acumen while advancing a spirit of innovation and solutions-driven change within their respective fields. Aside from this dedicated time and space to expand my knowledge base, I was drawn to London by the opportunity to test my operating assumptions about Black *community* in a global, diasporic context. And with the Olympics coming to London in 2012, I was equally eager to study the role of art and artists in driving alternative economies of cultural production surrounding global events.

During graduate school, I worked as a researcher at the Museum of Everything, "the world's only wandering institution for the untrained, unintentional, undiscovered and unclassifiable artists of modern times," as its website proclaims. I also participated in artist Tino Sehgal's *These Associations,* the first live commission for the Tate Modern's Turbine Hall. While the experience at MoE left me with unanswered questions about who constructs art world identities and to what end, Sehgal's project left me full of hope that artist- and community-led interventions could transmute the often hard, oppressive architectures of museums into soft, discursive spaces for collective belonging, learning, and growth.

I returned to the United States in 2014 and ultimately landed back at the Studio Museum, first as a communications consultant developing narrative around the museum's then-imminent 50th anniversary and later as director of the newly established Public Programs and Community Engagement department. I was excited by the opportunity to reinterpret the museum's mission through these new professional lenses and build out a holistic community-engagement strategy for a museum reimagining its local citizenship as part of its building project.

During this time, I launched my consultancy and began delivering cultural strategy and curatorial guidance to artist-entrepreneurs, cultural institutions, government agencies, and philanthropic foundations. I also picked up adjunct professorships at Barnard College and Hartford Art School that allowed me to continue investigating museum work on a continuum between art history and contemporary practice. The syllabi for both courses bridged theory and production; encouraged hyperlocal engagement among students; and steered them toward community resources beyond the confines of the classroom.

After five additional years learning from the rich cultural ecosystem of Harlem, I left the Studio Museum in 2019 to serve as inaugural executive director of NXTHVN, a then-nascent arts and business incubator in New Haven,

Connecticut. Having worked at the Studio Museum for most my career, it was with immense gratitude that I dove headfirst into this next chapter of institution building, cultural stewardship, and arts entrepreneurship. Another artist-founded space, NXTHVN was where I both sharpened and implemented the tools I'd gleaned along my journey and learned the ropes of building, quite literally, a culturally specific nonprofit from the ground up.

While this book was conceived during this most recent transition, its core consciousness has roots in the many experiences that preceded it. The threads of BIPOC arts advocacy, community empowerment, cultural entrepreneurship, and institutional critique that weave these experiences together *also* bind the distinct elements of this book into one cohesive volume. And its central argument—that in order to mobilize a people-powered arts-and-culture ecosystem, we must *first* decenter the museum's perceived authority over it—is derived from firsthand experience building and working within people-powered institutions over the past two decades.

My intentions in opening this book with an abridged professional biography are threefold. One, since I don't currently identify as a museum worker, it felt important to disclose my evolving relationship to, and intimacies with, museums and other cultural nonprofits. Two, because my path through museums was willfully nonlinear, it also felt necessary to caution that this circuitry is designed into this book's very construction. And three, since I share authorship with over 40 cultural innovators and changemakers in contemporary art that I've had the privilege of building with along this journey, it felt appropriate to name the milestones that mark where our respective paths have converged. While this volume initially emerged as a platform to document their work bringing cultural institutions into better alignment with community needs, the book quickly outgrew this early objective, both out of necessity and by design.

A PIVOT

> *This is precisely the time when artists go to work. There is no time for despair, no place for self-pity, no need for silence, no room for fear. We speak, we write, we do language. That is how civilizations heal. I know the world is bruised and bleeding, and though it is important not to ignore its pain, it is also critical to refuse to succumb to its malevolence. Like failure, chaos contains information that can lead to knowledge—even wisdom. Like art.*[3]
>
> —Toni Morrison

During the production of this book, a series of global events transpired that drastically changed its course, not only because the world we were writing about had changed but also because we, too, had changed—irrevocably. Seemingly overnight, our visions for reimagining the museum paled in comparison to the mounting threats of a global pandemic, domestic terrorism, police brutality, and the comorbid health, housing, and economic crises accelerated by COVID-19. Our daily commitments to scaffolding equity and justice within museums now felt like tending to only a symptom of the systemic racism that empowered police to murder George Floyd in broad daylight and Breonna Taylor in her sleep. And as our communities and institutions struggled to transcend the utter shitstorm, so did we. However, as Morrison asserts, artists, creatives, and cultural innovators met the moment by leaning in, learning from the new facts of our environment, and offering creative tools to unite our communities despite stay-at-home orders and widespread fear.

As people working to build equity on fronts both personal and professional, we continued to read, learn, plan, organize, create, build, and dream of a future beyond our circumstance. We did this not only as a means of spiritual survival but also to realign our work with the expanding and evolving needs of our communities. And together we confronted systemic injustice—and museums' roles in upholding it—in the streets, on the page, and through our respective platforms for advocacy.

Given the gravity of the situation and the new perspectives and priorities it yielded, I made space for the book's contributors to revisit what'd been written, out of due respect for the moment. Some of us had moved on to new positions, while others had been "moved on." Some had doubled down on their commitment to transforming museums into agents of social change, while others—out of care for their own mental health and well-being—packed their boxes and left the museum field altogether. And some had carved a path through our wildly transformed ecosystem, while others simply needed breathing room to process their fears and frustrations aloud.

As such, this volume evolved from a site of documentation and dissemination to one of celebration and affirmation, of both our humanity and our resilience—from transparent accounts of radical yet quasi-historical work to retooled recommendations enhanced to meet the urgency of now. The candid roundtables, case studies, and interviews included herein lay bare said recommendations yet are also transparent snapshots of our responses to this unprecedented moment of individual, collective, and systemic transformation. Let their coexistence in this volume serve as evidence of shared struggle, yes, but also—and perhaps most importantly—of our capacity to transcend it, together.

NOTES

1. Harvey, Emily Dennis, ed; Friedberg, Bernard, ed. June Jordan as noted in, A Museum for the people; a report of proceedings at the Seminar on Neighborhood Museums, held November 20, 21, and 22, 1969, at MUSE, the Bedford Lincoln Neighborhood Museum in Brooklyn, New York. Arno Press, 1971.

2. Lukov, Zoe. "Renato Rosaldo, 'Cultural Citizenship.'" Hemispheric Institute, September 21, 2018, https://hemisphericinstitute.org/en/enc09-academic-texts/item/681-cultural-citizenship.html.

3. Morrison, Toni. "No Place for Self-Pity, No Room for Fear." *The Nation*, December 23, 2019, https://www.thenation.com/article/archive/no-place-self-pity-no-room-fear.

INTRODUCTION
A Crisis of Relevance

The museum industrial complex is at a critical juncture: in mounting public distrust in governance, widespread movements that seek to redress historic injustices, and the prevailing work culture of museums, a popular desire for change is evident. This provocation is not to negate individual strides made by museums within the ecosystem over the years. Rather, it is to assert that the entire ecosystem *itself* is ripe for change and that this metamorphosis will be no greater than the sum of its parts. Alongside a sense of urgency and unrest, a series of existential questions emerge from this moment of heightened institutional critique and moral reckoning, which reached fever pitch amid the global events of 2020.

Will museums learn to embrace real-time change and adapt their programs and operations to meet the evolving needs of a rapidly shifting sociopolitical landscape? Will museum publics stand strong in their insistence that museums deliver on their commitment to the public good? Will museum workers continue to mobilize and hold their institutions accountable to advancing social justice, both internally and externally? Will museum leadership hold onto outmoded infrastructure and hierarchy, or will it embrace nimbleness and collaboration as vital practices of sustainability? And will museums across the board unite to address the crisis of relevance they face, by learning from critical perspectives beyond their echo chamber? Or will they continue to uphold the myth that the solutions they seek are endemic to their own spheres of influence and control?

While these questions guide this book's threads of inquiry and discussion, they are unfortunately not new. And while the pervasive threats of a global pandemic, domestic terrorism, and police brutality produced the untenable conditions in which this book was produced, previous generations had their *own* challenges to overcome, which similarly exposed the roles and responsibilities of institutions in relation to larger systems of control.

In the late 1960s, a community museum movement—mobilized by the founding of the Anacostia Neighborhood Museum in 1967, MUSE: The Bedford Lincoln Neighborhood Museum in 1968, and the Studio Museum in Harlem in 1969—audibly questioned the public duties of museums to engage diverse communities. A seminar on neighborhood museums, titled *A Museum for the People*, took place in New York City in 1969, in which "representatives of community-based cultural institutions met to interrogate how to make museums more accessible, how to decolonize the collections and how to foster leadership that reflected the institutions' communities."[1] This convening produced a seminal publication by the same name that documented the perspectives and strategies shared to help move museums toward necessary structural and cultural transformation.

That same year, the Black Emergency Cultural Coalition (BECC)—a group comprised of over 70 Black artists—was founded in response to the Metropolitan Museum of Art's controversial exhibition *Harlem on My Mind: The Cultural Capital of Black America, 1900–1968*. The exhibition, which featured no Black artists and treated legendary photographer James Van Der Zee's depictions of Black life as wallpaper instead of fine art, presented Harlem as an anthropological case study and *not* a rich site of living, cultural production. The BECC, alongside other groups born from the social justice movements of the day, protested the exhibition and the racist practices and systems that emboldened its creation. This was over a half century ago.

In the decades that followed, mainstream museums continued to mount racist exhibitions, born from both willful ignorance and a desire to effect an optics of diversity in lieu of putting in the necessary resources to transform their very constitutions. And at each affront, artists and communities of color continued to speak out, organize, and build their *own* cultural spaces while demanding more than surface-level change from their public institutions. Because this history is vast and nuanced and demands more engagement than I offer here, I would refer you to three seminal texts for further research: Mabel O. Wilson's *Negro Building: Black Americans in the World of Fairs and Museums* (2012), Susan E. Cahan's *Mounting Frustration: The Art Museum in the Age of Black Power* (2016), and Aruna D'Souza's *Whitewalling: Art, Race & Protest in 3 Acts* (2018).

In 2000, Lonnie G. Bunch III, founding director of the National Museum of African American History and Culture, tied museums' ongoing struggle with relevance to their persistent lack of diversity in his essay, "Flies in the Buttermilk," published in the July 2000 issue of *Museum News*. In it he states,

"Museums all seek to develop long-term, mutually reciprocal relationships with a dizzying array of communities. Yet why should these groups really believe our rhetoric of cultural transformation unless we are willing to exert the energy and make the hard choices that accompany the creation of a meaningfully diverse profession?"[2] He argues that for museums to build trust with their communities, they must *first* muster the will to know themselves—to introspect, identify inequity, and commit to internal transformation. They must move from self-importance to self-awareness, and shape their community of staff and visitors to, at the very least, resemble the diversity of the American people.

Flash forward to the 2015 American Alliance of Museums annual meeting, where field leader Johnnetta Betsch Cole doubles down on this position, pulling the escalating crisis into sharper focus when she states, "If we are to be relevant in this ever-changing world, to stay artistically and financially viable, all of our museums must boldly, indeed bodaciously, commit to reenvisioning what takes place in our museums, to whom our museums belong, and which colleagues have the privilege of telling important stories through the power of science, history, culture, and art."[3] Professor Cole supports her call to action by citing numerous field reports that evidence widespread and ongoing inequity in museum hiring and governance practices. She builds on Bunch's argument for change and even provides a clear road map to get there—reimagine museum practice, build museum belonging, and decolonize museum scholarship. This book takes up Bunch's road map for building museum relevance as a central strategy.

In the years since, numerous museum conferences have convened a global network of practitioners and field experts to address the precarious future of museums. At these annual gatherings and during rogue sessions in between, I, alongside numerous contributors to this volume, have presented case studies, built vocabulary, shared tools, and discussed strategies. The tone at these convenings has been one of urgency, and the message clear. Museums must learn to define, engage, and serve their communities or risk falling short on their duty to the public good. They must innovate *now* or risk falling behind other cultural and social institutions that have adapted to respond to our ever-changing world as it changes.

In 2019—on the 50th anniversary of the convening of *A Museum for the People*—the Anacostia Community Museum hosted a symposium to discuss how museum best practices had evolved over the last half century. As a presenter and participant in the room, I felt the immense power of the legacies of radical work that I, a relative newcomer, was so privileged to learn from and carry forward. And while it was energizing to hear directly from so many heroes, mentors, and peers as they discussed both the wins and the persistent challenges, my sense was that we were often preaching to the choir as many of us represented culturally specific institutions with missions to build equity, within both our communities and the field at large. Notably absent from the discussions, however, were representatives from those majority-white cultural institutions that had produced the conditions of exclusion and erasure out of which many of our organizations were built as a response. I state this not as a critique of the organization of the event, but rather as an affirmation of where—and with whom—tried and tested tools to advance innovation and equity in the museum field currently reside.

Most poignant for me was a comment made by Kinshasha Holman Conwill—deputy director of the Smithsonian's National Museum of African American History and Culture—in which she advocated for the reallocation of funds from unconscious-bias trainings to resilience trainings. Her argument was that, in many cases, the bias is, in fact, *conscious* and that the money would be better spent supporting those cultural workers who, like us, had committed to the arduous, lifelong work of structural transformation. I was particularly moved by Conwill's provocation, which—alongside those recommendations made by Bunch and Cole—helped pull the premise for this book into focus.

A PREMISE

ONE: a wealth of innovation, tools, and solutions emanate from culturally specific nonprofits. Born from a paradoxical oath to public service yet conditioning toward a scarcity mindset, culturally specific nonprofits transcend disparity by producing an abundance of cultural innovation. That's to say, the existential need to reframe resources, engagement, and service beyond a consumer-capitalist framework—beyond *whiteness*—often ignites the radical creativity that engenders the solutions the museum field so urgently seeks. In my experience operating within these professional contexts over the past two decades, the outcome is a lean yet highly considered, targeted, and relevant program. This book is oriented toward elevating and learning from the unparalleled ingenuity of practitioners of color.

In presenting this expertise, the tools shared often take the form of case studies and anecdotes, *not* a list of direct recommendations. This is to ensure that readers put in the necessary work to value slow, nuanced processes of institutional transformation and assess their own readiness to effect change where they are. It is also to resist co-optation and tokenization by insisting upon a process that centers the perspectives and strategies of those most harmed by the issues being addressed. Therefore, a primary objective of this volume is to spark radical yet actionable creativity in its readers, offering a multitude of frameworks for application built predominantly by women and people of color.

TWO: the application of these frameworks is a slow, iterative, and cooperative process. With its focus on structured collaboration and skills sharing across silos, this book demonstrates the potential of working through a collective impact model. It argues that to transform museums into culturally relevant spaces that are for, by, and of the people, the field must (1) shed its preferred hierarchical ways of working, (2) look to other sectors to learn new practices and strategies of adaptability, and (3) enact these strategies within long-term, reciprocal relationships built upon shared trust and accountability. For those looking to act without listening, to lead without following, or to find stopgap solutions for issues literally *centuries* in the making, this book is not for you. Alternately, for those invested in nuancing their understanding of the issues, finding and building allies, and more fully stepping into their respective role in their social change ecosystem, read on.

THREE: museum scholarship must be decolonized if the field is to learn from, engage in, and add to ongoing social justice conversations. For this book to succeed at redirecting professional attention and resources toward institutional strategies emanating from practitioners of color, museum scholarship *itself* must be decolonized. That's to say, the majority-white field of museums must learn to, as Bunch said, embrace *diversity*—of personal background, professional experience, and political opinion—as a core strength and not merely as a measure of compliance. And in the words of Cole, they also must consider "which colleagues have the privilege of telling important stories."

Ushering in critical perspectives from other fields—and elevating often overlooked voices from *within* the museum field due to longstanding hierarchies—this book invites changemakers from across the arts-and-culture ecosystem to share tools for reshaping museums into more vital and relevant forms. It also amplifies voices at all levels of leadership and not merely of those few leaders of color at the "top" with access to scholarship-building opportunities. As such, this book prompts each of us to critique our own biases and trusted sources of information, forging necessary space for the influx of fresh voices and perspectives.

A METHODOLOGY

Part 1 consists of seven roundtable discussions that reimagine the essential forms and functions of museums. In these candid dialogues, contributors share tools to liberate the museum from traditional paradigms and build more synergy between art and the everyday. The roundtable format is used to amplify multiple, at times conflicting, perspectives at once, and their lightly edited transcripts preserve the texture and tone of heartfelt discussion. We are neither neutral narrators nor emotionally distant from the mission-driven work we've poured our collective energies into. We emote, we listen, we question, we rant, we preach, we cuss, and we give gratitude. We also model radical transparency and vulnerability, because those are precisely the qualities our nation's institutions must adopt as they, too, set out down the path to change.

Part 2 features four case studies that encourage museums to decenter their perceived authority over the arts-and-culture ecosystem and embrace cross-sector collaboration and community partnership. The featured projects not only focus on touting successes in radical museum practice but also consider what can and must be learned from the missteps. To lay bare both the processes and outcomes of experimentation takes courage, and I group these discussions together not to essentialize them but rather to amplify their collective courage and clarion call to action. We discuss the essential DNA of these endeavors while remaining open in our vision for how these case studies might be scaled, adapted, and applied by others.

And Part 3 features four interviews in which field leaders share strategies for addressing the structural challenges of today while building inroads toward a more equitable future. The interview format is used to invite an expanded exploration of key topics explored elsewhere in the book. This is not to position these four brilliant Black women as soloists in front of the choir. Rather, it's to add additional depth to the sheer breadth of our dialogues and case studies. Because this book sets out to clarify, diagnose, and triage a system of interlocking issues that are as vast as they are deep, our dialogue in each section is designed to be as layered as the solutions we envision.

A FRAMEWORK

In the chapters that follow, we'll imagine the museum as a nexus, medium, citizen, apprentice, bridge, advocate, and stakeholder. Sensitive to, yet unbound by, traditional definitions of museums, this book positions existing structures and roles from everyday life as hypothetical frameworks for restructuring museums into people-powered spaces. In so doing we ask, *How might the metamorphosis of the museum build relevance by opening new pathways for engagement? Who, by extension, might the museum learn to serve, and how? And how might reconstituting the essential DNA of the museum recalibrate the power dynamics between communities and institutions, producing a sustainable model for engaged cultural citizenship?*

This *museum as framework* also produces a new compass through which to orient the museum's work—*within, through,* and *beyond*. In other words, instead of anchoring museum work to its traditional location within the confines of the establishment, we are also freed to imagine vital cultural activity taking place through—and at times altogether beyond—the museum space. This is essential because as museums learn to meet and serve new audiences where they are, they must also learn to enter those community spaces as fellow citizens and as equals. This book offers strategies for building the trust that undergirds and nurtures those relationships.

As you engage this framework, you will often come across the word *tools* to describe its numerous recommendations for dismantling inequity, building relevance, and transforming museums into more accessible forms. *Why tools?* If a tool is "an object that can extend an individual's ability to modify features of the surrounding environment,"[4] then consider this volume an extension of change-making tools already at your disposal. While gleaned from and sharpened through our collective experiences, the tools shared are meant to be adapted, scaled, and recalibrated to best serve your unique context and role. And while we steer them toward dismantling what we perceive to be the most broken parts of the museum system, the choice is yours as to how, where, and whether you apply them. Consider this *tool kit* an infinitely evolving repository of actionable ideas rather than a static set of objects to draw upon. And consider this book's existence as evidence of an ecosystem *already* undergoing rapid yet necessary transformation, both under our feet and by our own hands.

NOTES

1. Diamond, Anna. "Fifty Years Ago, the Idea of a Museum for the People Came of Age." *Smithsonian Magazine,* December 26, 2019, https://www.smithsonianmag.com /smithsonian-institution/fifty-years-ago-idea-museum-people-came-age-180973828.

2. Bunch, Lonnie G. "Flies in the Buttermilk: Museums, Diversity, and the Will to Change." In *Diversity, Equity, Accessibility, and Inclusion in Museums,* edited by Johnnetta B. Cole and Laura L. Lott, 6–7. Lanham, MD: Rowman & Littlefield, 2019.

3. Cole, Johnnetta B. "Museums, Diversity, and Social Value." In *Diversity, Equity, Accessibility, and Inclusion in Museums,* edited by Johnnetta B. Cole and Laura L. Lott, 18. Lanham, MD: Rowman & Littlefield, 2019.

4. "Tool." *Wikipedia,* April 27, 2021, https://en.wikipedia.org/wiki/Tool.

I

DIALOGUES ON DECENTRALIZATION

1

MUSEUM AS NEXUS

How to Cultivate Community Engagement through Artist-Powered Platforms

INTRO

> *The Studio Museum in Harlem is the nexus for artists of African descent locally, nationally, and internationally and for work that has been inspired and influenced by Black culture. It is a site for the dynamic exchange of ideas about art and society.*[1]
>
> —The Studio Museum in Harlem

The Studio Museum in Harlem's mission delivers vital vocabulary to the exercise of reimagining the essential form and function of museums. In *nexus*, we're given a framework for mapping fluid yet interdependent relationships between communities and institutions; in *dynamic exchange*, we're encouraged to experiment with how these relationships coexist in space to produce a shared sense of cultural place; and in *art and society*, we're dared to imagine the museum as an engaged citizen, one who is part and parcel of the broader cultural ecosystem. It was an attraction to the richness of this mission that drew me to museum work in 2006. And now, fifteen years later, it is my lived experience of it that inspires the dialogues on radical museum practice that follow.

At the Studio Museum, nexus is embodied in a circuitous network of relationships between artists, cultural workers, partner organizations, and art audiences, to name only a few key stakeholder groups. A home for *work that has been inspired and influenced by Black culture*, the nexus has also functioned as an incubator, actively cultivating the ongoing professional development of generations of artists and arts administrators of color. For every cohort of

Artists-in-Residence, there is an attendant network of curators, educators, programmers, and others who support those artists in building bridges between their studios and the public. It is important to name the nuances of this work, as *nexus* is perhaps too nebulous a term to carry the full weight of the Studio Museum's commitment to art and artists, a commitment embodied most visibly in its Artist-in-Residence program.

The Artist-in-Residence program was envisioned by legendary artist William T. Williams in 1971, shortly after the museum's founding in 1968, and gives the museum the word "Studio" in its name. While the program has certainly evolved over the past half century, its core commitments have endured: to cultivate the professional development and advancement of emerging artists of color by offering them dedicated time, space, and resources. Throughout the year, residents engage the museum's diverse communities through public and educational programs and, in so doing, animate the museum's mission to serve as *a site for the dynamic exchange of ideas about art and society*. At the culmination of the yearlong engagement, residents work with staff to produce an exhibition and accompanying catalogue, and select artworks are then acquired by the museum for its celebrated permanent collection.

What sets the Studio Museum's Artist-in-Residence program apart is its cultivation of an active community of practice, and its incubation of careerism, creativity, and criticality as interdependent practices. In other words, it invests equally in the art and the artist to ensure these two evolve and travel together within the ecosystem, and it advocates for an art market economy that places as much stock in the advancement of Black artists as it does in the consumption of their work.

As art historian, curator, and educator Susan E. Cahan states in her book *Mounting Frustration: The Art Museum in the Age of Black Power*, "Museums exist within a self-perpetuating system of mutually reinforcing judgements that create informal consensus about the relative importance of a given artist or group of artists." She goes on to state that "for artists of color there has not yet been such a thing as a life membership."[2] Like other culturally specific museums, the Studio Museum transcends the often-insular judgments of the mainstream echo chamber, and it offers *life membership* to countless artists and museum professionals who go on to impact the museum field in profound ways. This is evidenced in the museum's ongoing mentorship of curators of color that move on to leadership positions in a majority-white field, the midcareer surveys and retrospectives the museum mounts in service to its Artist-in-Residence alumni network, and the ever-expanding constellation of contemporary scholarship and cultural production that orbits the museum.

As a case study, the Studio Museum and its Artist-in-Residence program offer a useful framework through which to (1) imagine what ideal cultural citizenship and institutional belonging looks like and (2) qualify the sociocultural value of centering artists in core aspects of a museum's operation. It also exposes how relevance is built through a network of interdependent relationships that must be cultivated and nurtured over time. But how is artists' labor within museums more broadly quantified and compensated? As ambassadors for museum engagement, how do museums resource artists in building reciprocal, sustainable community relations that ultimately enrich the museum space? And what safeguards are in place to protect artists, and the communities they engage, from tokenization?

In a recent study, the Alliance of Artists Communities correlates the increase in artist residencies in the public realm—including "parks, government agencies, universities, museums, cultural centers, libraries and other spaces designed for public access"—with an increase in public awareness of "the role artists can have in civic life and how artists can shape the ways the public engages with the natural and built environment." However, when discussing museum-based residencies in particular, the tone shifts to one of deference as they state, "For artists working in museums, added inspiration comes both from museum holdings, staff and curators as well as museum visitors they have the opportunity to interact and engage with. In successful programs, the museum itself functions as an energizing source for artists in residence (AIRs). Not only are AIRs able to engage with and educate the public, but they are presented with new opportunities to develop professionally, to connect with curators and potential collectors. The museum-based residency programs provide AIRs with the opportunity to establish relationships that might otherwise take years to cultivate. The support, resources and public exposure that a museum-based residency offers has the potential to grow careers."[3]

While these findings focus on the museum-based residency's benefits for artists—and offer significantly less data to support how artists add value back to the museum—they do expose three essential yet often unspoken truths: (1) that building relationships through the museum is an essential activity that demands an investment of time and energy, (2) that artists must take an active role in shaping their *own* professional development by leveraging the museum's formal and informal resources, and (3) that it is in fact the museum's duty to support them, a primary stakeholder group, in this work.

With countless museum-based residences across the country funded to support artists, what does this support actually look like? And while it is easier to quantify the artist's award—X programs + $Y + Z months and so forth—why is it seemingly more difficult to quantify the value of the artist's impact on the museum? Unfortunately, very little professional attention has been paid to the reciprocal exchanges that transpire through the museum-based residency platform. This is because, of course, it benefits the field to profile artists as a service group in need of support that can be fundraised for. To name them as cultural laborers building relevance and innovating on behalf of the museum would invariably upset the understood power dynamic between artists and institutions.

In the roundtable that follows, I invited four artists to help build metrics for quantifying *and* qualifying their impact as resident artists on their hosting institutions. Jordan Casteel, Shaun Leonardo, Miguel Luciano, Lina Puerta, and I transparently discuss our experiences navigating some of the field's most coveted museum-based residencies, investigating the opportunities and challenges of the platform itself. Together, we concretize new metrics for its value that foregrounds the pricelessness of peer mentorship, nontransactional partnerships, and authentic community engagement. We decenter museum authority over these relationships and proffer that, for the socioeconomic value that artists create to endure, museums must invest in community engagement by carrying these relationships forward, beyond artists' often seasonal engagements.

ROUNDTABLE

JORDAN CASTEEL has rooted her practice in community engagement, painting from her own photographs of people she encounters. Posing her subjects within their natural environments, her nearly life-size portraits and cropped compositions chronicle personal observations of the human experience. Casteel is an assistant professor of painting in the Department of Arts, Culture, and Media at Rutgers University–Newark. The artist lives and works in New York.

SHAUN LEONARDO's multidisciplinary work negotiates societal expectations of manhood—namely, definitions surrounding Black and Brown masculinities—along with its notions of achievement, collective identity, and experience of failure. His performance practice is participatory and invested in a process of embodiment. Leonardo is codirector at Recess and is a Brooklyn-based artist from Queens, New York City. He received his MFA from the San Francisco Art Institute.

MIGUEL LUCIANO is a multimedia visual artist whose work explores themes of history, popular culture, and social justice through sculpture, painting, and socially engaged public art projects. His work is featured in the permanent collections of the Smithsonian American Art Museum, the Brooklyn

Museum, El Museo del Barrio, the Newark Museum, and the Museo de Arte de Puerto Rico. Luciano is a faculty member at Yale University School of Art and the School of Visual Arts. He is currently a Civic Practice Partnership artist in residence at the Metropolitan Museum of Art.

LINA PUERTA examines the relationship between nature and the body. She utilizes a wide variety of materials in her sculpture—concrete, clay, resin, wood, foam, fabric, artificial plants, paper pulp, and handmade paper. With these materials, she creates textural forms and compositions that blend the human-made world with the natural, and she explores notions of control, consumerism, and life's fragility. She was born in New Jersey, raised in Colombia, and lives and works in New York City. Puerta holds an MSEd in art education from Queens College/CUNY and has exhibited internationally.

The following discussion took place between Jordan Casteel, Shaun Leonardo, Miguel Luciano, Lina Puerta, and nico wheadon via Zoom on June 8, 2020.

> *The artist has a role to play in our communities, and it would be best were we to create a climate where artists are not all going to one place to live and function. If artists were to disperse among different communities and became invested in those communities, functioning as both purveyors of aesthetics and as role models, then there can be an alternative way of seeing the world, an alternative thing that art makes kids think about. . . . It gives them more insight into what it means to be human, and the ways we can express ideas about the commonality of people.* [4]

> —William T. Williams

nico wheadon: Prior to convening, I circulated the above quote by William T. Williams, the legendary painter, educator, and creative force behind the Studio Museum in Harlem's Artist-in-Residence program and the Smokehouse Mural Collective. In the paradigm he describes, artists are innovators who work against the grain to produce new, shared realities. They are natural and necessary leaders in our communities, and their art a tool for social transformation. In response to Williams's hope for artists as role models, how do each of you understand your responsibility to community, and where do museums support or hinder you in deepening civic engagement?

Shaun Leonardo: I would reflect here on my experience both working and exhibiting at the New Museum in a residency capacity. Whenever I carry a community engagement role at an institution, I try to approach it as an artist first, which allows me to ask questions of the institution that they have not faced before, namely around "community."

For example, when I started working at the New Museum, the first question I asked was, "Who do you consider your community?" They'd been on the Bowery since 2007 and couldn't answer the question. I considered that the first challenge.

NW: Well, Shaun, yours is a particularly interesting perspective as you—in your own words—have worked "on both sides of the fence," first at Socrates Sculpture Park as a community engagement practitioner and director of public programs and later at the New Museum, inventing the programmatic space of community engagement, R&D Summers, alongside Emily Mello, the associate director of education [see figure 1.1]. The circle comes back around in that you later participated as an artist in the very residency you helped design there, enabling you to evaluate the platform from a 360-degree perspective. In addition to that first question, what other questions did you ask to better understand how the relationships between artists, communities, and institutions manifested on the Lower East Side?

Figure 1.1. Shaun Leonardo guides youth enrolled in the Teen Apprenticeship Program during a visual storytelling workshop for *Mirror/Echo/Tilt*—a collaborative performance and pedagogical project with artists Melanie Crean and Sable Elyse Smith—for the New Museum's 2019 Summer Art and Social Justice residency and exhibition. Photo by Rey Londres, courtesy Shaun Leonardo.

SL: The New Museum's mission statement is "New Art, New Ideas," so I began by questioning, *Who are you stating these new ideas are coming from? Do they follow the same Eurocentric lineage of the artists that have been presented? Who in our immediate surroundings would bring new ideas to a necessary conversation around the work? What conversations does the work itself evoke? Who could bring their own brilliance to this space?* Question asking is the way I enter these roles. If we're contemplating *new art* and *new ideas*, what we're really talking about is an exchange, not some sort of top-down methodology of teaching.

As an anecdote, I was told early on, "We have an outstanding partnership with the Bowery Mission." I asked, "What does that look like?" and was told, "Our staff members often go there to serve supper." *But we're a museum! How is that a way of interchanging ideas?* Within my first two months, I had 60 homeless men touring the galleries at the New Museum. Certain members of the administration were not pleased, and I defended the work by proclaiming, "Actually I'm doing my job. I'm doing the very thing you hired me to do." So, in the process of creating engagement platforms, I decided against arbitrarily selecting audiences that I thought would somehow "benefit" from the institution, because I think that is when white supremacist values start to leak into the work.

NW: It strikes me that, in the scenario you just described, you performed the emotional labor of building valuable, local relationships for the first time while at the same time being critiqued by the very institution for whom you were shouldering the burden of historic complacency. It's an odd line to tow—driving the change that the institution asks of you yet is perhaps unready to embrace! Maybe this gets to the heart of my original question, which is, *How do we measure the value of artists' work, both* within *institutions and often as the bridge* between *that institution and its so-called community?*

SL: I think when I'm more clearly identified as an artist in museum spaces—for example, the New Museum residency—I'm actually empowered to be much more specific in terms of who the necessary publics are, because I'm engaging that conversation through the lens of my own practice.

NW: Right—you are situated more firmly in the driver's seat. Jordan, perhaps you can chime in on your experience driving community engagement at the Studio Museum in Harlem through the portrait series you made while in residence in 2015 [see figure 1.2]. In those portraits, you communicated *precisely* who you wanted to see in the museum—the street vendors who contributed to the vibrant culture of the street yet rarely crossed the threshold into the museum. Many of the Black men in your paintings—I'm thinking of James in particular—were moved beyond belief to regard themselves as art. I get emotional even now recalling the pride and ease with which he and Kevin the Kiteman moved through a space once seemingly beyond reach. Did you begin the residency knowing that you wanted to engage the citizens of Harlem in this way? As a new kid on the block, how did you build the reciprocal relationships that produced these portraits, and what can museums learn from your authentic approach to community engagement?

Jordan Casteel: I was raised to get to know the people who've come before me, wherever I go. I remember the first time I moved to New York, I found this apartment in Bed-Stuy. I was already terrified by the idea of moving to New York, and I couldn't find my mom, who'd come to help move me in. I found her outside smoking with these old men across the street who were sitting on their stoop. What she was teaching me in that moment

Figure 1.2. *Tenses: Artists in Residence 2015–16*: Jordan Casteel, EJ Hill, Jibade-Khalil Huffman (installation view). **The Studio Museum in Harlem, July 14–October 30, 2016. Photo by Adam Reich, courtesy The Studio Museum in Harlem.**

was that these were obviously the people on the block who've been here before. So the first thing you do when you arrive somewhere is say hello, sit, have a drink, and get to know the people who are going to be looking after you. That's where it starts—with real engagement around our values and whatever it is that brings us to a certain place.

If I think back to my experience at the Studio Museum, that was one of the first times when I was deeply engaged in my practice as it related to the community that I was living in. When I showed up at the museum, I asked myself, *How do I engage the work that I'm doing inside these walls with the work that's been done by someone before me? What is the intent of this space, and how do I mimic that energy or bring that to the forefront by honoring it in my actions?* It was a constant work in progress for me, anchored in asking others to reflect on how they were practicing what they preach as their values. If you say you care about the community, why are you not out there on the streets introducing yourself and inviting your neighbors inside? I noticed a slight disconnect between the institution and the people on the street who didn't recognize the museum as being for them. Even among people of color, there was a disconnect between what those values were.

NW: I find that it's a disconnect that many museums face, even culturally specific ones. This, for me, is where the notion of decentering museum authority comes in, as the relationship between a museum and its publics must be reciprocal and rooted in shared values if it is to stand the test of time. So how can museums better uphold the momentum of the conversations you initiate through your work while in residence, and carry those local relationships forward? What might motivate them to lend resources and infrastructure in support of artist-led community engagement more broadly? And how might those values shared between artist and community continue to show up within the institution, not just as one-off exhibitions but as ongoing and active cultural citizenship? As I ask this, I have an image of a museum sitting on a neighbor's stoop smoking cigarettes!

ML: Those are big questions, nico! I just want to say that I love Jordan's example. It seems so obvious—those connections between institutions and communities—that it makes me ask why that wasn't happening all along. It also makes me question how institutions sustain those kinds of relationships after artists provoke or inspire them. The nature of our residencies and projects is temporary, so I always question the potential impact of our work to lead to sustainable relationships that can change or expand how institutions genuinely connect with communities. In other words, how do you transform the culture of an institution through these gestures? Ideally, these gestures would continue on and become more complex and developed over time, but institutions are really slow to transform and change.

I'm currently working with the MET, one of the biggest institutions that is probably the slowest to change. The MET's new experimental artist residency, the Civic Practice Partnership, was designed to support artists in leveraging the resources of the institution in service of the work that we're already doing in our communities. So how does the institution become a partner in that work? I recently wrote an email to some of my colleagues wanting to put some caution into the air about how we protect that work. I say "caution" because we know that institutions are trying to move very quickly into these conversations about social justice, racial equality, and institutional racism. As such, they've been scrambling to create programming, and I don't want the work that we do to be co-opted in the moment. I also don't want it to be presented as a quick answer to something that's slow work.

Lina Puerta: Miguel, I'm curious to know which communities you're working with through your residency at the MET.

ML: I live and work in East Harlem. The research I've been doing has been focused on the relationship and history between the Puerto Rican community, the Latinx community more broadly, and the MET. It's been interesting to investigate the history of representation at the museum, past and present. *Harlem on My Mind* was the exhibition in the late '60s that set a historic precedent. While it was full of problems, it was the first time that the MET tried to exhibit beyond European history—to reach into Harlem and present Black culture.

Its major failure was that it didn't include any Black artists (i.e., painters, sculptors). Despite its many failures, the exhibition marked a shift as the museum tried to catch up with the times, and it paved the way for the 1973 exhibition *The Art Heritage of Puerto Rico*, produced in collaboration with El Museo del Barrio, which was the first and only survey exhibition of Puerto Rican artists in its history. Sadly, it didn't lead to major acquisitions or sustained relationships. This history and the ongoing struggle to create greater visibility for Puerto Rican and Latinx artists at the museum has been the focus of my work and research.

LP: But East Harlem doesn't represent the community of the MET, does it? I guess I'm going back to Shaun's question about who is the community that the museum serves. Right now, I'm in residence at the Sugar Hill Children's Museum, and I came there with all these expectations and ideals about community. I thought of the community as the neighborhood surrounding the museum but learned it's also members and patrons and that they drive decision-making that can impact the community. Also, since you still have to pay an entrance fee to come into the museum, not everyone in the neighborhood is necessarily able to be part of the museum's community.

NW: In my opinion, members, patrons, donors, and the board constitute only *part* of a museum's decision-making community. However, museums have this default behavior of creating silos among their stakeholders to more easily advance an agenda, target a message, or articulate parameters for engagement. I think it actually does museums a huge disservice to not treat *all* museum stakeholders as necessary and equal contributors to an ecosystem that is complexly interwoven and interdependent. Without artists there is no gala; without educators there is no program to fundraise for; and without community there is no public service or public good. So what would it take for artists and creative communities to be seen as integral to the overall health, sustainability, and strategic growth of the institution?

When I served as inaugural executive director of NXTHVN, I actively wove these considerations into the expansion of the professional development curriculum for the studio and curatorial fellows. For every collector or gallerist added to the roster of visiting mentors, I added an established artist, educator, curator, writer, or cultural leader as a counterbalance and to illustrate the diversity of roles that comprise the ecosystem. It was also an important reminder to the fellows in the program that not only those with disposable income determine the value of your work.

Another thing I considered was how to ensure balanced representation within the space at all times. While NXTHVN was under construction and closed to the general public, the majority of visitors the neighbors would see were the early supporters of the project. And while these private, hard-hat tours for foundations and donors were certainly important ways to honor that investment, I felt they must be counterbalanced by equal opportunities for our neighbors to engage. The stoop became an important threshold in which to initiate hyperlocal conversations, build trust, and welcome a broad cross-section of future stakeholders. Of course, the hope was that those iterative interactions would produce not only trust but also a sense of belonging that would lead to deeper, prolonged engagements in the future. It's so much harder to build relevance and repair the perception of exclusivity once it's been built up, especially if trust is broken in those neighborly moments on the street.

ML: That's why the work you are doing, nico, is so important. Leveraging the resources of patrons, investors, and collectors is a skill set very few people have or can
do gracefully, in service of larger, more inclusive community values. That's where the
market and the influence of capital can become very corrupting in a lot of museums,
unfortunately. So much of the work we're doing as artists in residence is not com-
modifiable—it doesn't turn into an object or product necessarily; it's participatory,
experiential, often temporary, and it's often harder to fund because it can't be bought
or supported in traditional ways.

SL: Within my practice, the work that has been situated within the museum residency
space has *always* been performance. So while there is a video product, I never have
the expectation that something is going to be collected afterward, which allows for an
advantage because it asks museums (and those I'm working with within the museum) to
more clearly see the purpose of whatever's happening in that time frame. That purpose
is quite often the conversations that would not traditionally be held in those spaces but
also the relationship-building, to put it more plainly.

What's beautiful about the residency as a platform is the way in which whatever I
come to the museum with can evolve over that space of time, and it is allowed to change,
even when it involves an exhibition format. By inviting social practitioners and projects
that are unfixed and continuously evolving, museums are forced to reshape themselves
around the projects. However, while there are possibilities that might remain, the hierarchical structures of the museum as an institution are never disrupted. Still, the work
can point to structural changes, because you're opening up possibilities that are not
comfortable within the museum space. Museums want something to come up and then
stay that way. There's not the same kind of labor and effort once the show goes up, but
in the residency model, what we're saying is, "No, the work is continuous!"

NW: I love that. I think encyclopedic museums have so much to learn from contemporary practice in terms of the *continuity* of the work as you put it—the value of live cultural
production as the pulse of the museum. Miguel, in your experience in residence at the
MET, what's your take on the effectiveness of residencies in shifting entrenched institutional practices and animating art history's contemporary relevance? The Civic Practice
Partnership arrives 150 years into the museum's life, and I'm curious to hear you discuss
the growing pains and the learning curves.

ML: Well, you can't have a short-term residency and expect it to yield long-term results.
One of the things fellow resident Rashida Bumbray and I did from the beginning was
advocate for an expansion of museum resources, and talking to you last week, nico,
was really inspiring. It helped hearing how you were responding to the needs of your
fellows at NXTHVN amid the COVID-19 crisis, by extending their fellowship year,
increasing their funding, and other immediate gestures. All these institutions now want
to lean into supporting artists that are doing political work, but are they willing to *invest*
in that work?

CHAPTER 1

In recent months, I've heard the director speak about the MET commissioning Wangechi's beautiful sculptures and Kent Monkman's glorious paintings, both being really bold gestures to redefine the institution's priorities on its 150th anniversary. But how do you talk about white supremacy at an institution that has probably done more to uphold the legacies of white supremacy in visual culture than perhaps any other institution in the city?

NW: Great question! I mean, as much as I love Wangechi and Kent's work—and as important as it is that the MET acknowledge their rightful place in the canon—I'm not sure I see their display on the museum's façade and within the ticketing lobby, respectively, as *progress*. In my opinion, there's an optic, and maybe even a tokenism, to positioning these works in such a hypervisible way, when the power structures and inner workings of the institution remain functionally intact. It reminds me of how museums hire staff of color for front of house positions—security, bookstore, etc.—for the *optics* of diversity yet fail to diversify senior level staff, their board of directors, or their donor base. So while these gestures are important as you say, where within the institution does accountability to stewarding equity and inclusion throughout the entire museum live, and what role do artists play in that?

ML: I will say this and leave it here—what made our work and platform impactful was that we had a really powerful advocate in Sandra Jackson-Dumont. As the chair of education, she had a strong institutional influence, and people listened to her, all the way to the top. She was a champion for so many of us, which underscores how important it is to have people in these institutions with the power to influence change internally. She created our residency, invited us in, and gave us the keys.

SL: That is a big conundrum in terms of the permanence and sustainability of these practices within institutional infrastructure, leadership, and philosophies—the way that projects reverberate during their time but then are so quickly removed and/or contained when key people leave. That's been an issue I constantly think about, because the residency model in particular was the space where artists could question the practice of the institution, yet it also calls the institution to be responsive in ways that work completely against its traditional models.

LP: It seems to me—from listening to your experiences and also recalling my own—that museums want to do social work and bring the community in but rely on education departments to execute that work. Decisions and directives coming from the board seem more concerned with the aesthetics, the glamor, and of course the funding. But when it comes to actions of social change, which are important, they are often relayed through the education department.

I recall a residency I did where I had the opportunity to work with the community through a number of workshops. Since a significant percentage of the community was of Latinx descent, I suggested offering a workshop in Spanish, not solely for families that didn't speak English but also for those who, aside from making art, wanted to practice, learn, enjoy, and even celebrate the Spanish language that enriches the neighborhood.

Unfortunately, the idea was shut down because the institution's education department felt there were members who would feel excluded and most likely complain.

Miguel, I'm wondering if you consider El Museo de Barrio to be *your* museum?

ML: I do—I feel like it's my hometown museum. I have a deep love for the museum and its history, despite my frequent disappointments with how it's been run in recent years. That's an important distinction, because El Museo is historically a "for us, by us" institution whose foundation and history was created by artists, activists, and educators in this community, and I'll always love it for that. It's the first museum that I could ever go to see Puerto Rican art, even before I lived in New York. It changed my life to be able to see Puerto Rican artists from the island and the States in the same gallery—people I looked up to, admired, was influenced by, and who became my friends and mentors later in life. I'll never forget that experience there, and I'll always fight to make sure the museum honors its history and its responsibility to our community.

It's had so many problems with its leadership and its board over the years. I'll always be part of holding the museum to account as a stakeholder in the community. It's been a difficult and painful history; I'm not excusing any of their errors—on the contrary I'll be the first to critique them. But I also want to see them succeed and to be a place that gives the same inspiration to other young Latinx artists that it gave to me.

JC: The Studio Museum is that place for me—it's one of the few places that has truly continued a certain amount of investment in me, which comes and goes at various points. But I feel like it's a space that I can access, where I can show up crying at the front door, say I need help, and somebody would help me inside and give me whatever resource I needed or at least direct me to where I could get it. From the beginning, the Studio Museum asked what I needed, as opposed to making assumptions about the needs of an entire community. That community includes artists and staff and begins with the person you meet when you walk through the door and flows all the way up to those big offices at the top floor, and every step of the way exists people who have needs. Whereas it has been a different experience at the institutions where I have had solo exhibitions, where I felt I had to fight my way through assumption after assumption, on behalf of all people of color.

NW: I'm struck by this notion of artists—as *role-models* and *purveyors of aesthetics* in the words of William T. Williams—being uniquely positioned to hold museums to account through the projects and exhibitions that they mount, sure, but *also* through the questions only they can ask. However, the question remains: Is it your responsibility to do so? And what do you gain and risk in the process?

JC: This question ties back to a conversation that I had just this morning about this moment,[5] in which everybody's coming to their Black tokens to represent an entire movement, and institutions are hoping we'll fill space on their behalf. I was asked to participate in a town hall forum that's supposed to take place this week, and I sent them this series of questions that I didn't feel they were prepared for, like, *Who's the audience and who's your community? If you're going to take my value and my time, how is it that you're investing back in the communities that you're soliciting labor from? Where is the monetary exchange?* I held them accountable to what they were asking me to do.

As we've been talking, I've also been thinking about the location of these institutions and what it means for the Studio Museum to be located in Harlem or the New Museum in the Bowery or the MET in the Upper East Side—how does that location shift the audience and who the museum is accountable to as a result? Before I knew anything about art, I knew the Studio Museum existed because my parents had a poster in the house that they'd gotten from there when they were in their 30s. I acknowledged that it must be a space that I belong to and that belongs to me, because it existed on my walls.

ML: I think you have to stay involved, and we all have to get invested; there's a lot of ways to do it. When I proposed partnering with El Museo del Barrio in my public art project *Mapping Resistance: The Young Lords in El Barrio* [figure 1.3], there was no director at the museum at that time. I took a risk in that moment, but I felt strongly that El Museo should be the institutional partner for the project because I wanted to implicate the museum in the activist history of East Harlem and to hold them to account in teaching it.

Figure 1.3. *Mapping Resistance: The Young Lords in El Barrio*, 2019. A public art project organized by Miguel Luciano, featuring the photography of Hiram Maristany. Billboard image: *The Bronx March* (1969), Hiram Maristany. Photo courtesy Miguel Luciano.

JC: I've had the recent experience of putting up my first museum solo show in New York at the New Museum, where I was expecting authentic collaboration, which wasn't always easily achieved. The institution had their motivations in framing the work, and it often pushed against the facts of my practice. I always care about language and context and found myself constantly needing to revise and edit—or even ask for the opportunity to revise, edit, and at the very least contribute to—the language used to frame my work.

ML: When I think of Shaun's projects, like his performance at the Guggenheim, and Jordan's exhibition at the New Museum, there's something disruptive about the act of exhibiting—I feel like it's a disruptive act in these institutions. Part of it is that we come with our people, our communities, into these spaces to disrupt them. I seldom go to the Guggenheim, even though it's walking distance from where I live. But, for me, one of the most gratifying parts of going to Shaun's performance at the Guggenheim was seeing all of our people in that space. We show up for each other like that, and that's part of where the love, impact, and influence are for us. Your Studio Museum residency experience is such a special example, Jordan, and it makes me happy to hear about your relationship there—I wish El Museo had a residency program that was similar and that we had these kinds of legacies there.

NW: We've all alluded to *this moment* a few times in our discussion, so why don't we be explicitly clear about what we're referring to. How do the social, cultural, and economic impacts of COVID-19—and the recent, empty solidarity statements issued by museums in the wake of George Floyd's murder—reveal cracks in the foundation upon which our arts ecosystem is built? And, inversely, where might the responses from our field actually affirm shared values and priorities?

All the messaging I've received is from majority-white institutions that are like, *You know what, OK, yes, we see it now—racism is real. And of* course *we don't like police brutality. But we also don't like looting, so be upset but not too upset. Be outraged, but please just don't direct that rage over here!* It's an acknowledgment of a preexisting problem accompanied by zero commitment to action. What are y'all experiencing?

SL: nico, you're pointing to it. I think in both very interrelated crises, what has shown itself is the ways in which many white institutions have struggled to gather both language, relevance, and programming because they hadn't been actually doing the work. So they fumbled through maintaining connections with diverse audiences, Black and Brown people, because, and I've shared this widely, much of the existing programming that you would codify as community engagement was very surface level and meant to just simply check the box.

So I have found that the few institutions that really were able to gather momentum quickly and establish or reestablish a connection virtually with their core audiences, those audiences that were most craving dialogue and most in need of a creative outlet, are the institutions that were already putting that programming out in the world.

JC: It's an interesting time because everybody is talking about pulling off the Band-Aid, and COVID-19 revealing all the systematic downfalls, neglects, and horrors that have taken place in marginalized communities and communities of color for generations. We've all been talking about not getting adequate health care, not getting the access to the things that we need, that we feel silenced, or that we can't communicate with our doctors because they don't believe that our pain is real. It's the same thing when I enter an institution and say this doesn't feel good to me. The institution's responsibility is to acknowledge that the pain is real to me whether they see it themselves or not. If I say that this is wrong, then acknowledge that it's wrong—there needs to be a shift in trust.

As I approach a show with an institution, I go in with a lot of hope but also hesitancy because trust has been broken in the past. All I can do is try to be transparent from the beginning and hope that meaningful, reciprocal relationships will emerge. Having your work exhibited at a major institution is a big deal—a career milestone; however, by the time of the opening, I often find myself exhausted as opposed to celebratory. As much as the day is supposed to be about me, the work, my community, and the sitters, I am frequently pulled in another direction, obliged to be present with those who are, in fact, less familiar to me, and a part of the institution's community.

A Black square on Instagram or exhibiting the work of Black artists is simply not enough. We are asking for more than a seat at a table—I am calling for institutions to get into the trenches to do the hard work of creating meaningful and sustainable change, both on a daily basis and long term.

LP: This COVID-19 crisis and what's happening right now with the Black Lives Matter movement is showing us that, even though some museums have made room for Black artists and all these issues we're discussing, they're definitely not doing enough, and the community is not feeling it. I like what Jordan said—that you have a museum that you can call home and is a safe space for you. Museums should be that, or we should at least strive for them to be safe spaces, especially for communities that are at a disadvantage—that should be central to all museums.

This conversation also reminds me of that period after the 2016 election, when I realized how much we have [regressed] as a country on so many issues. I was particularly disturbed by this rhetoric against immigrants, especially with Trump calling them names and referring to them as criminals. When he won it was such a shock for many of us, but that's when I started thinking about the importance of bringing art to other areas of the country to start a conversation.

NW: That's a good point. So far, we've only focused on New York City museums in this discussion. So let's go there for a second because I think you're onto something important, Lina. Tell us about your experience being commissioned as an artist in residence by the 21c Museum Hotel in Bentonville, Arkansas.

LP: The 21c Museum Hotels are a museum and boutique hotel model, with its museum free and open to the public 24/7. It was founded by an art-collecting couple based in Louisville, Kentucky, with the mission of bringing contemporary art to the southern US.

The Southern Foodways Alliance—an organization based in Oxford, Mississippi, that studies culture through food in partnership with 21c—awarded me the residency and commissioned my project, *Latino Farmworkers in the US Tapestries Series* [see figure 1.4]. This series was initially exhibited in Oxford, Mississippi, as part of the SFA annual symposium and then traveled to the 21c Museum Hotels in Bentonville, Arkansas, and Louisville, Kentucky. Five of the tapestries became part of the 21c Art Collection.

This series highlighted the different social issues faced by Latino farm workers in the US. I was surprised by how many people were eager to learn more about art and were really open to conversation. I think that's something to keep in mind—that art has this power to transcend boundaries and different communities.

NW: I love that the 21c Museum Hotels democratize access to contemporary art and artists in parts of the country where contemporary art museums are certainly outnumbered by historic houses and encyclopedic museums. This question of access returns me to the opportunities and challenges of our current moment—I'm curious to learn if

Figure 1.4. Lina Puerta, *Tomato Crop Picker*, 2017, 54" × 35". Pigmented cotton and linen paper pulp, lace, velvet ribbon, sequined and metallic fabrics, trims, beaded and embroidered appliqués, fake fur, feathers, gouache, and chains. Included quote: "In a 2012 report, Human Rights Watch surveyed female farmworkers, nearly all of them had experienced sexual violence, or knew others who had." Human Rights Watch. Photo by Jeanette May, courtesy Lina Puerta.

the emergent Zoom culture brought on by COVID-19 has supported or hindered you in discussing your work with an expanded audience.

JC: As an educator with an autoimmune disease who has an invisible illness, I'm constantly struggling through meetings, events, and talks that ask for my physical body to be present, and the real labor that it takes for me to be present in the way I'd like. Now I feel some relief— because we're all in the same place, technology has created accessibility for all sorts of bodies, not just Brown ones, not just young ones, but able bodies and disabled bodies, all of us can be a part of something.

NW: I also appreciate how time has slowed down and prescriptions around productivity have shifted in healthy ways that I hope we'll hold on to as practitioners engaged in what Miguel called *slow work*. I'm grateful for the privilege to hover in this procedural place, where art and ideas are in a constant state of becoming and adapting to whatever it is that we wake up to. And I love that, whether they want to or not, larger institutions are going to have to embrace nimbleness and adapt to this new way of working!

Since we're imagining life on the other side of social distancing and self-quarantine, what advice would you give to younger artists navigating the future arts-and-culture ecosystem for the first time? What tools can you share on how to leverage the capital, cache, community, and leadership of the museums in which these artists might be in residence one day?

SL: I think what's unique about entering the museum space as a social practitioner is that it has become inherent to the process to work with nearly every department in the museum and to understand that, as the scope of work. So in both recent cases, the New Museum and Guggenheim, I can tell you that I personally carved out time and space to work with security, visitor services, marketing, certainly education, up to the executive offices. I believe implicating as many people in the museum as possible nourishes the work, by moving them closer to its intentions and further from the role of host.

We've been talking a lot about the ways in which we make demands—I have also found it important to really understand for myself what I *don't* want as much as what I *do* want. I'll give you a few examples—I ask that the publics engaging with my work don't have to go to the visitor service desk, and I ask that marketing not use certain words in describing my practice. It's these little shifts, where I don't tell them how to work but ask them to work harder.

NW: Also, just to call it what it is, you're stepping into your agency to make those demands and outline the lane of participation that best serves the work. I think that's something that most people, especially women artists and artists of color, don't wake up feeling they are entitled to. It takes strength, and I admire each of you for taking the risk to flex those muscles—these small gestures and acts of resistance actually *do* transform institutions.

JC: In some ways I think demanding is important, but you only become more comfortable demanding as you get to know what your needs and wants are. I think learning how to sustain is really important too. So finding allies early is important, even if it's the front desk staff. You can make demands, can kick and scream, but there's so much institutionalized racism and systemic privilege—especially in the museum system. I believe that, as Miguel said, this is a long haul, we're not going to get the change overnight, and we have to invest in self-care as a radical act, finding the spaces in which we can rejuvenate in order to take this on.

Also, ask everybody *why*. *Why am I signing this contract? Can you explain this language to me?* If people can't explain something they are asking you to do, then you're in a better position to say, *This makes me feel uncomfortable. Until we get to a position that we both agree on the "why," I'm not going to sign anything.* And you should read everything.

LP: Jordan, what do you do to not just get discounted as a diva, because that happens so often with women of color—you just get brushed off like, *We're doing so much for you; how dare you ask for anything else?*

JC: It's exhausting. I showed up the day of my opening, having just bled myself on behalf of others. Through my experience, it became clear that a positive relationship with your gallery is instrumental in navigating difficult terrain. Veronica, the director I work most closely with, is a white woman who takes a lot of the "Black girl diva" burden off of me through understanding the circumstances at play and having the hard conversations on my behalf. Again, it's finding an ally so that we're not carrying the burden alone.

ML: I think mentorship is an important part of the work too. One of the things I have really admired about a lot of my friends is how incredibly generous they are in terms of connecting us to one another. I try to do the same thing with younger artists, and I've never forgotten the people who've done that for me. Unfortunately, there are still a lot of spaces where people feel intimidated and alone in this work.

NW: So, I've heard knowing what you want, learning what you *don't* want, making informed demands, leaning on allies, and engaging in peer mentorship—any other parting thoughts?

JC: My parting thought is *thank you* for creating this space, nico! I'm excited about how the book will live as a document of our conversation, in and of this time, for eternity in a very specific way. It's only a portion of the conversations that exist in the world and hopefully are happening intimately, as you said, Miguel. I think the intimacy part of it is really important, but the bird's eye view into that intimacy is a gift that I wish I had as I was stepping into this work, and you're giving that to all of us.

NW: This space literally wouldn't exist without each of you, so thank you for your generosity! I know this level of transparency is hard because we're critiquing systems and institutions that have both nurtured and, at times, oppressed us. They are definitely difficult but important conversations to have.

ML: There's momentum for things to shift, and this is the time to apply pressure in these spaces. You're setting a powerful example, nico!

OUTRO

> *Because artists often gravitate to what is missing, many have committed themselves to creative events that connect people and ideas in the public sphere because they discern that what is missing now is public discourse about the relationship of individuals to society.*[6]

—Carol Becker

It's no coincidence that the first practitioners invited to share tools in this volume were artists—this orientation toward artists as social innovators who drive culture, democracy, and our collective imagination forward is a foundational premise of this book. As such, it felt most authentic to begin a discussion about art's power to drive engaged cultural citizenship with the *makers* of art, discussing their role building belonging within and through museums.

In our conversation, Jordan, Shaun, Miguel, and Lina shared how their experiences navigating museum-based residencies are symptomatic of far greater challenges of intimacy currently faced by museums. If museums struggle to support a single artist in their desire to authentically engage community, what does that say about the institution's capacity to serve entire publics? And if, as Becker states, artists gravitate toward what is missing, why don't museums trust that artists' pull toward community is movement in a necessary direction?

These Associations

Recently, I've been reflecting on a transformative museum residency that I participated in almost a decade ago that achieved the radical intimacy we discussed toward the end of our roundtable—Tino Sehgal's *These Associations*, at the Tate Modern in 2012. In this first live commission of the Turbine Hall, Berlin-based artist Sehgal brought hundreds of Londoners together to scaffold this non–object-based artwork. I, alongside dozens of other participants, showed up to the museum every day to activate the piece—a *nexus* of spatial and dialogical relationships between me, my fellow participants, and that day's visitors.

Since the work relied on a social contract to which I'll feel eternally bound, I will not divulge too much about the necessarily invisible architectures of the piece. However, what I *will* share is that my job was to shed all conversational pretenses and formalities and approach visitors by launching into conversations that began with our shared vulnerability—me as divulger of personal information and them as dialogue partners who helped transform my personal musings into something shared and universal.

Here I found and built community among others seeking to engage the museum as a platform for connection. The piece empowered anyone that engaged it to tap into its rich undercurrent of collective memory and learn more about what binds than what estranges us as humans. I walked away from the experience wholly transformed by the generosity, kindness, and trust I was shown by visitors that I met only briefly and will likely never see again.

Toggling at all times between public performance and private conversation, the piece asked important questions of both the museum and its publics. How is belonging constructed within and through institutions? What role do art and artists play in constituting these associations? And can community dictate its own lanes of participation within the museum space? Let's carry these questions with us—in addition to the insights so generously shared by Jordan, Shaun, Miguel, and Lina—as we step into the next chapter, which investigates the museum as a medium for new models of sociospatial engagement.

NOTES

1. "About." Studio Museum in Harlem, February 16, 2021, https://studiomuseum .org/about.

2. Cahan, Susan E. "Introduction." In *Mounting Frustration: The Art Museum in the Age of Black Power*, 2–3. Durham, NC: Duke University Press, 2018.

3. "Residencies in Museum." Alliance of Artists Communities, https://artistcommu nities.org/publicrealm-museums.

4. Hadler, Mona. "William T. Williams." *BOMB*, February 19, 2018, https://bomb magazine.org/articles/william-t-williams-by-mona-hadler.

5. Our discussion took place amid the global COVID-19 pandemic; the ensuant public health, housing, and financial crises; the 2020 Black Lives Matter protests that took place across the world; and the mass museum layoffs and solidarity statements issued in support of the movement.

6. Becker, Carol. "Microutopias: Public Practice in the Public Sphere." In *Living as Form: Socially Engaged Art from 1991–2011*, edited by Nato Thompson, 67. New York: Creative Time, 2012.

2

MUSEUM AS MEDIUM

How to Liberate the Museum from the Designed Hierarchies That Entomb It

INTRO

> *The "where" of our sensory experience in the world have a profound influence on our ability to create individual and collective identities—to become, know, and name who we are—primarily because "space comprises the social arena in which individuals reproduce or challenge their experiential boundaries of action and interaction." It provides us what Aspa Gospodini has referred to as a spatial membership, a type of place-based identity provided "to almost all individuals and social groups of [the same] society." Space then—one's ability to perceive it, access it, etc.—becomes an essential element in the construction of identity and, concomitantly, entire societies as well.*[1]
>
> —Craig L. Wilkins

Between 2010 and 2014, I conducted fieldwork on arts-led innovation while pursuing a master's degree in creative and cultural entrepreneurship at Goldsmiths, University of London. As a curator seeking tools to build culturally relevant spaces, I developed an interest in architecture, human geography, urban planning, and other fields that map the myriad relationships between communities and institutions as appendages of the built environment. In my research, I first came across the scholarship of architect Craig L. Wilkins, who radically transformed how I understood architecture's role in mediating the construction of social belonging.

As discussed at the end of chapter 1, my research extended beyond my formal studies to include my participation in Tino Sehgal's *These Associations*, a case study in an artist serving as a visionary architect of public space. I was interested not only in how artists' interventions might adapt or repurpose pre-existing spaces (i.e., Tate Modern's notoriously sterile Turbine Hall) but, more importantly, in how they might construct altogether new, *intangible* spaces (i.e., the associations between subjects and objects) through which to mobilize cultural citizenship. At the time, I found myself questioning the materiality of the inherited structures that comprise the arts-and-culture ecosystem, the efficacy and accessibility of their designs, and the role of artists in transforming these often cumbersome, material forms into more accessible mediums for civic participation.

Upon my return to the States in 2014, I sensed a profound synergy between my own experimentations with *spatial membership* and those taking place within cultural institutions more broadly. As I shifted my professional attention from curatorial to community engagement—"architect" of aesthetic space to engaged citizen of it—museums were also beginning to restructure their priorities. Community engagement positions were being developed in museums across the country, and adult education departments were being resourced to develop an engagement methodology that addressed ongoing challenges of accessibility and relevance. It was amid this sea change that I rejoined the Studio Museum in Harlem as the manager, and later director, of the Public Programs & Community Engagement department.

The department was established on the eve of the museum's 50th anniversary to help expand and deepen conversations between the museum and its *local*, *national*, and *international* diasporic communities, among other key objectives. Concurrently, the Studio Museum was embarking on a building project that would, at least temporarily, unmoor it from its 125th Street facility, a former bank adapted into a museum by the late African American architect J. Max Bond Jr. In this moment of radical transformation, I saw the opportunity to both collaborate with experts to envision a museum for the future and gain experience designing and building institutional infrastructure. A few guiding questions at that time were, How can a museum without walls continue to serve as a cultural anchor in and of a particular place? How might an itinerant museum renegotiate its place-based identity and hyperlocal citizenship? And how does working in a decentralized way open new possibilities for arts-led civic engagement to take place organically, in the public sphere, and on the public's terms?

Architectural firms David Adjaye and Associates and Cooper Robertson—in partnership with Studio Museum leadership, stewarded by Director and Chief Curator Thelma Golden—encouraged staff to reimagine the orientation of their work during this moment of institutional reflection and strategic planning. I was co-lead of the task force inHarlem, an interdepartmental working group comprised of leadership from across the entire museum, and we set out to define an interim program for our museum-without-walls. (See part 2 for two in-depth case studies of this work.) We led interviews and focus groups with field leaders who'd undergone similar change; participated in local community board meetings, as both neighbor and presenter; deepened existing school and community partnerships; held co-ideation sessions with new partners already doing amazing work in our neighborhood; and initiated open lines of communication with our neighbors through the establishment of the museum's Community Advisory Network, which I'll discuss in the next chapter.

I begin here—with my experience of the Studio Museum's approach to dematerializing its own *experiential boundaries*—to lay the foundation for how I, a novice, enter a dialogue about museums and architecture. Despite my four years of research and the five years spent engaging architects in the exercise of designing a purpose-built museum, my primary investment was in the process of co-ideating designs for culturally responsive space, *not* in the delivery of a shiny, new museum. It was in the opportunity to collaborate with and learn from experts from other fields whose skill sets and ways of seeing were wholly different from my own.

This chapter is an extension of that brainstorming and skills-sharing exercise. In the discussion that follows, I'm joined by architects Mario Gooden, principal at Huff + Gooden Architects, and Deborah Berke and Maitland Jones of Deborah Berke Partners, as we look at the entire superstructure of the museum, who designs it, and who ultimately articulates its highest and best use. We interrogate how the medium of the museum itself dictates who the space is for and, alternately, who is excluded by design. We consider how dematerializing the spatial enclosure of the museum might, in turn, empower the arts-led community engagement we discussed in the previous chapter to flow more freely. And we look both backward into the annals of art history and deep into our present moment to imagine what museums—and the architects that design them—might learn from the artistic, social, and political movements of today. By pulling back the veil on the covert ways that museums both elect and benefit from elitist infrastructures, this chapter unpacks the social injustices that are often produced as a result.

ROUNDTABLE

DEBORAH BERKE, FAIA, LEED AP is an architect, educator, and the founder of New York–based architecture firm Deborah Berke Partners. Deborah leads the firm alongside her ten partners. Among the firm's most significant works are the Residential Colleges at Princeton University, the Cummins Indy Distribution Headquarters, the Rockefeller Arts Center at SUNY Fredonia, the Yale School of Art in New Haven, Connecticut, and the 21c Museum Hotels across the South and Midwest. Deborah is the dean of the Yale School of Architecture, the first woman to hold the position. She has been a professor at Yale since 1987.

MARIO GOODEN is a cultural practice architect and founding principal of Huff + Gooden Architects. His practice engages the cultural landscape and the intersectionality of architecture, race, gender, sexuality, and technology. Gooden is a professor of practice at the Graduate School of Architecture Planning and Preservation (GSAPP) of Columbia University, where he is the codirector of the Global Africa Lab (GAL). Gooden is the author of *Dark Space: Architecture, Representation, Black Identity* (Columbia University Press, 2016). Gooden is research associate at Visual Identities in Art and Design (VIAD) at the University of Johannesburg (South Africa).

MAITLAND JONES, AIA, LEED AP, joined Deborah Berke Partners in 1992 and became a partner in 2002. Over the past decade, he has served as both a critic and a lecturer at the Yale University School of Architecture. As design partner at DBPA, Mait has worked on numerous projects ranging in type from custom residential to commercial and institutional, including the Yale University School of Art, the Rockefeller Arts Center at SUNY Fredonia, and the High Street Residence Hall at Dickinson College. Currently Mait is working on a pair of new residential colleges at Princeton University and NXTHVN, an arts incubator in New Haven, Connecticut.

The following discussion took place between Deborah Berke, Mario Gooden, Maitland Jones, and nico wheadon via Zoom on June 30, 2020.

nico wheadon: First, I must disclaim that I know very little about architecture. Sure, I'm a participant of the built environment and have even played my part in a few museum-building projects. But how cultural institutions are dreamt, designed, and then *materialized* is certainly beyond me. So being in conversation with you three brilliant architects is both exciting and terrifying.

I'm particularly excited to discuss if you think it is your responsibility as architects to encourage museums to envision altogether new spaces for art and community to intersect—museum alternatives that don't subscribe to inherited design hierarchies and that value the production and display of art in equal measure. As someone who's had the privilege of operating within spaces such as these that you've designed, I'm also excited to learn more about how you bring progressive design philosophies to life. But before we go there, let's ground our discussion by each sharing a formative experience within the traditional museum settings we're collectively working to subvert.

Deborah Berke: I certainly know that for me, as a kid who grew up in Queens but had a mom who was an artist, museums were a rite of passage. My mother would take me into the city, and we would go to events at MoMA or the MET. It was transformative to look at art with my mom, hear her opinions, and learn from her. It was also a rite of passage in a negative way in that I quickly learned that what we did as creative people was lesser than what we were going there to see. We had to pass through this kind of important portal—the grand lobby at the MET comes to mind or the intimidating understatedness of MoMA to my nine-year-old eyes as an outer borough kid—those memories shaped how I saw museums well into my young adult life and shape how I think about creating spaces to view and make art today.

Maitland Jones: I have the same artist mom and was taken to museums endlessly as a kid but not enough for it to demystify that threshold moment you described, which is to say, going into a museum was to enter a kind of site of wonder and awe. I, like you, Deborah, footnote my own sort of creative instincts now in that experience, meaning I see the line delineated by nico in the prompts between museums as sites of presentation and museums as places of production. Or places where, today, that boundary between art making and presenting might be blurred. I do see my own creative urges as originating in going to museums and hearing my mom talk about how things were made.

Mario Gooden: I think the past several weeks have been challenging in a number of different ways, and I'm not sure that the way in which I've thought of museums in the past, or what they are, still holds. I won't say it's no longer valid, but I think that's all called into question. Museums, like libraries, have historically been based upon a European epistemology of organizing knowledge, understanding knowledge, and presenting that knowledge. It's not always for knowledge production but for understanding the rest of the world as a colonial project or an imperial project and somehow bringing that back and putting that on display.

Take the MET, for example. Think about the Egyptian collection and where these works have come from. They were all part of a colonial or imperial project not only in terms of how the West understands the rest of the world but also in terms of how Europe and America situate themselves in relationship to the rest of the world. Architecture has really been complicit in that. Most architects love working on museums. However, within the history and theory of architecture is embedded not only a European epistemology but also the European white male body as its subject and protagonist. Vitruvius takes this ideal subject and inscribes it within architecture. The museum has somewhat continued that line of thinking and conceptualization. For me, thinking about what a museum is must be evaluated in light of the current social revolution. I think it calls all of that into question: How do we begin to think about the relationship between architecture and the body in a different way?

DB: It's so interesting that everything you've described, which is completely true, is primarily from the vantage point of the museum as the holder, the storyteller, the presenter, and the organizer of the goods, which I guess is what I was trying to get out of my childhood experience—the control of the experience of seeing the goods. The way they tell me, you, Mait, or nico the history of Egypt is as much a part of how our experience is controlled as is how they got the stuff in the first place. I feel like the problem you're addressing is actually a two-sided problem. It's their role in presenting it and their role in having it.

MG: Absolutely. To stick with the MET, or a similar kind of encyclopedic museum, the way in which that work is presented, and the experience that is constructed, has been very important because it's also being presented for a certain kind of body. Going back to the Vitruvian subject, whom Leonardo da Vinci rendered, and thinking about the construction of perspective drawing, which is a tool of architecture. The perspective drawing as a mode of representation is conceptualized around that ideal subject, so the ideal subject and the presentation of the experience become complicit. So, yes, the experience is presented to a body, but that body is also implicit in the way in which the work is seen.

MJ: This reminds me of an observation Leonard Barkan made in the introduction to one of his books[2] that might take the eye away from the little apex of the Alberti construction. If you peek behind that veil and regard the museum as a system, like an archive, you can maybe see all of the principles that led to the assembly of all those goods, that cultural trove of stuff, and the child in me never saw that. I've only been made aware of that recently, but you know, museums-as-a-kind-of-archive-of-knowledge are also putting on display the system of their assembly. Therein lies the structure of power that I think many people who are put off by museums, or are troubled in their presence, are perceiving. I guess what I'm inviting us to do is, if you look behind that veil that separates the person who goes to the museum from the work, you see the mechanics of the ordering of knowledge, of goods, of possessions, and their accumulation. Am I going out on a limb here?

MG: No, I don't think so. I think it goes very deep because even when we're visiting the museum, we only see a small percentage of their collection. There is much more that we don't even see or perhaps that we aren't aware of. There are multiple layers to that veil.

NW: This reminds me of the work of artist Fred Wilson, and his landmark artist intervention *Mining the Museum*, at the Maryland Historical Society in 1992. Of it, art historian Kerr Houston writes, "Working with objects in the collection of the MHS, Wilson unsettled the museum's comfortably white, upper-class narrative by juxtaposing silver repoussé vessels and elegant 19th-century armchairs with slave shackles and a whipping post. Texts, spotlights, recorded texts, and objects traditionally consigned to storage drew attention to the local histories of blacks and Native Americans, effectively unmaking the familiar museological narrative as a narrow ideological project."[3] I'm struck by the fact that an independent artist led this exercise in deep institutional self-reflection. I'm curious if you can think of examples where the provocation comes from the institution itself and doesn't rely on the artist to perform the labor of making the museum's holdings more accessible.

MJ: I'm going to make this conversation very literal for a second. The MET tried (and now everyone followed) with their own kind of collection rooms. Where you go down and you see the stuff on the racks. It tried to allow you that "peek," as it were. It tried to demystify or somehow make available the artifacts in the storage rooms downstairs. But that to me only accentuated the issue. Now it's revealed that not only do they have one of these cool silver chalices, they have 600 of them that no one ever gets to access! What are these things for?

MG: And how did they get there?

MJ: And why did they get number 599?

DB: That's right. If they are that important, why aren't they sharing with 599 less fortunate museums who need a chalice to tell a story?

MJ: So, that's something disquieting.

DB: I have a question. I feel as though you're both completely right, but you're referring to the viewer's ability to be critical of the story that's being told by the museum. I feel there's another part to the architecture of most museums, which is that the building is intimidating and makes us feel less than, and question if we have a right to be there. Do we have the right to go up those big steps and walk between those giant columns and stand next to those 25-foot-tall bouquets of flowers before we even see the art? I bet that if a child were asked to draw a museum, it would look exactly like the MET.

I think that we can be critical because of the privileged knowledge we have, and maybe nowadays, because of all that's happening, more people can be critical. But I'm also interested in how the museum, as a building, has for so long tried to make the visitor actually feel inadequate. Do you guys feel that way, or is this just me?

NW: The thing that shocks me most is not that these monoliths with their cultures of aggrandizement exist but that many are choosing to construct new contemporary art institutions in their image. That they are *choosing* frontal modes of address that subscribe to those old typologies you just named, Deborah, while simultaneously boasting more progressive programs to fill and activate these spaces.

MG: To Deborah's point, I think architecture has a role to play in that because, as you were saying, nico, the design of architecture has been complicit in maintaining those systems, whether or not it's an issue of style or typology. But I also think that the signifiers that architecture puts out there are read differently by different people. There are degrees of comfort, and I think different people can also read that language, but it may read in a much more exclusive way to some people. So what is architecture's role in dismantling that language?

DB: I completely agree.

In the case of the library or the museum, what was once a place of certainty, an orderly deposit of knowledge arranged in familiar and agreed-upon categories, has been eroded by the onrush of media, consumer culture and telecommunications. Architecture's capacity to represent and shelter that collective memory has in turn withered. To design a library or a museum today is to contend with an entirely new set of expectations. Above all, it means to recognize an ever-increasing uncertainty about what constitutes knowledge, who has access to it and how it is distributed.[4]

—Stan Allen

NW: Deborah, how does your design for the 21c Museum Hotels dismantle that language and, in so doing, democratize access to contemporary art? What's the backstory there?

DB: Steve Wilson and Laura Lee Brown are these rather extraordinary art collectors out of Louisville, Kentucky. They've built this group of hotels called the 21c Museum Hotels, that are located in tertiary cities across the United States. The model of the hotel is *comfort meets art*, and the public spaces of the hotels—which display contemporary art exhibitions drawn from their collection—are open 24/7, 365 days a year. Steve and Laura Lee's collection includes works by celebrated contemporary artists but also commissions work by local artists that are political, particularly about race, equality, sexuality, and issues of gender preference and presentation.

Close to 20 years ago, Steve and Laura Lee went to the Speed Art Museum in Louisville, Kentucky, and said, *We will give you our extensive collection, which is only going to continue to grow, but you need to build a branch downtown because we do not believe that the museum should be remote from where people are. In fact, we want to help seed the revitalization of downtown,* which was essentially destroyed not so much by urban renewal but essentially by parking lots that were making more money than buildings. The museum said, *No, we love your collection, but we don't want to be downtown. We don't agree with your critique and analysis.* And so they decided to rethink the kind of place that the arts should be seen in. The inspiration to rethink how you show the collection sponsored this unusual path, because what the traditional, local fine-art museum wanted to do was not consistent with how they envisioned it.

This is a hotel that is a museum and a museum that is a hotel [see figure 2.1]. People who might be eating there, sleeping there, or having a drink there would see these very provocative artworks, and many of these people would never go to a traditional museum. They would never walk up the steps of the MET or under the giant, magically cantilevered awning at MoMA—they just wouldn't do that. But in Louisville, Lexington, Durham, or Oklahoma City, they would encounter art they wouldn't otherwise see. It was really turning a museum inside out and making interesting, difficult, provocative work available to people who might never seek it out, and both challenging them and welcoming them at the same time.

NW: In an earlier roundtable, I chatted with Lina Puerta, who was an artist in residence at the 21c Museum Hotel in Bentonville, Arkansas, in 2017—it was interesting to get a

Figure 2.1. The 21c Museum Hotel, Louisville, Kentucky. Photo by Catherine Tighe, courtesy Deborah Berke Partners.

360-degree perspective of the platform by understanding the artist's experience of it. She was excited by the level of access it provided—that someone could see her work at any time, day or night, and that her work is now part of a national collection that travels to parts of the world where critical, contemporary art conversations might be harder to come by. She felt as though her work took on new meaning in those contexts.

With the 21c Museum Hotel model, there is a bit of a bait-and-switch—the bait is the comforts of "home," and the switch is an invitation into a difficult conversation initiated by art. There does, however, appear to be an underlying trust—the hotel entrusts its public with unfettered and unmediated access to world class art, and guests trust the context enough to enter into conversation with difficult work.

MJ: In my limited experience, the trust is two-directional. The clientele is not surprised by the art. It's not sprung on them, and they don't recoil from it—their interaction with the art seems to be mutually beneficial. It's not like the founders of this are saying, "You will see this art, like it or not." It produces a kind of symbiosis between people who might not otherwise go to museums, or see this kind of art, and the art itself that might never have this audience. It's very sincere.

DB: I'd love to hear Mario discuss the building project that's taped up on the wall behind him. That is a museum that you're designing, right?

MG: Yes, it's the Dr. Carter G. Woodson African American Museum in St. Petersburg. We started working on it about a year ago, but now we have a new site. We're in the process of conceptually rethinking it.

I've recently been thinking a lot about Arthur Jafa's work. Just over the weekend, for example, his 2016 film *Love Is the Message, the Message Is Death* was being streamed by 13 museums all around the world for 48 hours for free. It was pretty remarkable. It's just an eight-minute film, but there were several things which struck me about that and about the work. That it was being streamed globally by 13 different institutions is a way of breaking the bounds of enclosure, decommoditizing the artwork, and throwing into question the notion of ownership. The piece itself is a visual juxtaposition—a collage using found footage that brings together elements of the sublime, the horrific, and the beautiful. Thinking about that film made me also want to think about the museum as a space of abolition. So not only turning the museum inside out but maybe even having to rethink what the museum is, and maybe that word "museum" will no longer even apply.

The project that we're working on in St. Petersburg was looking at some work by Romare Bearden—one could say it's somewhat similar in terms of using juxtaposition and collage. What I'm interested in with AJ's work is that it is not easily categorized in terms of the object or the frame and that each time that you see it, you see something a little bit differently, or when it's juxtaposed to a certain context, it just kind of totally changes the way that you see. It's something which is constantly in production, I would say.

So is there a way in which the museum could perhaps be more of a space about production than a space about the object? Or could the museum become more of a medium than an object? I don't know what that means in terms of the building design, but that's what I'm interested in now. Again, maybe the word "museum" goes away. Perhaps the building is no longer a typology.

DB: I love the idea of breaking down the typology. It's all the stuff that the three of us were talking about at the beginning of this conversation—the dictates of the typology itself on our own response. Perhaps if the physical topology gets broken down, the word becomes a little less important and we will expect different things when we go to the museum. It would no longer be dictatorial in its experience, and I think, in a way, the success of the 21c Museum Hotels is at the outset. It's both fabulous and ridiculous—like, your bed's upstairs, you can have a drink in your hand, and there are like 70,000 square feet of gallery space, but it's spread across eight different cities that might be thousands of miles apart. I think what we can do as architects with well-informed clients is to help break down the expectations of typology.

MJ: I think there's an insight in identifying the museum as a thing constantly in production. This idea has obvious pathways to the museum becoming a place where we share in the making of meaning, or history, instead of becoming consumers of history as it's been benevolently put together for our consumption. The museum is a "medium" to me. It rhymes with things we hear from clients. We haven't designed a museum, we've designed museum-like spaces like NXTHVN [figure 2.2], and a dozen projects. We are helping Williams College program their teaching museum, a very active place and a site of art production, not necessarily containing messy studios or an artist in residence, but it will be understood to be a place of activity, always being renewed so that, when you go back, you will perceive it to have been a medium, to have changed in the interim, and that you're going there to participate in the construction of its meaning. Again, this is a study and we're programming it, but it's appealing to hear them describe more places where stuff happens than places where art is displayed.

Figure 2.2. Rendering of NXTHVN, New Haven, Connecticut. Image courtesy Deborah Berke Partners.

MG: Early African American museums functioned more like social and community spaces, actually. One of the first ones was in Detroit, and my colleague Mabel O. Wilson writes about this in her book *Negro Building*. Now, it was a mobile museum, a trailer that went around the city. It was the International African American Museum, which is now the Charles Wright Museum in Detroit. But that started out really as a community and social center. African American museums traditionally have taken that on and, let's say, *rolled* within the communities where they were always involved in politics and social production. It was a place where the community met, a place where the community organized, and a place that was about care.

DB: In that history, Mario, were the art objects treated differently than, say, a stone taken from Egypt, to go back to our early example of the MET?

MG: A number of them actually did not have permanent collections to start with, and those that did began with someone's private, small collection. So it wasn't the kind of collection that we think of now that requires the climate-controlled storage space. Again, they functioned as a place to distribute knowledge.

NW: I really appreciate you introducing the lineage of African American museums, Mario—you do so brilliantly in your book *Dark Space: Architecture, Representation, Black Identity*, which is actually one of the texts that got me excited to invoke architecture in this book in the first place! In my experience, every museum is propelled by its own unique mantle that, in turn, is shaped by the conditions of its founding and its overall culture of acquisitions.

While at NXTHVN, I often considered what the organization's responsibility to collecting was, as a cultural intuition with a museum-caliber gallery, on the one hand, and a studio wing of practicing emerging artists, on the other. I was curious to imagine how the organization could balance investing in both the production and the display of contemporary art in equal measure, since—within most cultural institutions—that balance is just so heavily weighted to the latter. And for a modular organization designed to benefit from the fluidity of its architecture—I'm nodding at you here, Deborah—I really questioned whether or not bearing the weight of accumulation that comes with a collection was a strategic move in the right direction. That's why I'm really excited by Wilson's analysis of the mobile museum, or the Underground Museum in LA, for example—these museum alternatives that stay light and nimble by shedding the bureaucracy of operating a culture palace like the MET!

MG: nico, the Underground Museum is a fantastic example, and they do have a relationship with the Museum of Contemporary Art, Los Angeles. But they're in a different part of LA, intent on serving a local community that's Black, Brown, and Asian.

NW: That's right, and MOCA surely visited and immediately saw the value of partnering with such an abundant community resource. However, yet again, I see artists—in this case UM founders Noah and Karon Davis—as the innovators driving the change in how and where mainstream museums operate, and MOCA as a beneficiary of that work.

So if what we're ultimately discussing is a redesign of the museum space—and reimagining of the social and spatial relationships that comprise it—what is the essential DNA that must remain for it to still be considered a *museum*? Perhaps now would also be a great time to discuss the expansion of museum practices into the public sphere.

MG: Well, I think it's also why I'm interested in thinking about the museum as a space of abolition. Before COVID-19 and the current social revolution, we would still be talking about the museum as a place to try and make more diverse or inclusive. Now, it seems to me, the question is, *Diverse from whom or from what?* Or, *Inclusive of whom?* So somehow there's still a kind of othering that's happening there. Abolish the word "museum," and abolish the typology; then maybe it can become a space of abolition, and we can discontinue the othering.

DB: What I think is interesting about your question about public space, and Mario's observation about getting rid of the museum, is I think we should worry right now about public space actually becoming *more* like the museum. Which is to say that it's a surveilled space. We want to imagine that we didn't have to pay admission or identify ourselves—however, we were only allowed to be there by virtue of it being surveilled public space. I would certainly like to say that the museum understands it *should* be public space, meaning that anybody can go in and out whenever they want and not feel either threatened or intimidated or unwelcome. I think what we're experiencing now is the downside of the positive demands for change, and now public space itself is becoming a place to which you need access. You need identification, you will be documented as being there, you will be controlled in the way you can be there, and I think we need to be very wary of our public spaces becoming *museumized*.

MJ: The control test would be to design a museum that resembles a community center or what we used to think of as "public space." I think art school is a very nice kind of community center where there are things to do and few barriers to participation and use. I think art school quite literally, of course, is a very exclusive phenomenon, but at its best its structures offer clues to how institutions may grant permission to use experimentation and participation: that which the campus communities called "engagement." We're currently working on two projects where there is an explicit requirement that we disrupt what Mario identified as the commodification of identity or a regime that reifies the dichotomy of otherness.

In one, Princeton has asked us to design buildings that cease to send the messages that are otherwise encoded on campus. They came to us because I think we could do that art school talk and explain the benefit of architecture that holds back a little bit but is nonetheless visible (which are the two ingredients present at NXTHVN). Princeton hopes the project will drive belonging in advancing their goals and disrupt the predominant iconography and symbolism found elsewhere on campus. This project is not a museum (the project is to design residential colleges), but I think the way these colleges will operate resembles the museum-as-a-community-center.

So, our "museum as medium" is a site of renewal and continuous production. I think we will then draw on that experience and use those same words. I'm intrigued by that discovery I made today about the museum as community center. Maybe we won't even call it that. . . . Deborah, I think that becomes a place free of surveillance, or the kind of museum that, in its best manifestation, would be public space, which obviously is that thing that's most hotly contested right now.

NW: Unfortunately, I think people have come to expect museums to control and mediate their engagement with art, regardless of the precise context. Our agency and autonomy as curious subjects are repeatedly denied (i.e., don't touch, don't stand too close, don't photograph, etc.), and museums strive to impart knowledge that's actually ours to create! We're often, through didactics, beaten over the head with the prescribed value of art that leaves little space for our individualized interpretation. What worries me most is that, more and more, public art is now arriving in public space with all these same cues that disrupt natural instincts and processes of observational learning. What would it mean to just pare all of that back and trust people to engage art on their own terms? And what does the future of public art in the built environment look like, in a culture hellbent on controlling the narrative?

MJ: Here's a naïve question. Are there museums that do not attempt to tell you what you're looking at? No labels, no show titles?

NW: I mean, I tried it once and it didn't go so well.

MJ: Who opposed the idea?

NW: Honestly? Everyone! Particularly the departments that wanted the value of the project to accrue back to the institution, or—in some cases—even them as individuals. Now, mind you, some fears were super valid—I understand how, without branding, there *could* be a missed opportunity to forge an intimate connection with a passerby that could blossom into a future, lifelong engagement. However, I tend to place my trust in people to do the hard work of making meaning, bridging knowledge gaps, and connecting to the places and people that matter to them.

MG: I also wonder if we can think about art that works across media and eradicate the emphasis on art as objects? Or art as a thing? And that might even become a model for thinking about art in the everyday, in terms of how it goes in public space, if there was a way of dematerializing the enclosure around this art and this public space. But what if they could be one and the same? Art gives us clues about how we might live or how we might engage public space. I do think that there is now a fear of the museumization of public space, and we can see that in New York City and Manhattan with these Plazas along Broadway. What I find interesting is that, over the last few weeks of protest, there has been some surveillance, but protestors also have strategies around this surveillance. They start off on one route, but then they split up. I was in a march this weekend which split into like two or three different directions and then merged again. I was like, "Oh, what just happened here?" I think maybe there are some strategies for resisting that museumization.

MJ: I asked my children why everyone wears the same clothing in marches, and they were like, "So that no one stands out!"

DB: What we're discussing touches on a number of issues, namely, the monetary value of a work of art. I think some of the traditional museums that we've been analyzing also treat the work of art like a diamond—it's either valuable because of its materials or it's valuable because of its age or it's valuable because of who made it. Like, Picasso made this, or Goya made that. As we think about the space in which we view these objects, how do we separate out the monetary value of something from its other values, its values of communication, for example? This film that you're describing, Mario, that could be shown around the world to everybody at the same time is the opposite of going to see the *Mona Lisa*. The *Mona Lisa* might be one of the most valuable pieces of art in the world if you have to put a dollar value on it, right? You can't put a dollar value on it. I guess I'm asking us as architects, where in the story that the building or the nonbuilding tells does it address dollar value?

MJ: You would love a museum where the question was never raised somehow, where the public stays floating in and out and you were not even aware of the threshold moment, and there was no moment of transition from museum to public space and back again, or vice versa. As a kid in the museum, I always looked at the weird little screws that were behind the painting and thought, *How did they get those there? That must be a very valuable painting that it got screwed to the wall.* Somehow, if a museum didn't have any of that and could deny the difference between those objects that were especially valued and those that were not, I think that would be a more interesting and slippery public space, but that would be to say that going to the museum is not about seeing objects of incredible scarcity or value, and maybe that's a different kind of value. Are we trying to get rid of them?

DB: I don't know. I'm just asking the question. I think, because particularly in the late 20th, early 21st century, you're seeing maybe it's always been like this. It's just more visibly ugly that high-end clothing brands have exhibitions in museums or museum trustees pay for an exhibition and then collect the work of that artist and the exhibition has increased the value of their work. I think there's a lot of complicated territory here. I guess I'm asking, in Mario's abolitionist, antimuseum, is there also a getting away from this giant lockbox that protects the things that you can't be trusted with? How do we get away from saying that through the building?

MG: Well, I do think that these objects in and of themselves have not assigned their own value. It's the institution which somehow constructs the value around the *Mona Lisa* or around the *Water Lilies* or what have you, and that is at the service of the prestige of the institution, that is at the service of value creation for the institution in that it has holdings. I think practically, the placement of the thing in the museum is a part of how that value is constructed. So not only that it has a vitrine around it, but that the *Mona Lisa* is located here, and you have to go there to see it and that only so many people can get up close to it. That's all a part of that construction of value, and the architectural design is a factor in that construction and the making of such of rarefied settings. Well, that was at the old MoMA.

DB: It still has a ta-da moment at the new MoMA.

MG: Yeah. It's a ta-da or what have you, which is all about that construction of the value, and the architectural details such as lighting. So maybe in terms of Deborah's question, it has to do with how we think about viewership. How we think about spectatorship is a little bit different than how we think about the relationship between the body and the thing in that space and how one sees the thing. Maybe there are other ways of seeing and understanding.

NW: OK, my turn for a naïve question—when you hand over a museum design to a client, do you also hand over recommendations for how to operationalize it? Is there a world where you can say, *Here's this design; however, in no way is X, Y, or Z going to happen that reifies this type of object in this way?* My question comes from a desire to understand how much of what Mario described can be purposefully designed, and how much is left up to the interpretation of the institution.

MJ: The architect embarks on the project with either a "program" provided by the client or after the development of a program with the client that articulates both spatial objectives and operational ones. The building is designed and then is set afloat into the future. One often discovers later that the success of that project depends very much on how you did or did not bind it to that moment in time, because surely the operations, and all those things that might happen there, change faster than you expected. Our most successful projects are those where we're told later, *We were able to evolve, and so much changed and happened in the interim.* This both obliges us to think of the myriad ways in which things will happen in the space or the building, and to operationalize it in our head on day one, but also to let go of it and let it thrive and evolve. Somehow that is related to public space or the founding of community, which is to say the best architect allows community to be born in the building.

MG: I think it depends on the clients. For the last two decades since the Guggenheim Bilbao, all museum clients wanted an iconic building, but what that really meant was an iconic-looking object with gallery spaces that were as neutral as possible. The architect didn't have any hand in curating where anything went but just designed a blank space or blank cube for the temporary exhibitions here or for these permanent exhibitions there. In terms of the specificity in which the architect was involved with the curatorial strategies, I can think of Castelvecchio by Carlos Scarpa, in which he designed every detail for how every artifact would be presented (but it's a much smaller institution), or Museo Canova, which is a very small building, again, where he had a hand in the placement of every piece. But that way of designing . . . that ship has long sailed. Maybe at MoMA the architects were able to get a little bit of agency, but I don't know how much they were given in terms of programming the relationship of objects.

DB: I wonder if part of the undoing of *museum*—and at least getting the big *M* down to a little *m* and maybe then the whole word goes away—is to shrink the massiveness of the undertaking because in a way that might also take away the massiveness of the assumed authority, such as the MET. I don't mean to keep picking on the MET; it's a place of joy some days, but it assumes a global authority about all it has. But when you talk about a small museum of ceramics or a small museum of sculpture that's outside and with a few vantage points, I think the relationship between the viewer and the art, and the institution is much more in balance.

NW: Yes—I couldn't agree more. However, to decenter that authority and recalibrate the relationship between museums and their communities, museums across the board would need to (1) acknowledge that the disconnect people are experiencing is real and (2) own their role in producing and maintaining that distance for their own gain.

MG: Well, there've been lots of these statements of solidarity over the last few weeks coming from art institutions, museums, and galleries. I wonder what happens when the rubber hits the road, so to speak. What happens when the sentiment of *Let's put out a statement to look or sound good* subsides? As I've been speaking with colleagues, artists, and creatives, we all agree that there's no going back to normal after this. The disparities have been laid bare. Then what does that mean for the museum? What does that mean for these institutions? There should be no going back to normal, which is why I also raised the question of thinking about the museum as a space of abolition, not just as a space of more diversity or more inclusion but somehow that it actually has to be undone—the whole concept has to be liberated.

OUTRO

I'm struck by the fact that three architects—who presumably sustain a living designing and constructing physical spaces—spent a great deal of our conversation advocating for the dematerialization of the museum and its reconfiguration as an abolitionist space. They, through a belief in the transformative power of their chosen medium, advocated for architecture to work harder and in some cases toward its own obsolescence. And we concluded our discussion with a direct call to action—for architecture to confront its responsibility to undo the designed hierarchies and inequities of museums. In imagining what Berke described as an *undoing of museum*, I was curious what a first step might look like and what role artists might play in that process, given Arthur Jafa's impact on Gooden's approach to designing a museum today.

Ruffneck Constructivists

In 2014, the Institute of Contemporary Art at the University of Pennsylvania launched an exhibition entitled *Ruffneck Constructivists*, guest curated by artist Kara Walker. The exhibition "focuse[d] on structure and space as it is made and remade by policed bodies and identities" and, in Walker's words, "return[ed] a viewer to the questions of modernism, architecture, urbanism and the resistant bodies who reshape it."[5] Featuring Pope.L, Dineo Seshee Bopape, Kendell Geers, Arthur Jafa, Jennie C. Jones, Kahlil Joseph, Deana Lawson, Rodney Mc-Millian, Tim Portlock, Lior Shvil, Szymon Tomsia, and Kara Walker, *Ruffneck Constructivists* was far more than a contemporary art exhibition. It was a stick of dynamite implanted within the hegemonic structure of the museum to implode it from within. It, too, was an entire *world*, designed by artists—"defiant shapers of environments"—who built themselves into it "one assault at a time."[6]

From Deana Lawson's repurposed family portraits—staged in front of an indoor mural of a seaside getaway, that document her cousin Jazmin's visits to see her boyfriend Erik at the Mohawk Correctional Facility—to Arthur Jafa and Malik Sayeed's short film, *Deshotten 1.0*, that lyrically depicts a drive-by shooting from the perspective of those involved rather than surveillance footage, the exhibiting artists inhabit institutionalized space on their own terms. They, too, through depicting Black life unfiltered by the white gaze, disrupt the museum's understood orientation of margin and center, revealing that space, like race, is a social construct that can be dismantled and built anew.

In his catalogue essay for the exhibition, architect Craig L. Wilkins—like Gooden, Berke, and Jones in our roundtable—liberates architecture from its historical prescriptions, stating, "The principal medium of our work as artists might surprise you. It is not so much the visible object—the museum, the concert hall, the gallery, or library, as stunning as that may be—but the not so visible, the space within. We shape space. We mold it, bend it to some purpose—many of my colleagues might argue a higher purpose. Space is the essential material of our profession; sculpting it is what we do."[7] Here, Wilkins delivers us back to a central thesis of this chapter—that space is a medium that, like all others, must be sculpted to bring form into alignment with function. In Wilkins's refusal of the authority of the *visible object*, he frees us to imagine all the ways a museum might then exist, unburdened by its own objecthood. As we move on to chapter 3 and deepen our investigation of public spaces *beyond* the museum, let's carry this orientation toward their interstitial and invisible social spaces with us.

NOTES

1. Wilkins, Craig L. "Space—Place." In *The Aesthetics of Equity: Notes on Race, Space, Architecture, and Music*, 7. Minneapolis: University of Minnesota Press, 2007.

2. Barkan, Leonard. *Unearthing the Past: Archaeology and Aesthetics in the Making of Renaissance Culture*. New Haven, CT: Yale University Press, 2001.

3. Houston, Kerr. "How Mining the Museum Changed the Art World." BmoreArt, May 3, 2017, https://bmoreart.com/2017/05/how-mining-the-museum-changed-the -art-world.html.

4. Allen, Stan. "Field Conditions (1999)." In *Constructing a New Agenda: Architectural Theory 1993–2009*, edited by A. Krista Sykes, 130. New York: Princeton Architectural Press, 2010.

5. McClister, Nell. "*Ruffneck Constructivists.*" Institute of Contemporary Art, May 2014, https://icaphila.org/exhibitions/ruffneck-constructivists.

6. Walker, Kara Elizabeth. "Ruffneck Constructivism." In *Ruffneck Constructivists*, by Kara Elizabeth Walker and Craig L. Wilkins. Philadelphia: Institute of Contemporary Art, University of Pennsylvania, 2014.

7. Wilkins, Craig L. "Cuirass Architecture." In Walker and Wilkins, *Ruffneck Constructivists*, p. 18.

MUSEUM AS CITIZEN

How to Engage the Commons and Build a Public Art Pedagogy

INTRO

> *So, ours is primarily a cultural crisis—rather than an eco-*
> *nomic or environmental one—resulting in the inability of*
> *institutions to question their ways of thinking, or the rigidity of*
> *their protocols and silos. It is within this radical context that we*
> *must question the role of art and humanities and their contin-*
> *gent cultural institutions of pedagogy, production, display, and*
> *distribution. A more functional relationship between art and*
> *the everyday is urgently needed, through which artists can act*
> *as interlocutors across this polarized territory, intervening in*
> *the debate itself and mediating new forms of acting and living.*[1]
>
> —Teddy Cruz

In the previous chapter, architects Deborah Berke, Mario Gooden, and Maitland Jones empowered us to liberate museums' forms and functions from
the space of enclosure. This act of radical imagination produces a new set of
considerations that we will now explore: As a free entity, where else might the
museum's work live and thrive? How do its essential building blocks map onto
a more fluid environment? What happens to institutional hierarchies when
dispersed into the commons? And how might the museum best embody an
engaged citizen, of both its local community and the global cultural ecosystem?

Teddy Cruz, professor of public culture and urbanism at the University of
California, San Diego, offers his insights in *Living as Form: Socially Engaged*

Art from 1991–2011, a volume edited by Nato Thompson and published by public art pioneers, Creative Time. He proposes that, for cultural institutions to broker healthier relationships between *art and the everyday*, they must first loose the shackles on their own capacity to innovate, shedding *the rigidity of their protocols and silos*. In other words, to actively participate in a more inclusive cultural citizenship beyond their walls, museums must first cultivate a culture of participation, collaboration, and belonging within them.

inHarlem

Between 2014 and 2019, I served as co-lead of the Studio Museum's inHarlem initiative, "a dynamic set of collaborative programs" produced in partnership with "a variety of partner and satellite locations in Harlem."[2] From public art exhibitions in historic Harlem parks, libraries, and schools to public programs presented in partnership with local grassroots organizations and social service providers, inHarlem became an important vehicle for the museum to reimagine its local citizenship.

In preparing for this deeply cooperative work in the public realm, the inHarlem working group first set about transforming how collaboration took place *within* the museum. Comprised of leaders from the curatorial, education, public programs, communications, operations, director's, and development departments, our working group met weekly to develop a vision and strategy for hyperlocal projects, map the existing and potential partnerships vital to their success, brainstorm the opportunities and challenges of adapting our work from within the museum to contexts beyond it, and articulate a shared vocabulary and budget for how the museum would approach these priorities as a unified force.

Because this was the first initiative of its kind at the Studio Museum—and because the precedents for museums sustaining a full program while undergoing total structural transformation were few—we had a lot to learn. While museum departments collaborating on large-scale projects is certainly not new, what sets this initiative apart is its decentering of an exhibitions-driven program to make space for rich, interdepartmental collaboration on the *full* breadth of the museum's work. Similarly, this enabled us to, at times, decenter our own expertise as a museum altogether and look to our partners and neighbors for best practices in cultural production already at play in public spaces throughout the neighborhood. Because inHarlem is an evolving, cooperative project—and because the above is my biased characterization of it as someone involved in its inception—I would encourage you to track its evolution, as it has certainly taken on new and different meanings since my involvement.

The Community Advisory Network

In support of inHarlem, my team launched the museum's Community Advisory Network (CAN), a group of roughly 20 individuals who either lived or worked in Harlem. These included local artists, business owners, cultural leaders, and government officials, to name only a few stakeholder groups constituting our diverse cohort. Our covenant was simple: to bring more transparency to our work, inviting collaboration from our neighbors on key initiatives and feedback on how to design a more locally relevant program.

In our quarterly convenings, space was held for the participation of museum staff across all departments and at all levels of leadership. This helped to generate internal buy-in and collapse the distance between the feedback we received from CAN and those who might implement it. Some meetings began with a museum presentation on proposed or in-progress projects, where staff invited comments, questions, critique, and feedback. Others began by inviting advisors to state a community challenge and brainstorm solutions for addressing it, leaning on the cohort's diverse expertise and the museum's resources wherever possible. Regardless of the point of origin, our discussions were candid, impassioned, and action oriented. I offer this final and abbreviated case study of my work at the Studio Museum as a point of entry to this chapter's roundtable—both inHarlem and CAN are cited in our discussion about how to build a public art pedagogy.

While not all museums can or should develop a public art program, those with a community-vetted vision for broader access to—and deeper engagement with—art beyond their walls might benefit from considering such an endeavor. In the roundtable that follows, I invited four practitioners in public art to build vocabulary that can support museums in making this determination and nuancing their understanding of best practices for how art enters the public realm. Together, Eric Guy Booker of the Studio Museum in Harlem, artist Maren Hassinger, Kendal Henry of the NYC Department of Cultural Affairs, Diya Vij of Creative Time, and I build a pedagogy for public art practice; demystify the policy and procedure surrounding it; name key players in the process, including artists, communities, museums, and government officials; and riff on how museums can better participate in, and learn from, the politics of public space.

ROUNDTABLE

ERIC GUY BOOKER is a curator and writer. His work makes space for less visible artists and for narratives that challenge dominant histories. Booker is currently the assistant curator and exhibition coordinator at the Studio Museum in Harlem, where he works on a range of exhibitions, performances, and site-specific installations. Booker is currently at work on his first book about the Smokehouse Associates mural collective, for which he is the recipient of a 2019 Graham Foundation grant.

MAREN HASSINGER lives and works in New York. She received her BA from Bennington College and her MFA in fiber structure from the University of California, Los Angeles. She has exhibited widely in both the United States and abroad with recent public installations: *Monument*, in Washington, DC, through the Smithsonian's American Women's History Initiative; and *Nature, Sweet Nature*, at the Aspen Art Museum, slated to travel to the Oklahoma Contemporary, Oklahoma City.

KENDAL HENRY is an artist and curator who lives in New York City and has specialized in the field of public art for over 30 years. He illustrates that public art can be used as a tool for social engagement, civic pride, and economic development through the projects and programs he's initiated in the US and internationally. He's currently the director of NYC's Department of Cultural Affairs Percent for Art program and an adjunct professor at New York University's Steinhardt School of Culture, Education and Human Development.

DIYA VIJ is the associate curator at Creative Time, who critically investigates the evolving role of public art in politics and civic life. Over the past decade, she has held programming, curatorial, and communications positions at the High Line, the New York City Department of Cultural Affairs, and the Queens Museum. As the associate curator of public programs at the High Line, she organized dozens of live events and performances with artists, activists, practitioners, and healers. She received her MA in art history from Hunter College in 2015 and her BA from Bard College in 2008.

The following discussion took place between Eric Guy Booker, Maren Hassinger, Kendal Henry, Diya Vij, and nico wheadon via Zoom on June 30, 2020.

nico wheadon: Maren, you are one of the first artists I learned of who was using the public sphere as a laboratory for both artistic experimentation and social commentary. In particular, I'm thinking of your 1982 performance *Pink Trash*, which interrogates the intersections of public space, human use, and ethical citizenship. Eric, I had the honor of serving as your colleague at the Studio Museum in Harlem, where you helped to organize Maren's public art exhibition, *Monuments*, in Marcus Garvey Park in 2018. I was so impressed by the depth of the questions you were asking to ensure alignment between the Museum's objectives with the project, and its hyperlocal impact and relevance.

A few years earlier in 2016, I participated in a public art walking tour of Harlem organized by the NYC Department of Cultural Affairs that you led, Kendal, where we were joined by artists Jorge Luis Rodriguez and Gabriel Koren, who discussed their public artworks in situ. I was so struck by the way your guidance through a once familiar space yielded altogether new insights and observations. And Diya, around that time, you invited me to serve as a juror for the NYC Department of Cultural Affairs Public Artists in Residence program, where we selected Rachel Barnard, Onyedika Chuke, Ebony Noelle Golden, and Tatyana Fazlalizadeh to be in residence across four different city departments. We have since worked on any number of programs together, and I have always admired your dual commitment to artists and communities in manifesting these contemporary art projects in public space. Let's start with some simple introductions.

Kendal Henry: I'm an artist and curator. I run the Percent for Art program at the NYC Department of Cultural Affairs, where we commission the permanent public art for all city properties. I also work with other city agencies on temporary art, like the Department of Transportation, Times Square, Madison Square Park, etc.

Eric Booker: I'm the assistant curator and exhibition coordinator at the Studio Museum in Harlem, where I work on a variety of exhibitions, performances, and site-specific installations. For the past four years I've been deeply involved in the museum's inHarlem project, which organizes public art projects at a variety of partner and satellite locations in Harlem, including the four historic Harlem parks and libraries throughout the neighborhood. I have worked closely with you, nico, and of course with you, Maren, on your public art exhibition *Monuments*, which we produced in Marcus Garvey Park in 2018.

Maren Hassinger: I'm a visual artist working primarily in sculpture but also performance and video. I began my career in New York City in 1980 when I was an artist in residence at the Studio Museum in Harlem. My works are connected to nature, to people's connections to nature and each other, and to culture in general, but to New York City in particular. I worked with Eric on *Monuments*, who was wonderful in organizing this project that I thought was going to be small but turned out to be expansive!

Diya Vij: I was recently associate curator of public programs at the High Line, where I was in charge of all live events, performances, festivals, etc. Before that, I worked at the Department of Cultural Affairs and launched a program called the Public Artists in Residence that embeds artists into city government to use their creative tools and their practice to advance policy or to think about how systems change can interact with art processes and practices. I worked closely with Kendal while at the Department of Cultural Affairs on several initiatives, that being one of them, reviewing and commissioning public monuments being another. I'm about to start a new job at Creative Time as associate curator.

NW: I think the tie that binds this group is a commitment to building "unmuseums," or museum-like platforms that exist beyond the confines of traditional museological structures and paradigms. So, first and foremost, thank you for the work you've done to enrich the public sphere—I believe that the case studies we'll discuss today exemplify what the future work of museums should look like as they strive toward accessibility and relevance.

Maren, . . . a pioneer and innovator in public art. I'm very honored to have you here to help ground us in the history of the practice. Over the years, we've seen you experiment with your personal and professional relationship to public space. In your opinion, what constitutes public space, who builds it, and who owns it?

MH: When I was doing *Monuments* in Marcus Garvey Park [figure 3.1], there was an alternative piece that I wanted to make. During my research, I went up to one of the guys who was a denizen of the park, so to speak, and said, "I'm thinking of doing these banners that will hang off of polls, post and trees. They will have photographs of all the people who use the park!" And he looked at me and he said, "Photographs? No, no photographs!"

And then I realized in a snap, *Oh, he's a drug dealer, he doesn't wanna be photographed.* I also realized that might be true of a third of the park and that I didn't know *anything* about the people who use it! So we scratched that idea, since I'd never thought of that perspective and wanted to respect it.

And as far as who owns the park—the people who use the park own the park. While we *all* pay the taxes to support it, it really belongs to the people who use it.

EB: Maren, I wonder if you could talk about that decision-making process a little more and how people were brought into the making of the work. You described the initial proposal—which progressed, morphed, and ultimately changed into something that was abstract, not figurative. I think the abstract quality of your work has an open-ended, natural element to it that allows ample space for the viewer to own their experience of the art and the space it creates. Your initial proposal brings to mind another historic project: John Ahearn's sculpture casts of residents in the Bronx, which received a mixed reception in that community.

MH: Yeah, I think my work has an abstract quality, but it's always based on something that *is*. . . . And so, when I decided to make sculptures out of branches collected from all over the park—a familiar material native to the park—I was trying to draw attention to the place in which the branches would exist and the shape that they would take in that new existence. I don't know whether people paid attention to that or not, but it certainly was something that inspired me. I made something round for a round space, and a little mountain below a rocky outcropping above it. The works mirrored their surroundings.

Without the volunteers, the project would have never been completed. It was really labor-intensive, and the volunteers actually wanted to be part of the process, many of them being members of the Studio Museum's extended family. People were relaxed and were doing something with their hands and bodies that gave them a chance to engage in conversation.

Figure 3.1. Maren Hassinger: *Monuments* (installation view), 2019. Marcus Garvey Park, New York, New York, June 16, 2018–June 10, 2019. Photo by Adam Reich, courtesy The Studio Museum in Harlem.

KH: How much interaction did you have with people in the park in terms of developing the second proposal, and getting their opinions on who owned the park?

MH: Not as much as I'd hoped for. The one place where I had some conversation, and at times I thought too much conversation, was with the guys who played chess there every day. I built a piece next to them that was a cube with a grid that mirrored their table. And their comment was, "You should have made a sculpture of us playing chess here!" Most people think of figures when they think of a public sculpture, but unfortunately for him, I'm not a figurative artist!

KH: One of the things that I have encountered a lot in doing public art is that, regardless of whether the work is figurative or abstract, you have to involve the public in some way. Right, that's the deal—you have to either make it with the public or consult with them and channel what you learn to create something. But a lot of times, what happens is that you do all that is right, and then you put something out there, and it's all wrong.

So, when creating public art, the holy grail is to find an artist in and of the community, to involve the community, and to craft work that's about the community. And, because of that, it's a great work of art in the end—it's up to the standards of the museum and the artist's own work. However, it seems that a lot happens throughout that process! Maren, you shared perfect examples of this. So yeah, the question is, Whose space really is it? And who do you listen to in creating the work?

And so, I'm gonna go back to the John Ahearn piece, for example, because I was actually there for that. That space belonged to those people who were represented in the artwork—they saw that as their space, their community, their neighborhood, and *they* determined the three people that were going to be represented. It was all theirs. And even at the police station, and despite what you read, the people who created it were like, *Yeah, this is what we want.* But when the work was actually installed, outsiders were like, *Wait a minute, wait a minute, wait a minute. Why are these people here?* It raised questions about representational differences between "the Bronx" and that particular community.

I still have difficulty determining how one determines whose space it *really* is. Is it a geographical understanding? Does it belong to the entire city? And how do we enforce whatever definition of whose space it is that we put forward?

MH: Well, those are really legitimate questions in the public sphere. Those are absolutely *the* questions.

DV: I think it's important to go dig a little deeper into "the public sphere." Because I think that a certain thing happens when the government is the commissioning body and it's a "public" public space, like taxpayer-funded public space, versus when a nonprofit arts organization is the commissioning body in a public space or a privately owned outdoor space. I think that kind of structure behind how artwork even enters a space and what that space is has so much to do with the process that's employed and the public's reaction to it.

Working for the government, thinking through public art, we just hit controversy after controversy because of this question[:] . . . *Who owns the space?* Who does it belong to? How can you ever define one community when there are hundreds of thousands of people that live near this one park and have very different experiences? There is a map of power that enshrouds those spaces.

For example, the High Line has a really robust public art program, but those kinds of questions are not really at play for a lot of reasons because it is a publicly owned, privately operated park. It sits above street level, so there's already a barrier to your everyday experience of that space, and it's just understood that it's basically a museum outside. It's not like Marcus Garvey Park or the John Ahearn bronzes outside of the police precinct in the Bronx. It's a really separate thing with its own sense of ownership. And I think that happens a lot.

People are acutely aware of these structures of ownership, maybe because it's legible through the function or architecture of a space. People really understand those invisible structures that go into the process by which art comes to public space, but I find it to be a very different process, in terms of public input and reaction, when it's government-run and on government land.

EB: I appreciate these distinctions, Diya, and it brings up two things for me. One is the invisible structures that bring art into public space, and two is how that space is maintained and what that implies in terms of who might be welcome or not. That is definitely something that's visible in the landscaping and the manicured environment of the

High Line and also to an extent in Marcus Garvey Park. The latter also exists in a very particular space that's embedded within the history of Harlem. What we've learned as we've worked across the four historic Harlem parks is that each has varying levels of governance. Marcus Garvey has its own governance body called the Marcus Garvey Park Alliance. While the museum attempted to do a lot of legwork in understanding the landscape and the social structure of the park before we ever *entered* this space, we did rely heavily on the knowledge and advocacy of the Alliance. They're the ones that are working there day in and day out, having volunteers take care of the park, and really understanding which spaces are used and how.

So at the advent of Maren's project, we walked through the park with the Alliance and really talked about this use. Like, *OK, this is where baseball happens, and this is where they retire after the baseball game, so you don't want to put a sculpture in the middle of their resting space.* We also learned that Marcus Garvey Park is one of the most well-served parks in the neighborhood. So that's why, over the arc of inHarlem, we've made a point to not just work in one place but rather spread our attention and efforts across the parks and libraries to engage with various communities in the neighborhood.

MH: Diya, I remember seeing artists' works around the High Line and thinking that they were all really prominently known artists and that, in many cases, the pieces that were shown were not specific to the site—they were pieces that had been made for museums that came from that installation and moved to the High Line for a short period of time. I believe that who something is made for, how long it remains there, and who's in support of it really make a difference in what the thing actually *is*.

DV: That's such an interesting point about the temporality of it. Having an understanding that the works change over makes people a little less attached to ownership as control over the space or the artworks that go in it.

KH: When we talk to artists, we tend to separate the public artwork into two categories, and that's not to say that one is better than the other. We call one "art in public place," which is exactly what you just described—art that is just placed there because it needs a home. And there's nothing wrong with that because, again, most people don't go to galleries or museums, so just bringing it out into the light is fantastic.

And then we have another definition for "public art," which is infused with site specificity. It defines works that are created for a particular audience, environment, or space. So going back to your questions, nico, it's like, How do you put a definition to it? We resolve it by acknowledging these two separate forms.

NW: Kendal, I'm intrigued by the fact that you prefaced your definitions by saying that there's not a negative connotation in how you draw those distinctions between *public art* and *art in public place*. I imagine there is, however, a distinction between how value operates in these two contexts—or that the default is to assign a monetary value to art in public place and a cultural value to public art. Is that true and, if so, can you tease that out for us a bit?

KH: It's all public art when we talk about it among ourselves internally, however, these distinctions are mostly used with people outside the organization. We establish these definitions alongside others like *community* and *site-specificity*. Interestingly enough, we do think about monetary value when we describe the two. So let's stick with well-established artists, for example. To purchase an existing sculpture by Kehinde Wiley and put it in public place is *much* more expensive than commissioning his work for that same space. This is because the approach, the process, the way of thinking about the work tends to be very different. And so an artist's studio work is more expensive than a commissioned work. For a commissioned work, the breakdown is usually 20 percent for the artist's fee and the rest goes toward actually making the physical object. To purchase that same work is 100 percent, split between the artist and their gallery.

When it comes to what the work means to the community, I place a higher value on public art as we define it, versus art in public place. This is because it responds to the audience and really draws valuable context from the site. Whereas if you've just taken something that you created for a museum show and pop it out in the public sphere, a lot of that process is not integral to the piece itself.

MH: That difference is very, very important, because actually the art may not even be what's done when you're finished working with the public. Maybe the real art is the getting together.

KH: And I'm glad you say that, Maren . . . we don't call it "art" anymore, we call it the "artifact of the art." So you're right—the sculptures are the artifacts of community coming together. That's the real art.

DV: This idea was actually the impetus for launching the Public Artist in Residence program at the NYC Department of Cultural Affairs, in which we invited artists to support the process of gathering, of being together, of creating situations that could inform or push policy.

EB: This brings me back to the temporality of public art. The art in public space category follows a legacy of a particular type of sculpture or monument that permanently inhabits a space. And we're seeing now that those things degrade in cultural value over time. For the inHarlem parks projects, we collaborated with the New York City Parks Department. NYC Parks stipulates that nothing can be installed in a public space for more than one year. While we would've loved to consider something beyond this period, I think that requirement relates specifically to this conversation. If the work is just left there for years and years at a time, perhaps that starts to work against it. This is very much the case with Maren's project, since the work was made out of organic material that would degrade over time. So I feel as though temporality and value have an intrinsic relationship here.

DV: That makes me think of Kenseth Armstead's recent piece, *Washington 20/20/20*, in Union Square, in which he made this fence around the statue of George Washington of tar, feather and some other materials. And what he explained to Kendal and I, when we went to see it, was that originally the fence was supposed to be opaque and would cover the statue of George Washington. The Parks Department said that he could do that but then could only leave it up for a week or two. However, the more translucent he made the fence, the longer he was permitted to keep it up, which was really interesting. So at the end of it, it was a fence you could see through that mildly obstructed the statue so that he could have it up for several months instead of two weeks. In this particular situation, the prescribed value was so one-to-one, and its protection revealed a lot about how the Parks Department considers these figurative sculptures.

KH: I think that, as a result of all these rules and regulations, artists are allowed to really speak to the contemporary issues that are affecting us today. Because they know their work won't last in the public sphere forever, artists can be more flexible with their materials and can speak to this moment in a more visceral way. When you put things in public, of course, then you have more interaction, which makes controversy more likely. And then, when the controversy happens, you can respond with, *It's gonna be gone in a month. No big deal!* So I think it gives artists better tools, or more flexibility in the tools that they use, to create these kinds of works, which is I think is a plus.

And, just as a side note—the one-year thing is somewhat arbitrary. If a project extends beyond the year, then the project just has to go through an extra review process that nobody really wants to do, but it's possible.

NW: Your knowledge and transparency around the public art process is so valuable, Kendal. I'm curious to know how much of the bureaucratic process that you've shared is laid bare for the public. I'm thinking back to Simone Leigh's imbas as the first inHarlem project in Marcus Garvey Park [figure 3.2], and that being a real learning moment for the Studio Museum. In fact, I think it actually paved the way for your project, Maren, to take place in a much more participatory, transparent, and engaged way.

Prior to that, I don't think we totally understood what removing those imbas would mean to the public, who began to exercise real ownership over them. From the Community Advisory Network, we learned that to have those taken away without clear communication around the timeline and deinstallation processes was a real shock to some in the community. Eric, I'm wondering if you can discuss what you and the rest of the curatorial team learned through this experience, and how you translated these lessons into a different approach as you entered into *Monuments* with Maren.

EB: Simone's project was our first foray into the public sphere, and it was also the artist's first public art commission. Entitled *A particularly elaborate imba yokubikira, or kitchen house, stands locked up while its owners live in diaspora* (2016), the project allowed Simone to expand her sculptural practice, which later led to her monumental commission for the High Line and beyond. The work was wildly successful in Marcus Garvey Park because the artist thought deeply about the unique cultural landscape in which her work was being situated. The project spoke to the complicated multiplicity of the African diaspora. People would walk by and immediately identify with the iconography she was referencing in the material and form of the work.

Figure 3.2. Simone Leigh: *A particularly elaborate imba yokubikira, or kitchen house, stands locked up while its owners live in diaspora* (installation view), 2016. Marcus Garvey Park, New York, New York, August 25, 2016–July 25, 2017. Photo by Adam Reich, courtesy The Studio Museum in Harlem.

While we were fabricating the imbas, two men from Burkina Faso happened to walk by. They immediately recognized that we were working on these structures that they knew from back home and they were like, *Oh yeah, we've done thatched roofs before.* Since we were quite unfamiliar with this process and having such a hard time constructing these roofs, we actually ended up hiring them to complete the work!

That was, of course, a dream scenario in terms of public art engaging the community. Another aspect of Simone's project was that, after we took down the work, people began to replicate it—the imbas began to crop up everywhere, like in a mosaic for the park's community library. It had these various afterlives in the park.

Like you said, nico, it helped us to learn from our work on *A particularly elaborate imba yokubikira* and carry it forward. That project was very much a conversation between the museum, the artist, and the Marcus Garvey Park Alliance. For *Monuments*, we built upon this so that we were working with the public in a more inclusive way. The community was invested in realizing the work from the beginning, physically and conceptually contributing to the success of the project.

KH: I would have loved to see both of those projects in another park! There are so many different communities, or pockets of communities, that would respond to those. Maren, where did the pieces from Marcus Garvey Park end up after the show came down?

MH: Back to nature, I guess. Well, actually, two went to deCordova Sculpture Park in Massachusetts. But by now, the original core of the work is probably gone, since it was made from degradable materials. Also, it's not as significant there, because it's not site-specific to that location as it was in Marcus Garvey Park.

NW: In an earlier roundtable, architect Deborah Berke introduced the concept of the *museumization* of public space—the banners, extended wall labels, and QR codes which are all, of course, the soft architectures that one would expect to encounter *inside* the museum. I'm wondering what the effects of the museumization of public space are on our natural practices of observation. Maren, in your opinion, what's good about extending museum practice into the public sphere, and what's dangerous about it?

MH: There is a big difference between art inside a museum and art outside on a meadow, or even on a wall that's outdoors. Certain people don't have a history of being inside of museums, but they do have a history of being in parks. As an artist, it's not that you're trying to appease everybody, but you kinda have to realize that some people are not going to go into a museum, even on a free day! They're gonna be uncomfortable inside with all those people pushing and shoving to see some Picasso, because that artwork doesn't mean anything to them on a personal level.

And it's not to say that doing art outdoors in a park is speaking down to somebody; it's just an entirely different language. Encountering art in museums is an entirely different experience that requires a certain intellectual leap. So I really think it's important to know where you are and who you're dealing with and that the work, as it is to be public, is a conversation between you and the people who are going to be seeing it. Acknowledging the communication differences among strangers is a huge responsibility and a huge step.

KH: I think the expectations are different. Diya, I'm remembering when we were discussing the problematic monuments across the city. A lot of that discussion included propositions like, *Why don't you put it in the building? Put it in the museum!* So the expectation was that, once it's in those four walls of the museum, artworks can be made acceptable that simply aren't in the public sphere. So it's an interesting case when museums are intentionally putting work outside for public consumption—what is the goal there and what is the expectation?

To respond to Maren, I'm ashamed to say that, until a couple of years ago, my own mother wasn't going to a museum! It was not for her. It was just not a place that she felt comfortable due to the intellectual barriers and lack of representation. So I think museums are beginning to try and speak to constituents that they want to see come to the museum by putting the work out in the public and having that dialogue as a bridge.

EB: With public art, people meet the art on their own terms as opposed to the terms that are set forth in a museum or a gallery space. I think that the Studio Museum's sensitivity to the culture of inclusion that permeates our staff, and our history of upholding an artist-centric mission, shapes how we as an institution interact with the public, both inside and outside the museum's walls. When we break down the hierarchy that exists around the production of knowledge, we're able to connect with people in a very real way.

NW: Is there a world where more reciprocity exists between museums and communities, and there is a genuine trust between the artist, the institution, and the public to produce that knowledge together?

MH: The museum would have to learn to trust in the idea that everything will work without so much language—to trust that the sculpture has its own language. They'd also have to trust in people's ability to see and learn from an artwork being built. That could go a long way. I think the museum is afraid that this form of communication is not going to exist without their intervention—that nobody will understand what they've done, and it will just be a waste of everybody's time. And that, by having this text here, people will understand. But maybe a better way of doing it is to have the artist come out and fix the piece once or twice a month while staging a conversation. Or maybe the actual piece is just these Saturday afternoon conversations. I think the conversation piece is much more powerful than signage. That's what this pandemic has exposed among other things—we're all very isolated and need to be together more and communicating more across the board.

DV: I totally agree. I feel like a flipside to your question, "How do museums trust the public enough not to overinterpret?" is, How are museums trustworthy in the first place? I think a lot of that contextual interference of the artwork is often around fears of how the public will receive it. Was this a waste . . . was this too controversial? It can also be about that text serving as justification for the work, and for the museum, being in that space in the first place. I think we see a lot of that, too, with controversial public monuments, where one of the first things people do is put up a plaque explaining what it is and why it's there, instead of having those dialogues and exchanges that really get to the root of what about the piece is so upsetting.

So I think those museum tools don't necessarily translate into the public space for so many reasons, and that's one of them. I think another is that a lot of people also see museums as part and parcel of the same lineage of some of these monuments. I think that's why it makes sense or feels right to send those controversial monuments *back* to museums to contextualize there.

NW: Diya, exactly! Also, I should admit there was a subtext to my question—I find that, oftentimes, the didactic framing of public art is a museum power grab to claim it, ensuring its assumed value accrues back to the institution that "created" it. The irony is that the museum only supported its creation. I would argue that, in fact, the *artist* created it in partnership with the museum, and others. I'm fascinated by how a mere step outside of traditional viewing paradigms exposes these assumptions about ownership and control.

EB: The "museumization" of public space reflects the museum trying to reconcile with the fact that it already exists within an economy that challenges many of the things we're talking about. So the purpose of wall labels is to educate the public in the gallery and then, by extension—or rather necessity—the museum's funders and other stakeholders.

That's the underlying economy of how museums are shaped and run. It is also one of the inherent problems with museums, which I think is why our work in the public space produces this productive tension. Despite the social drive of museums in this moment, and the attempt to meet that call for social justice and action, museums are still tethered to those who they must report to. At the Studio Museum, we are trying to place trust in the artists' voice to hold us accountable and to push us in ways that aren't necessarily familiar or comfortable.

MH: Yeah. Well, we all have responsibilities. Every part of the project has its responsibilities, and I realize that, in my work indoors, I'm doing all this work with people that's becoming more and more like a sewing bee. We're just all sitting there twisting things and having a conversation and letting it go wherever it goes, but we're together doing that. And that is tremendously satisfying. Really, it's wonderful just to have a conversation with people.

NW: Eric and Maren, I think you are hinting at something similar, which is, how do we harness the power of art to not only educate, but to also connect, communicate, and amplify preexisting conversations? Maren, do you remember the public program we did for *Monuments* across the street at the Harlem Library with Lowery Stokes Sims? That was one of the most well-attended programs my team ever produced at the Studio Museum. I have this video of you conducting over 100 visitors of all ages as they ripped newspaper at the same time; it sounded like we were making crazy, experimental noise music! For a brief moment, I think we all forgot that we were inside a *library*—a reified public space that, like a museum, is culturally coded to be silent and reverent. But there we were, librarians included, literally tearing shit up! I remember feeling a collective power in that moment, to set the terms for how we wanted to engage and reclaim a public space that we felt belonged to us.

So maybe this is a good segue to building a public art pedagogy. When I ask my students, "What is public art?" the first thing I hear is monuments or murals, despite the existence of a nuanced spectrum in between. Today, we've both defined and extended some terms for the practice, which is important because the more shared language we're able to develop, the more likely it is that a new generation of practitioners will find their way to the work. So how do we encourage more artists to consider working in the public sphere? How can communities play a more active role in determining the art that animates their public spaces?

MH: I think categorizing makes it difficult. As you were speaking, I imagined a bunch of people marching with Black Lives Matter banners in solidarity with several ideas, several political ideas, and that's kind of art too. A march or parade is choreographed movement, among like-people having like-ideas that they feel are somehow supportive of the entire community and that are leading us to a new understanding of our relationships with one another.

I think more people would support public art if we broke down these categories and instead focused on communication: How are we gonna communicate better with each other, and is this communication going to make something that's going to remain in a place that people are gonna come back to see? I definitely see the public protests as a form of public art that's gaining momentum.

KH: Yeah, I think that's a really, really great way of saying it, because it expands what it could mean to make public art. One of the hugest problems that we have when we start doing a project is exactly what you described, nico—immediately we start with a mural or a sculpture on a pedestal, and that's the furthest thing from our thought process.

And so, the first step is to really expand that definition as broadly as possible, to get people to think beyond that, and then to share knowledge about what you could actually do as an artist, what's available, and what's possible. And all these little bits of information are important in helping to shape people's interest.

When working with artists on public art, I always get the, *Oh, I didn't know I was eligible for that* or *I didn't know I could do public art*. That's because people assume you need particular types of experience, which is not the case at all. I'm happy to say that about 90 percent of the people that we commission have never done public art before!

DV: Maren, I love what you said about BLM. In these protests are collective gestures that encourage us to imagine differently and reorient space and how we use space, to think about a different kind of environment or set of conditions that are possible for us to live within. I think this was made clear in the powerful protest, Brooklyn Liberation for Black Trans Life, where 15,000 people gathered outside of the Brooklyn Museum dressed in white. Parades and processions and performances that traverse space have long been a tool for public artists, from Lorraine O'Grady to Pope.L and many others. Having more public art helps us bring in more ideas of collectivism and allows us to explore how people can have more access to create and participate in a reorientation of our space.

EB: I believe museums will continue to learn from public art, taking these lessons back to their galleries in order to reorient and decenter those spaces. It's really amazing to hear Kendal share the percentage of artists he's commissioned who haven't worked in public art before. While Maren has had an illustrious career working in public space, other inHarlem artists have not. So there was a learning process, both on the part of the museum *and* the artists. These lessons unfold in real time in such a way that feels distinctly different, and more exciting, than some of those conversations that might happen in the gallery.

DV: The opportunity for a museum to learn from the public is so much more present when working in public art.

NW: I couldn't agree more. However, I think we've mainly discussed commissioning bodies that are receptive to that learning. But what about large or private museums that are perhaps more entrenched in traditional ways of working? I fear that, without some guardrails, public art as a practice of access and inclusion might become colonized, and its practitioners more and more tokenized.

DV: Yeah, I think we also see that in the way real estate has taken to public art as marketing. Developers invest in public art preconstruction as a way to really drive market class. And now that artists of color are gaining prominence in the market, they have more access to these kinds of opportunities that have hugely negative effects on communities of color. I share your fear too, nico: we need to come to terms with how we're mediating harm within these new systems in which our art is able to exist. Although deserving of scrutiny, I still find value in government-commissioned public art, even with all of its red tape, because there is accountability in place, and public input in place, in a way that we don't necessarily see when museums or real estate developers are taking it on.

EB: An artist rarely presents public art on their own. As we've discussed, this is often realized, for better or worse, through a presenting institution like a museum. I think the responsibility that you bring up really falls on the organizer. As a steward of the work in the public sphere, a curator must have these conversations with the artist, ensuring that their work is properly situated in the public, and that the politics behind the work are carried through in things like educational programming. And while tokenization is a very real issue, I don't think this should put us in a place where we're saying, *Oh, we don't want more public art.* Let's continue to put the organizer or institution in that difficult position to answer these questions, and hopefully in turn that process holds them more accountable.

KH: But I also think having the work in public sort of opens the door to these conversations. So I think that's a good outcome. But whether or not the institution provides a platform for those conversations to unfold is another story!

OUTRO

The discussion with Diya, Eric, Kendal, and Maren prompts us to consider not only how public space is constructed and by whom but also how it is claimed or *reclaimed* by the citizens it is theoretically designed to serve. Let's zoom out for a second to investigate how public space is treated within the national arts landscape. Consider the National Mall, perhaps most visible of our nation's public parks and home to countless public memorials, monuments, and museums. Billed as "America's front yard" and a destination to "celebrate the United States' commitment to freedom and equality,"[3] it, too, bears a history of social exclusion and cultural erasure. The most recent addition to the Mall was the National Museum of African American History and Culture, which—before it took physical shape in 2016—was a 100-year proposition for how Black Americans might claim their rightful space in this country's history and within the national arts landscape. Architect Mabel O. Wilson puts this history into context in her book *Negro Building: Black Americans in the World of Fairs and Museums*:

After decades of racist elected officials rejecting citizen-led initiatives and debates about the efficacy of a national institution, the new 300,000-square-foot museum and research facility will finally rise on the last remaining unbuilt site along the National Mall across from the Washington Monument. Taking stock of these laudable advances, what does it mean for black Americans to claim a physical space in the nation's symbolic cultural landscape and a symbolic space in the nation's historical consciousness, two spheres in which their presence and contributions have been calculatingly rendered invisible and abject for over two centuries?[4]

—Mabel O. Wilson

In her resistance to brand NMAAHC's mere existence on the Mall as progress, Wilson reminds us that presence in space is not evidence of a free or equitable society at work—rather, equity is defined by the *right* to space, representation, and full participation in civic life. While Black history—and soon women's history and Latinx history—has found a home on the National Mall, it's been the evolution of hundreds of grassroots museums and cultural centers that precede the birth of NMAAHC by a half century that define Black America's will to, as the artists in *Ruffneck Constructivists* did, write ourselves into the story and build ourselves into the world.

Earlier, Wilson notes that it's been the relentless organizing efforts of "nonprofit organizations led by determined citizen groups allied with cultural commissions and local municipalities" that have produced and are continuing to produce "museums, memorials, interpretive centers, and historic sites" across the country—spaces that ensure our national institutions don't trade in the dominant historical narrative alone.

In the next chapter, we will qualify the value of contemporary "for us, by us" arts organizations that embody the living legacies of Black institution building laid bare in Wilson's *Negro Building*. We will investigate the practices of creative and cultural entrepreneurship that spawned them and continue our investigation of *people*, *place*, and *space*, with a focus on strategies implemented by those *rendered invisible and abject* by the mainstream to claim necessary space within the arts and culture ecosystem.

NOTES

1. Cruz, Teddy. "Democratizing Urbanization and the Search for a New Civic Imagination." In *Living as Form: Socially Engaged Art from 1991–2011*, edited by Nato Thompson, 58. New York: Creative Time, 2012.

2. "InHarlem." Studio Museum in Harlem, https://studiomuseum.org/inharlem.

3. "National Mall and Memorial Parks." National Park Foundation, https://www.nationalparks.org/connect/explore-parks/national-mall-and-memorial-parks.

4. Wilson, Mabel O. "Introduction." In *Negro Building: Black Americans in the World of Fairs and Museums*, 3. Berkeley: University of California Press, 2012.

4

MUSEUM AS APPRENTICE

How to Learn from the Cultural Entrepreneurship of People-Powered Organizations

INTRO

> *Dominator culture has tried to keep us all afraid, to make us choose safety instead of risk, sameness instead of diversity. Moving through that fear, finding out what connects us, reveling in our differences; this is the process that brings us closer, that gives us a world of shared values, of meaningful community.*[1]
>
> —bell hooks

> *One of the most vital ways we sustain ourselves is by building communities of resistance, places where we know we are not alone.*[2]
>
> —bell hooks

For over fifteen years, I have worked within Black, artist-founded organizations. From the Studio Museum in Harlem to Rush Arts Gallery to NXTHVN, my commitment has been to spaces designed by and for creative communities of color. But because community is not a monolith—and because all of these organizations define "community" on their own terms despite a shared, culturally specific context—my work building capacity, infrastructure, and programs within each has looked markedly different. The tie that binds these experiences, however, is my belief in *community* as the moral compass of a cultural organization and *art* as an effective engine for mobilizing its members toward social change.

Borrowing from the many wisdoms of author, activist, and professor bell hooks, I define "community" as a space of shared values. A social and at times physical place, *community* is where these values are sharpened into tools for individual growth, interpersonal connection, and collective resistance. *Community* is the sustenance needed to transcend the loneliness and isolationism perpetuated by dominator culture. And as we learned from architect Mabel O. Wilson in the previous chapter, *community* is precisely who stepped in to ensure dominator culture didn't prevail in authoring a biased and incomplete American story.

As I consider the living legacies of culturally specific institutions—and the conditions that must continually be overcome to ensure their endurance into the future—I am eternally grateful to have landed in a community of practice with artists and cultural leaders that dare to build the world in our image. In the conversation that follows, I am joined by Kemi Ilesanmi of the Laundromat Project, Jamaica Gilmer of the Beautiful Project, and Shani Peters of the Black School. All have, in their own right—and through their *own* definitions of community—embraced risk to build an arts-and-culture organization of, by, and for the people. In each case, their values-driven approach demanded that the construction of physical space follow, not lead, their strategic priorities, which is a rare occurrence in today's landscape of ever-expanding culture palaces.

While the roundtable that follows decenters museums in its very construction, it does offer perspective on how the majority-white museum field might learn from the organizing principles and people-powered approach of culturally specific organizations. Furthermore, it asks, *How might museums learn to keep pace with the innovation and radical creativity of social institutions beyond their spheres of engagement and influence?*

ROUNDTABLE

JAMAICA GILMER is a strategist, storyteller, photographer, and curator who has a 15-year background in creating and implementing curricula. She is founder and director of the Beautiful Project (see figure 4.1), an arts collective that centers Black women and girls as the authority over their own narratives. A graduate of Howard University's John H. Johnson School of Communications, she is a highly influential speaker, sharing insights and cultivating radical spaces of belonging. Jamaica is a passionate, bold thought leader and a revolutionary hope architect.

KEMI ILESANMI is executive director of the Laundromat Project, which advances artists and neighbors as change agents in their own communities. She has previously worked at Creative Capital Foundation and the Walker Art Center. In 2015, she was appointed by the mayor to the NYC Cultural Affairs Advisory Commission. She is on the board of the Joan Mitchell Foundation and the Broad Room. A graduate of Smith College, NYU, and Coro Leadership NY, she is also a Sterling Network Fellow.

SHANI PETERS is a multidisciplinary artist based in New Orleans, Louisiana. She holds a BA from Michigan State University and an MFA from City College of New York. Peters is a former faculty member at City College of New York, the Pratt Institute, and Parsons School of Design, focusing her teaching at the intersection of art, design, and social change. She is a codirector of an artist-initiated, experimental art school that has led 100-plus workshops since 2016.

The following discussion took place between Jamaica Gilmer, Kemi Ilesanmi, Shani Peters, and nico wheadon via Zoom on September 10, 2020.

Figure 4.1. In 2019, the Metropolitan Museum of Art premiered *Pen, Lens & Soul: The Story of the Beautiful Project*. A group of the Beautiful Project artists traveled to New York to see their exhibit. Photo by Eileen Travell, courtesy the Beautiful Project.

nico wheadon: Since we are family here, let's launch right in. I'd love for each of you to discuss your respective journeys as Black women founders and institution builders. In particular, I'm interested to hear you discuss the role of *people* and *place* in everything that you've built and will continue to build.

Jamaica Gilmer: The Beautiful Project is such a sweet place. For us, *people* and *place* started with people who *weren't* here. The project was born out of the pain I was in after my mother passed away and rooted in a conversation that I was having with her in my head. This conversation sustained me through a whole lot of sweetness, memories, love, and intensity.

I had just gotten married to my boo and moved to Durham, which became the place I grew up in my adulthood. But I didn't feel grounded in Durham and felt afraid without the grounding of my mom. So, while I'm from Maryland, Durham ultimately became this place that held me. I fell for Durham, and the people here became my home and helped fan the flame for my dream of the Beautiful Project over the past 17 years.

NW: Who were some of the first people you talked to about this dream? And what did some of those early conversations produce in terms of clarity of vision for the organization?

JG: Oh my gosh, some of the first people I talked to about it were super scary and terrible. At that time, creating programming intentionally for Black girls got a visceral response. I was often corrected in my language. "Really it's for all girls. What about our Black boys?" So after I talked to folks that were unkind when it came to Black girls, I started to find folks who got it and, usually, they were parents: parents of Black girls could often see that I was committed to ensuring their daughters know the power of their voice.

One woman comes to mind who is now on my board: Dosali Reed-Bandele. She is a mom, she's an executive, and I feel like she's been here before. She could see where we were heading, even when our snacks were all wrong. Her daughter was in our first year-round cohort—we met her when she was nine, and now she's a sophomore in college. It was around that time that I realized I was talking to my students like my mom used to talk to us. Which is to say, I was talking about money too much in front of the babies.

At one point in time, Dosali's daughter looked at me and said, "Can we *please* have a sleepover? Don't worry; my mom can buy the snacks!" I thought, "OK, I have to course correct. 'Cause I'm up here talking like Ida: 'Y'all better not eat them chips. I can't afford all these chips. You just had four bags of chips. You don't need more chips. Have a banana!'" You know what I'm saying? There was no budget. We didn't have funding for 10 years. We were just doing this because everybody that was drawn to the Beautiful Project, and drawn to me, knew our *lives* were on the line unless we could build a place where Black girls could be seen.

The ways that our families and friends and communities had shown up for us growing up is what we replicated in the Beautiful Project. And so Dosali and her daughter, were the folks who taught me how much of a trigger the Beautiful Project actually was, even for me. When you talk about Black girls or women, and *mean* it—without caveats—

it's a trigger for everybody. So I then had to cultivate the skill to manage this trigger without it taking me out. But the first pattern I saw of folks who could rock with us were the parents of Black girls.

NW: Well, kudos to you for navigating the naysayers with such grace and transforming their negative energy into positive momentum! In that regard, the Beautiful Project seems part and parcel of a long lineage of *for us, by us* institutions born from survival, yes, but also a desire to transcend the micro- and macroaggressions of institutional racism. I imagine you actually faced a double-edged sword—eking out a conceptual space in the collective consciousness for Black girls to thrive *and* building an actual physical space for them to come together under an umbrella of safety and care. What did it take to build and protect the early infrastructure of the Beautiful Project, and where are you today?

JG: So the physical space of the Beautiful Project was initially my home, friends' homes, and locations we could secure for free or with the small amount of funds that we had. To make the space ours wherever we landed, I locked arms with my core sojourners, Pamela Thompson, Erin Stephens, and Khayla Deans. We learned, over time, that the more children, volunteers, or staff came into play, the more you had to share your house, and the less your house could operate as a good programmatic space. We enjoy stretching out and laughing with our whole bodies! So we rotated through our homes, depending on what was happening in our personal lives, and from time to time, folks donated offices and conference rooms.

And then, eventually, funding hit. But from my perspective, things really changed for the Beautiful Project when Malia and Sasha got into the White House. Black girls then became this visible situation, at all times and on all sides! And I think their visibility did help deepen foundations' interest in us. "Well, who's working with Black girls?" And so, when we got some substantial funding, we started to get offices.

NW: That's such a poignant observation on the currency of representation and how it circulates in this country. OK, so flash forward 10 years to another milestone. What did it feel like to imagine, and then realize, the Beautiful Project's exhibition *Pen, Lens & Soul*, at the MET? How does that fit into this lineage of personal and professional growth?

JG: Man, there was a lot I knew about Beautiful when it was born in my heart, but there was also a lot I knew I did *not* know. I knew that I wanted to impact Black girls through photography. I knew from the very beginning that, in 10 years, I wanted to do a national travelling exhibition. But the rest I just knew would be my job to protect—it felt spiritual. Like, I would be the protector of those who were coming, because there was so much more that I couldn't see, but I could feel that this was bigger than what I knew and could see then.

The Beautiful Project became so much better than what I'd dreamed of because of the women who joined me, and because of their tendencies to hold up a mirror. It's through women in the Beautiful Project that I learned that people see me as relentless. And I didn't know that about myself; I just felt guilty and like I wasn't doing enough at all times.

Dorian Burton, one of the folks who believed in TBP's collective relentlessness introduced us to Sandra Jackson Dumont, former chair of education at the MET. We were telling her our dream of the travelling exhibition, and there was this back and forth because she's intensely honest and reflective. After telling her the plan to travel to 12 cities with TBP's exhibition, she said, "I don't want y'all to die."

When she said it, I instantly knew in my gut she was right. Then she said, "You can go around to the people. But when you do it right, the people will come to you."

The Beautiful Project finds the most success where there's a relationship. Even if the relationship is new—if it's real and it's good and it clicks, then there's some safety and trust there. The ebbs and flows and the ups and downs have a container. There were several places that we were thinking about having our exhibit, and later, Sandra said, "Y'all need to do the exhibit at the MET and stop playing! Like, what's up?!" She thought that we had hesitation and judgment around the MET because it wasn't a Black institution, which we did before meeting her. But the truth is, we just thought it was too forward to ask.

NW: That's an assumption so many of us have made in our personal and professional lives. As Black women, we are not taught empowerment and certainly not entitlement. We observe it in others and imagine it for ourselves, but it's a muscle we need to learn to flex more often! The question stands: How many safe spaces are there to actually do that? Jamaica, you've created a truly safe space for Black girls to express themselves through art and to find themselves within the collectivity of culture—thank you!

OK, Kemi. Tell us about the Laundromat Project [figure 4.2] and the journey of the organization as it's transitioned under your leadership. How do *people* and *place* show up at the LP?

Kemi Ilesanmi: The Laundromat Project was founded by Risë Wilson, a Black woman from Philly who started thinking about it in the late '90s, before we incorporated in the summer of 2005. I met Risë in the fall of 2004 and had only been living in New York City for about two weeks when we met at a brunch party. I don't exactly know how we started talking, but we did and immediately just vibed and connected.

She said, "I just got an Echoing Green Grant. I'm starting this organization called the Laundromat Project, and we're gonna work with artists of color and communities of color." Our interests aligned, as I had been working as a curator for six years in Minneapolis where I ran our residency program with a variety of incredible artists. I was really interested in how the arts intersected with the fabric of urban spaces and communities.

We decided to stay in touch, and when she incorporated the following July, she invited me to be on the board. I had since started a job at Creative Capital and wasn't sure how I wanted to show up in the world, so she actually had to convince me. I'm so thankful that she didn't give up on the first "Let me think about it." I joined a few months later.

The idea of *place* and *people* is just built into what the LP is by definition. So, the *Laundromat*, the name, was about meeting people where they were, in a place like a laundromat, which is a de facto gathering space for community. In cities like New York

Figure 4.2. Neighbors make art together outside of Fulton Street Laundry at the Laundromat Project's *Field Day* (2013) in Bed-Stuy. Photo by Ed Marshall, courtesy the Laundromat Project.

and Philadelphia where she first conceived this idea, it's a multiracial, multigendered, and multiclass space. So, if you're in the top 1 percent, you ain't coming to a laundromat! Here you had a number of different folks coming together in a pre-smartphone era with a lot of downtime. It was about using our culture to connect people to have conversations, and the people part was so key. We were interested in Black people specifically, and people of color more widely, depending on the neighborhood. The idea was to meet people where they were—where they already gathered—and meet them on their turf and their terms.

These folks all already had creativity, and it was a matter of inviting them to share that with themselves and with others. So if you identified as an artist, you were invited to share that at the laundromat. And if you didn't identify as an artist or didn't even think of yourself as creative, you were invited to connect to your creative self, to be in conversation with others, and to think about the beauty of community as conversation, culture making, and art making.

NW: So, how important was the physical site of the laundromat to the overall concept and operation? Were laundromats simply your programmatic partners in the endeavor or did you hope to actually own and operate a laundromat?

KI: When I was on the board, Risë was like, "We're gonna make, own and operate our own laundromat. People will come in to do their laundry and then we'll hit them with the programs in the basement, upstairs, and all around." But the reality at that time was, we were a board full of all Black women, and ain't nobody come with, "We gonna buy New York City real estate money!" So we had to pivot real quick. Once we realized that nobody had money to actually buy a building, we moved to a citywide model that spread pretty quickly. Our focus was, "Let's think about artists of color and communities of color and really see New York City as our canvas."

As a board, we were really excited by this idea of owning and operating a laundromat that would give off some profits to help fund the program. I was on the board for about five years, and we were testing the idea: Do artists want to work in community in this way? Do they want to be in a laundromat and connect with their neighbors? What do they need to be supported through that process?

The very first year, we told the artists, "Go do your thing, and let Risë know when you're done." And that wasn't really working, so then, after a few years, we started adding, "Actually, why don't you meet together as a cohort of three to four artists, chat, and support each other?" creating a peer-to-peer network and process. And that eventually evolved into our Fellowship Program, which we still offer today. It was at this point that I left the board for two and a half years to go to graduate school and then came back as our first, full-time, paid executive director, taking over the role that Risë had essentially done unpaid for a long time. And I *know* y'all recognize that role.

By that time, the world had changed. We now had smartphones, which led to Uber and the Uberization of many things. My neighborhood had seen several laundromats close down—and remember these are cash businesses with slim margins. We were no longer interested in running a laundry business. We were interested in connecting creativity and people. To your original question, nico, the people mattered, the art making mattered, and now we had a seven-year track record of doing the work, so we were like, "We don't want to pivot all our energy to figuring out how to run a laundromat and not be able to deliver on our mission!"

So it took some time for the board to work through that new reality. Shani actually had one of the few projects that was about the laundromat in a really essential way. It was the People's Laundromat Theater, a film festival for the laundromat. There were very few other projects that were that specific and organically in tune. Shani aside, most artists were like, "I'm not going to apply. I have a great idea for a project, but it just doesn't fit in a laundromat." And since our work is about being responsive and meeting people where they are, if the people and the projects don't thrive in a laundromat setting, it doesn't make sense for us to force them to do that. So that was our thought process—it was actually looking at what the artists needed, what they were saying, and then in a larger context, the way the world was shifting. So we arrived at a place of seeing the laundromat, instead, as a metaphor. Today, we work in community centers, local gardens, libraries, neighborhood festivals, on sidewalks, and some laundromats.

NW: In retrospect, that seems like such a natural shift; however, I'm sure it was difficult to navigate in real time. Can you talk about some of the early supporters and partners of the LP? Who helped you to build out the new direction for the Laundromat Project in this post-laundromat era?

KI: Well, we moved from the original idea of owning and operating a laundromat and anchoring in one specific community to mobilizing a citywide initiative very quickly. But what that one neighborhood idea represented was the idea of being able to build deep relationships. Each year, we held an open call for an artist of color working in a community of color; that was fantastic and on-mission. But what we had given up on from that original concept was the idea of a sustained, accountable, reciprocal relationship.

So one of the first things I did as ED was work with Lisa Yancey Consulting on our strategic-planning process. This started on my second week, and she helped us to transition our language. We began to see that we needed to be an "organization in residence" in particular neighborhoods. Lisa encouraged us to think of it as anchoring and having "anchor neighborhoods." We could still work citywide, but we'd have certain neighborhoods where we'd return over and over again and build out a long-term relationship. So if you saw me this year, you knew you'd see me again next year and you'd see me the year after that. Which is a very different relationship than, *We're just going to be here for three months and peace out. Maybe we'll be back next year if someone applies from your neighborhood, but maybe we won't.*

So that was one of the first things. The other thing that we did right away in the context of the strategic-planning process was limit our scope to the borders of New York City—not New Jersey, not Philadelphia. Instead, we beefed up our social media, activated our blog, and had more of a public presence. That encouraged people worldwide to go to our social media, where we shared our tools and our projects so others could make those work in their communities too. We let information be the driver, not necessarily physical presence.

Jamaica, it reminds me of your conversation with Sandra that you just described, where you said 12 cities might kill you! I was like, "We can't be in every city all the time and be all over New York City, y'all. Let's narrow down to three anchor neighborhoods." So, we selected Bed-Stuy—because that was our original home and idea. Harlem, because we had projects there from day one. And then the South Bronx, and particularly Hunts Point, because at the time we actually had an office and a two-year project there. Three seemed like the right number—it was a stool; it wasn't scientific. To do only one wouldn't have made sense just yet, since we were moving from working all over the city and the tristate area to just one neighborhood. Two would've been a comparative study. But three was like, *Oh, we've got a dialogue. We've got a situation!*

Throughout that seven-year period of being in three noncontiguous neighborhoods, the staff discovered the challenge of working this way! So we experimented and tried different things. We had a school partnership in Bed-Stuy and tried some after-school programs. (I'm looking at Shani, because Shani has been involved in *all* parts of the LP, in all ways, at all times. She's done everything!) We had an after-school program in Harlem, and then we eventually acquired a physical space on Kelly Street in the Bronx that grew out of an artists' project. When the project was done, the owner of this affordable housing development was like, "We have an extra apartment that we can't rent out; it's a basement apartment, it's not zoned for rental, but you can use it for arts programming."

So we said yes, before we knew where the money or staff to support it would come from. We just said yes! Because it was going to get as close as possible to that original idea of being embedded in a neighborhood. Before that, we had moved to being in and working across three, but we still didn't have a dedicated program space.

Last year, we concluded a new strategic-planning process, where we figured out three neighborhoods is too many. We can't show up equally, across all three with our full selves. We went through lots of discussion internally with our community, and it became clear that, one was now the correct number. We selected Bed-Stuy and found a space earlier this year, pre-COVID-19. So even though it's happening by Zoom, we didn't let quarantine stop us from building community and building life in Bed-Stuy.

NW: What a journey! It's inspiring to see how you've responded to what you've learned, from your artists and from your communities, in real time. And that, as a leader, you've invited these lessons to impact the structure, mission, and strategic direction of your organization. That level of responsiveness is just so rare. Thank you for your tenacity and for modeling how to position your communities as equal stakeholders in the work of your organization.

Alright, Shani. Let's hear about the Black School [figure 4.3] and how you've grown your organization over the past few years, carrying lessons from your work with the Laundromat Project with you.

Figure 4.3. The Black School. Photo by Sindayiganza Photography, courtesy the Black School.

Shani Peters: There are so many relations to this whole conversation that I'm gonna have to stop myself 'cause I could start at age five! I've been super informed and influenced by the LP, for sure. So maybe I'll start there. I actually finished my MFA doing community-engaged work and had a blind studio visit with Petrushka Baskin-Larsen, who was at LP before Kemi as program director. Before I ever heard the phrase *social practice*, she was like, "Oh, you're doing social practice?" And I was like, "What's that now?"

And so Petrushka and I did this weird online exhibition, which transitioned into me first starting to work with the LP. It was this perfect home for all the things that I wanted to do. There was an organization with offices in my neighborhood that was growing the concept of social practice. And so I was really supported in navigating this type of making that I didn't even know the name of. The LP has been super fundamental for me, not to mention all the Black women at LP . . . that's a whole other conversation! (Jamaica, your work, my goodness.)

But in terms of the Black School and *people* and *place*, our vision for people is informed by that original model that Risë had. When I was in grad school, I started working at this place called Harlem Textile Works that came out of the Harlem Children's Arts Carnival, that has an amazing history, Black arts community, and community art space. While I was there, I watched its demise. It's a space that invested a million dollars into its design yet couldn't keep the lights on, and now it's a real estate office in the Harlem neighborhood. So I was coming away from seeing an organization take that turn and then seeing this LP vision rise and was like, "That's genius. That's brilliant."

As an artist, my studio practice extended into a socially engaged practice and shortly thereafter into teaching. I've been teaching as long as I've been thinking of myself as a professional artist. Early on in teaching, I imagined eventually running my own teaching program. I realized that I actually *liked* teaching to subsidize my artist career, where a lot of people do it 'cause they have to. For me, I actually liked it, and it really brought a sense of balance to my overall practice. When the social practice work wasn't actually contacting people, which happens so often in the art world, my teaching always was. When the partnerships weren't doing what they needed to be doing, I knew that I was always rewarded by teaching.

So while I always loved teaching, I lost track of the dream to organize my own teaching program because I was just tired. I was doing too much, and teaching is exhausting. And then I met Joseph, who, as soon as I met him, was talking about this Black School idea. I was like, "What's that?" We very instantly bonded over this because I had also been dreaming of a self-led, Black, arts education program.

He started developing the idea while he was in graduate school, coming from an HBCU outside of Houston to New York, to the predominantly white Pratt Institute with no Black faculty and no community. He started leaning into Black radical histories, and he talked a lot about reading bell hooks's *Teaching to Transgress*. When we met through mutual friends, we instantly had a ton to talk about on those grounds. We started dating, and it was a little complicated to be collaborating with somebody you just started dating, so I was trying to be very hands-off. He applied for the Blade of Grass grant, and I was a collaborator on that application. I really wanted to give him space with that first grant because we were just dating. But by the time the funding came through, and by the time the programming was happening, we were more than just dating—we were cooking a child!

You know, you take on one life project, so why not two? Baldwin has facilitated a much speedier growth of the combined Black School because we had to learn how to raise a child together, and that's a real investment and commitment. Just seeing the way Joseph leaned into fatherhood told me what I needed to know about leaning into a partnership with him. So 2015, the idea was there; 2016, we started doing programming. We originally got that grant to have programming in a high school in Bed-Stuy that on paper looked like a perfect home. However, when the school year started, we could hardly get anybody on the phone. There were no students showing up, there was zero commitment from the school, and we had a $20,000 grant and an intricately laid-out plan with A-list artists ready to go. So we gave them three sessions and said, "This is not gonna work." So we had to quickly pivot to figure out how we were gonna make the best use of that grant. At that time, I was six or seven months pregnant.

Suhaly Bautista Carolina, who's at the MET now and helped organize the Beautiful Project's exhibition there, helped us compile a list of potential partners to reach out to. So we had this $20,000 program laid out and just needed a place and people to enact it. After reaching out to all of these schools and community spaces, we ended up partnering with 15 different spaces in that first year. The initial plan was to have a long-term relationship with students, but it wasn't happening, because we didn't have that one school home. We learned a lot moving between spaces, and I learned all about loading up your backpack and bringing the workshop to the people. So that's what we've been doing in New York.

All the while, from early on in our pregnancy, we started thinking about relocating out of New York. Joseph was born in New Orleans and lived there for a few years as a little boy. When his parents split up, he was in Baton Rouge with his mom, and then his dad moved to Houston and he went to join him. As an adult, he hasn't had the experience of living in this amazing city. I loved New Orleans before I even met Joseph—it was another feather in his cap to have that relation, so that made sense as a place to relocate to since we have a ton of family there. Trying to be a parent in New York without a grandmother, auntie—somebody—to call on is really, really hard. So we knew we wanted to be somewhere closer to family. I'm from Lansing, Michigan, originally, my parents live outside of Detroit now, and what can I say? New Orleans beat out Detroit. I'm sorry. It just did.

On top of that, there's this family legacy of teaching in New Orleans, and in general for us to build upon. Both of our fathers are educators, and I think in hindsight, this is another reason that we really connected. This is another reason that we're both artists and designers thinking about how to incorporate that into an education program. We are both from Black families that were like, *Education is important, jobs are important, stability is important—art is nice, but I don't know if that's really a* career. We both have undergrad degrees that are not in art because neither of us imagined it was a real career choice, like so many other young Black people. We just don't have this luxury.

Joe's dad is a principal in Houston, and was a teacher and later an administrator in New Orleans. He got his master's in education from Xavier, an HBCU, in a moment where the city of New Orleans didn't even hire Black teachers. He wound up teaching in the school district and becoming a principal, and after he passed, they actually renamed the school where he taught in his name. So there's a Joseph Cuillier Career Tech school in New Orleans right now.

As of now, we have partnered with over 50 organizations in nearly 50 different places. And when you look at other spaces, you get a lot of ideas about what you would do with your own space! So we first started thinking about that during our 2018 residency at the New Museum. And because there was a "space" theme, they invited the architect Mabel O. Wilson to come in for a talk with us. And a big part of her talk was the legacy of these Rosenwald schools. Those are called Rosenwald schools, but we like to call them Booker T. schools because it was Booker T. Washington's vision that Julius Rosenwald, a wealthy philanthropist from Sears and Roebuck, supported financially. Local Black communities enabled this vision, which started with those one-room schoolhouses that we see in the historical pictures.

Over 5,000 of these schools were built in the USA. And that model included putting the drawing plans for that one-room schoolhouse in a book and just taking it to people and saying, "This is how you do it. Do you wanna do it?" Communities committed to building the structures, and Rosenwald put in the other half of the money to realize it. So that's this other amazing legacy that we're part of—Black schools born out of slavery. How does the first generation of Black people out of slavery advance the construction of 5,000 schools!? It's incredible.

So now we're working toward building a physical home for the Black School in New Orleans. And we've been introducing the concept to people by first talking about that Rosenwald idea, and, as long as we've been doing the Black school and as long as Joe's been thinking of it, that visual of the one-room schoolhouse has always been the stimulus, or trigger, as you say, Jamaica.

Because we're experimental, we do all types of strange things. We're not trying to be like a charter school or meet state standards of education or anything like that. But it is so functional to frame our work by our collective understanding of what a Black school actually is, right? My dad grew up in West Virginia, presegregation, and he said that in those all-Black schools he went to, there was a teacher that would say, "Boy, when you look in the mirror, you're looking at the best person you're gonna see all day. Not any better than anybody else, but goddamn it, not any worse." Right? And that's what you get from a Black school, that's what you get from a space that is made of you and for you and by you.

We have this copy of the Rosenwald model book, and it's not just the building plans—it's also gardening plans, programming plans, and church plans. The Black School, in this model, is a community center. So the space that we are imagining and working toward will function more like a community center than a school. There'll be an open-access garden. On the ground floor, there'll be a gallery/event space, a library/meditation room that will hopefully open up to make one larger space. And on the upper floors, there'll be a wet room, workshop space, a media lab to house Black School Studio.

There are three arms to our work—we do the workshops, we have the design studio, and we do Black Love Fest. The design studio enables us to give tangible resources to the young people we work with. We train standout students that we meet through the workshops who are really engaged and wanna stay on with us. We pay them to learn graphic design and creative direction, after which they take on real-world clients for real-world money, and forge tangible creative careers. We know we can't really pitch this aloof artist career that not even *we* felt was open to us—so we learned that to get folks to stay on with us and give their time and energy when they could be working a part-time job and contributing to their household income, we gotta give a bit more motivation. So that's how the design studio functions and, in the long term, we hope to grow that and be able to support the school through the studio.

We also want to have a residency space and invite Black and POC artists into the space. If you're a Black artist right now, most residencies are with white organizations. For instance, I have no interest in going to Skowhegan, so we're creating this other avenue. You always hear about Black artists at Skowhegan forming these bonds because they've gotta travel in groups to the grocery store to avoid something crazy happening in this remote, white, Maine town. So yes, we're really interested in speaking to a lot of these issues in the art world, but specifically, we're looking forward to being locally rooted in one place and having those long-term relationships. New Orleans deserves it—it's the birthplace of so much of our collective national Black culture and there's this legacy to build off of. So that's what we're working on.

We started fundraising this summer because Joe has a lot of nerve and he's a man and he's socialized to have a lot of nerve . . . it's part of the way that we balance each other and pair so well. I'm really good at being crafty and fitting in wherever I can and taking whatever little scraps are there and figuring out what to do with that. That's my lane; I can do that. But just dreaming without barriers . . . that's hard for me! This summer, once the Black Lives Matter uprisings kicked off, we had a few friends that told us, "Y'all need to get a Venmo link up. Y'all need to get some of these coins that people are giving away right now." And we did it—we put something up at 10 o'clock at night and had $1,000 by the next morning. Then Joe was like, "We should fundraise for the whole thing on GoFundMe. We should take advantage of the moment." We got the campaign up and raised $100,000 in two weeks. Because you've got to ask!

NW: You've got to ask!

KI: You gotta ask.

SP: And you forget how great your own ideas are the longer you sit with them. They become normal to you, but other people are like, "Oh my god, this is amazing!" So that's where we're at—$200,000 of the $300,000 we need to raise and working on some other sources of income. So now we're planning to make the permanent move to NOLA and pretty soon we'll actually begin building the school. We've got an architect team, and it's all going down. It's amazing!

JG: I don't know what time it is, but I can't tell you how long it took me to not interrupt you by screaming, crying, and wailing! I was like, "Just calm down, let the woman talk, we're recording, nico's writing a book!" Oh my god!

NW: I could see it on your face the whole time though. I was like, "I can't wait to open this conversation up!" There's a lot that I saw you each responding to in each other's journeys that I would love to hear you discuss aloud.

KI: I would love to speak to *boldness*. I would love us to have a discussion about *boldness*. Because it is a muscle that I am pushing in myself, in my team, and in our community of artists. I think it is the mantle! I'm just like, "Be bold y'all; just ask!" And Shani, you gave us an amazing story, and it shows up in a lot of different ways. And, Jamaica, you're clearly already doing it. Boldness is an abundance muscle!

NW: That's right. But it also begs the question, *Who are you surrounded by as you flex that muscle for the first time?* Because if you have all your fears affirmed when you first step into that power, you might not do it again!

KI: But Jamaica kept going! Jamaica had folks who were like, "No, Black girls, I don't see it. I don't see it." And she was like, "Well, I do." *Bold.*

JG: Boldness is a great synthesizer. My mom was a revolutionary that nobody knew, and, because she was a child of the '60s, she was angry. She was also extremely hilarious and joyful, but she was also angry, and we were taught to relish in that thing. We didn't have the skill to not exercise our boldness to our detriment. Someone would piss us off, and we'd be like, "Oh, OK, *watch* me be bold." We were trained to fight.

NW: In that regard, boldness is perhaps another double-edged sword—a manifestation of strength that can be retooled against us by those fearful of our power. I'm thinking of the number of times I've been called *ambitious*. It's like, "I'm sorry, what? That doesn't feel like a compliment. Why am I not allowed to dream out loud? Why can't I experiment and innovate and push the status quo with confidence? Why do I have to ask for your permission to do that?"

So for me, it's about creating safe and intentional spaces—like those that each of you have built—where people that look like us are able to flex this muscle, in community, for the first time and for *forever*. When I think about the places I've worked, I must also acknowledge the privilege I've experienced. The Studio Museum has a history of stewardship by women of color, by Black women. And when someone tells me, "I like your ambition, but that's not your best idea," I'm like, "You're right. You're right! Thank you." The critique sits in a different place because it originates from a place of love and respect.

KI: I'll just tell a quick story about Thelma Golden. I first met Thelma in the late '90s when I was at our alma mater, Smith College, and later again at the Walker Art Center. I was very new to the field, and this was around the time she, alongside other women and women of color, left the Whitney Museum en masse.

So Thelma was working for contemporary art collector and philanthropist Peter Norton, who was convening this group of contemporary art curators from across the country at Bard College. I was part of the steering committee for a number of years, but at the beginning I was just invited as a guest. Thelma did not have an institutional job at the time but was critical in organizing this gathering for Peter. She was still figuring out what her next big move was going to be and told this room of 50-some-odd folks, mostly white, "I've hired a publicist."

She mentioned it in passing, and everybody was like, *Let's just put aside whatever we were planning to talk about and talk about this publicist!* Because of *course* you are important enough to invest in yourself like that. You have something to say, and the world needs to hear it! The whole room—of every ilk, age, color, etc.—was like, *What kind of Black girl magic is she?!* She was so clear on who she was and what she had to offer the world. And I've never forgotten that, as a fellow member of this field which was not built for us. The Thelma Goldens and the Dr. Kellie Jones and the Rick Powells are beacons for me to this day.

My father, who's Nigerian, moved to America as a celebrated young banker. He moved here from London because he wanted a college degree and wanted to try something different. He said goodbye to family without them even knowing it was a goodbye. He left on Good Friday 1969 and arrived on Easter Sunday and moved in with my Uncle Sonny in DC. Easter Monday, he was a janitor. He had dreams for himself, which in the beginning meant being a janitor. He went to Howard University that fall, and his journey took him back to Nigeria, where he's now a storied and retired civil servant.

In reverse, in 1977, my mother moves with two young kids to Nigeria, a country she's never been to, without any of her own family, to be with my father's and start a new life. We all, in ways that are not necessarily recognized, come from bold stock! People who did things like say, "I'm gonna be a teacher; I'm gonna get a degree in teaching; I know they don't hire Black folks, but this is what I wanna do; this what I'm passionate about." As Black women, as Black people, those are lineages that we need to tap into and muscles that we need to remember to exercise. Because we didn't get here by chance. The LP just secured our second million-dollar gift, and they didn't come to us offering a million dollars! I went to them and said, "It looks to me like you meant to add a couple more zeros." And they agreed! We have to be bold and know our worth.

SP: Ladi'Sasha Jones, who I met through the LP and [who] had a fellowship at New Museum before we did, taught me, *Whatever they offer you, ask for more.* And I take that philosophy to every engagement I've had since 2017. Every time I ask, I get more—'cause they've got it.

KI: And they don't expect you to ask, and they're never gonna put you in the million-dollar bucket—*you* gotta put yourself in the million-dollar bucket.

OUTRO

As a framework for cultural production, the "for us, by us" (FUBU) framework offers so much. First, it reminds us that in our consumer-capitalist society, there is always a maker and there is always a consumer—culture is not exempt from this *for/by* construct of power. In a FUBU context, however, there is a necessary reclamation of agency, resistance against cultural erasure, and reauthoring of the dominant narrative. Second, because the value of said narrative is not contested or undermined and is broadly understood, the resultant dialogue is able to reach full breadth and depth. In other words, when Black art need not expend all its energy making the case for its existence and inclusion in the canon, the work can spark a deeper conversation. And third, despite FUBU institutions' commitments to serving clearly defined communities, their work *actually* undergirds and benefits the entire arts-and-culture ecosystem. Their sustained investment in so-called marginalized communities is what ensures the broader culture that we all trade in remains authentic and inclusive.

In a museum field marked by *sameness*, the existence of culturally specific institutions holds us accountable to the important work of identifying and celebrating difference. Our call for *boldness* at the end of the roundtable is a multifaceted prompt that asks each of us to look both outward and inward, as Lonnie G. Bunch III prompted us to do at the beginning of our journey: to ask for what you need but also question your innate ability to address that need; to roll up your sleeves and do the work but also listen and pause if the work is telling you to do something differently; and to trust your instincts and vision for the impact you want your work to have, but never over the truths as evidenced in your communities' lived experiences of it.

NOTES

1. hooks, bell. *Teaching Community: A Pedagogy of Hope.* New York: Routledge, 2013.

2. hooks, bell. *Yearning: Race, Gender, and Cultural Politics.* New York: Routledge, 2014.

5

MUSEUM AS BRIDGE

How to Build Relevance, Equity,
and Sustained Engagement
through Adult Public Programs

INTRO

In the previous chapter, we considered the importance of spaces designed
by and for clearly defined communities. While the primary work of the
cultural organizations discussed is located *beyond* the museum space, each
boasts thoughtfully designed programs that run alongside or *through* it. In
Jamaica's work bringing the Beautiful Project to the MET, and in Shani's work
incubating the Black School within the Sugar Hill Children's Museum and the
Brooklyn Children's Museum, we're gifted two progressive designs for culturally specific space, both as a discrete entity and as a programmatic initiative
nested within the museum.

In the discussion that follows, I invited three museum professionals to share
their approaches to building similar dedicated space *within* the museum, identifying tools and strategies borrowed from innovation taking place *beyond* museums. With a focus on adult public and educational programs, Chayanne Marcano of the Studio Museum in Harlem, David Rue of the Seattle Art Museum,
and Lauren Argentina Zelaya of the Brooklyn Museum discuss the importance
of skills sharing, vocabulary building, peer mentorship, and building bridges
between the departments of a single museum and across multiple museums or
cultural institutions.

ROUNDTABLE

CHAYANNE MARCANO is an art worker, writer, and researcher of space, place, and belonging. As senior coordinator of Public Programs & Community Engagement at the Studio Museum in Harlem, Chayanne cultivates modes of public engagement with contemporary art and artists of African descent through live programs, performances, and community partnerships.

DAVID RUE is a dance artist and creative professional born in Liberia and raised in Minnesota. He is a graduate of the University of Minnesota with a bachelor's of individualized studies that combined journalism, English, and dance. He holds an MFA in arts leadership from Seattle University and currently works in the public engagement department of the Seattle Art Museum, where he conceptualizes and implements arts programming that helps adult audiences more deeply engage with the visual and performing arts using the lens of equity, excellence, and joy.

LAUREN ARGENTINA ZELAYA is a cultural producer, curator, and DJ based in Brooklyn, New York. In her role as the director of public programs at Brooklyn Museum, Lauren curates and produces public programs that welcome over 200,000 visitors annually to engage with art in new and unexpected ways. Lauren is committed to collaborating with emerging artists and centering voices in our communities that are often marginalized, with a focus on creating programming for and with LGBTQ+, BIPOC, and immigrant communities.

The following discussion took place between Chayanne Marcano, David Rue, nico wheadon, and Lauren Argentina Zelaya via email between the years 2019-2021.

nico wheadon: David, we met in 2017 when you visited the Studio Museum as part of a larger research trip to New York City. What exactly were you researching, and what made Harlem a site of knowledge production for you?

David Rue: I initially traveled to New York to learn how other museums conceptualize and implement multidisciplinary, late-night programs targeted toward young adults, the ways in which racial equity help shape these programs, and how that lens is applied to the program-planning process. I was drawn to the Studio Museum in Harlem because I wanted to learn more about Uptown Fridays, and I'd also heard real things about the museum (particularly its education staff) from my colleagues at the Seattle Art Museum.

NW: You later invited Lauren and I to speak on a panel titled "Building Relevant Public and Educational Programs Using an Equity Lens" for the 2019 American Alliance of Museums Annual Meeting. Chayanne—then a member of my team at the Studio Museum—ultimately replaced me on the panel. Can you talk us through your conceptual framework for the discussion and how you imagined programs at the Studio Museum and the Brooklyn Museum serving as case studies in equity pedagogy alongside your work at SAM?

DR: I was really interested in providing three different institutional perspectives on how to utilize public and educational programs to implement racial equity work both internally and externally. After meeting with both of you, I felt a mutual desire to continue a professional relationship of network building and idea sharing and thought that AAM would be a great opportunity to continue the rich conversations we'd started in New York.

I'd admired the work of the Brooklyn Museum and the Studio Museum from afar and trusted that the case studies discussed at AAM would beautifully communicate that equity-driven strategy leads to excellence and innovation. Within the museum conference circuit, I think SAM, Brooklyn Museum, and the Studio Museum all have reputations that precede them. I wanted to capitalize on that by bringing us all together to tangibly communicate the message that "Surprise! It's not just one museum doing this kind of work, and if you're not doing it by now . . . you look kinda silly."

NW: Lauren, what were your first thoughts when invited to speak on the intersections of equity, relevance, and education at—let's face it—a pretty traditional museum conference?

Lauren Argentina Zelaya: This was my first time presenting at AAM, and David reached out from a genuine and generous place of wanting to share strategies and build as people and professionals for the greater communities we care about. I respect the work he and his team do at SAM, and I admire David's energy and approach, so I was excited to share the mic. I knew it wouldn't be stuffy and that we could share our expertise as leaders in the field and have fun with it.

NW: David, in your titling of the panel was a potent subtext—that museum relevance and sustainability are tied to equity practices. Chayanne and Lauren, in your work at the Studio Museum and the Brooklyn Museum respectively, how do you operate programs as a vehicle through which to drive equity and inclusion? And where does the museum field at large fall short in supporting that work?

Chayanne Marcano: Programming, at its very best, is holistic and sees itself as a continual practice of making space for those "outside" of the museum. It requires those who lead this work to often act as liaisons between institution, administrators, artists, community partners, and publics—attempting to hold and honor each entity's needs in equal measure. This becomes an exercise in listening, transparency, and collaboration. All of which are critical values for equity and inclusion work at museums and, thus, tend to be modeled first by programming staff.

I've been fortunate to do this work at Studio Museum, with its forever relevant mission of championing Black artists [see figure 5.1]. Artists are often my primary collaborators when developing programs. Including them in the process means that they become privy to institutional ways of working, but there's also an opportunity to put much consideration and care toward what it means and looks like to cultivate an audience around their work. This gesture can have an impact down the line, as artists go on to work with other museums and art spaces and, perhaps, request more opportunities for responsive and thoughtful public engagement.

Figure 5.1. Participants make cyanotypes in *Studio Squared: Experimental Print-making with Tschabalala Self*, St. Nicholas Park, Harlem, July 13, 2019. Photo by Stephanie Aguayo, courtesy The Studio Museum in Harlem.

Where does the field fall short? In its ableism. I was thinking the other day about the seating in galleries, which is already rare, but they're usually metal and cold and flat and hard. It's like a cruel joke. Maybe you've been on your feet for almost forty minutes, and you see this bench, so you're like, "Woot! Finally, relief," but when you sit on it, it's not comfortable at all. You almost think you're better off standing.

Back in 2019, I attended a program at the Whitney with Carolyn Lazard, organized by their access and community team, which includes Justin Allen, who demonstrates so beautifully on Instagram what's possible with alt-text and image description, and Dyeemah Simmons, who I had the pleasure of meeting at AAM earlier that year.

The event was free, and we were a small group, gathering in the gallery for a collective reading of Audre Lorde's *The Cancer Journals*. There was live CART captioning, ASL interpretation, assistive listening systems, iPads, pillows and cushions, and physical copies of the book. Afterward, there was a small reception with light snacks, wine, water. I was completely struck by how taken care of I felt, and I wouldn't have known to ask for those amenities if they weren't made available to all who joined. Centering the needs of people with disabilities in museums, to the point where it becomes default, can completely transform the space.

LZ: There are many ways to answer this question! You can leverage public programs as a way to experiment and invite people to actively shape who and what museums are for and imagine what is possible. Producing public programs that offer multiple modes of engagement (conversation, making, dancing, watching, listening) are generous ways of inviting people in. Inviting people to dance in the museum is a huge way of shifting the culture. Some may think dancing is trivial, but I believe dancing in a museum is powerful. Not only are you validating the artistry of musicians and DJs by giving them rightful space in the museum but there is a transformation that is possible when people come together and dance. We feel free. In Brooklyn, where the historically Black and immigrant neighborhoods are gentrifying, holding space for people to socialize, see art, dance, and express joy for free is a big deal. It is a statement of affirmation that we value you and we have space for you.

I'm repping for the oldest museum here so I'll say it: we are capable of falling short in every way imaginable when it comes to equity and inclusion, because museums weren't designed with those concepts in mind. The residue of the colonial, white supremacist structure is everywhere. Oftentimes museums fall short, because we're unable to break free of tradition in order to embrace a collaborative, people-centered approach. Institutional critique is too often feared and avoided rather than seen as the beginning of a conversation. Like Chayanne said, everyone needs to be involved. Public programs invite the public to think critically and fine-tune their own expertise, which is also essential to true equity and inclusion.

NW: Much of the DEAI [diversity, equity, access, and inclusion] work I've seen carried out within museums rests on the shoulders of an individual at worst, or an under-resourced department at "best." How might museums learn to share this work and this responsibility across the entire institution? And furthermore, how do we continue to strive for equity within the museum space when there is not even equity in the world?

CM: This is hard! It's easy to slip into working in silos, but it's so important to collectivize and identify your allies in the museum. Speak with those colleagues who share that commitment to DEAI and learn what they're working on or aspire to do, as there'll be moments in the future to collaborate and "disrupt" traditional processes in favor of one that might allow for more equitable outcomes. Even if these connections don't translate to immediate change, there's groundwork laid for mutual support when things get tough. Camaraderie is one way I protect myself. My challenges are not my own or isolated but become shared and something to work through together.

DR: Cross-departmental institutional participation should be the standard from which this work is done, and I think much of that comes from the support of leadership. Writing equity-driven strategies into strategic plans and designating line items in a budget give this kind of work the longevity that's required for it to live on. Museums often exist within very hierarchical structures, so positions of leadership must set the expectation that working at a cultural institution requires cultural aptitude.

I protect myself (while striving for equity) by using whatever sliver of opportunity I have to provide access, support, and visibility to those that have been historically denied those things. This shows up for me by thinking critically about which artist, performer, DJ, or photographer to hire for a large-scale program I'm working on. It shows up by advocating for myself (and those around me) to not take on extra work because someone else who's just as capable doesn't want to do it. It shows up when I choose not to engage in conversation with proverbial tone-deaf individuals who want nothing more than to have their outdated way of thinking validated.

I also work in a way that centers joy and celebration, no matter what the circumstance. Not only is this approach better for the skin (I literally refuse to have stress-related wrinkles for no reason) but it also helps me pay homage to the people who came before me and helped make the work I'm doing now possible.

LZ: Yes to the reminder that many people paved the way, David! I'm fortunate to work at an institution where I'm inheriting the legacy of this work, and DEIA is perceived as mission aligned and so much a part of our identity. A lot of that is because of the decades-long commitment of people before me who made it a priority to center the artistic production of people of color and, by extension, invite their people into the museum.

I think we're at an interesting moment where a lot of museum professionals, especially in the US (in particular northern US), have harnessed the language. Our field is at a critical moment, post–culture wars, moving away from discussing identity politics, and moving beyond diversity to think about equity, but a lot of us use these words without checking in to make sure we have shared definitions and values.

I was talking with a colleague in the field recently—Amanda Carneiro (who is a curator in São Paulo), and she totally reframed the question, which I think is necessary. Now many of us have to ask, *How do we implement racial equity work when the stakeholders you are trying to convince act as if they are already convinced but perhaps aren't doing their part to invest resources in shifting the culture?* You might have members of leadership that quote Audre Lorde, but if you still have jobs that require tons of degrees to be in decision-making roles, is your institution really transforming?

As David points out, there are practical everyday ways to implement equity, and building that into institutional memory a lot of times means writing it into policy and collaborating across departments and hierarchies. It goes hand in hand with effectively doing the work, but an important part of caring for myself has also been finding my people—like all of you! It's essential to make the work sustainable. Prioritizing joy is key. You have to find ways to make it fun! I also have a life away from work—although I believe that a commitment to equity and justice has to come in all aspects of my lived experience. I love to recharge by reading, watching horror movies, and spending time with my partner, who is not in this field.

NW: For museums that are new to the social justice conversation—or are developing a political voice for the first time—what would you suggest as a first step to bridging allyship and action?

DR: There's so many articles, evaluations, and studies out there to recommend, but some of the most effective tools to begin with are honesty, bravery, and understanding. If you're just beginning to do this work, start by asking yourself (and your organization), *What took so long?* Begin the process by understanding that this work is necessary because institutional, structural, and historical racism (to this day) continues to negatively affect people's lives while so many others continue to benefit from it. Be brave enough to shift the culture of your organization by letting go of staff or volunteers that are in direct opposition to this change.

LZ: Finally, my chance to fangirl—the model that SAM's equity team has created is impressive and can be applied in other contexts! People have been harnessing creativity to make our world more equitable and inhabitable for a long time. Look outside the museum world for possible models. What strategies can we learn from social justice movements or community organizing? If you work in a big institution, take a look at smaller art nonprofits—such as the Laundromat Project in New York or Show Room in London. Notice how they are structured for collaboration and put resources behind artists.

Some people I recommend reading: adrienne maree brown, Nina Simon, Pablo Helguera, Kareem Estefan, Keonna Hendrick (one of my friends and mentors!)—all offer interesting perspectives and help us reframe the way we are thinking about power, participation, and what is possible in and outside of institutions. Race Forward offers resources and workshops on understanding the pervasiveness of racism and undoing it.

Listen! Ask, "Whose voices am I not hearing?" Redirect your listening to colleagues inside the institution and community members outside of the institution who don't have the mic. Young people's voices are essential. Follow their lead and be transformed by their honesty and curiosity. They will determine if museums stay relevant, and any attempt to shift the culture in museums without them is in vain.

CM: Yes, to Lauren's tip for listening. It is so, so key. Allow your thoughts, assumptions, and biases to rest, and truly receive what it is that you're hearing. Refuse the impulse to filter it through your own experience.

Now, as far as fangirling, Stephanie Cunningham of Museum Hue, Porchia Moore of Incluseum, and La Tanya Autry of #MuseumsAreNotNeutral are a few of my *big* sheroes. I so appreciate the ways in which their movements have made space for folks to address the very necessary internal work that must happen in museums in order for them to change. There was a blog post on Incluseum a few years back that completely changed the game for me. It described best practices in the workplace—one of which was answering emails promptly as a form of emotional labor. Even when you don't know the answer, let your colleagues know! "Don't give your peers more work." [1]

Calls for change can come outside the museum, but it must be actioned from within, and it starts with how we show up and respect each other as colleagues.

OUTRO

We build because audiences exist. We build because we seek to reach out to others, and they will come initially because they recognize themselves in what we have built. After that initial interaction, spaces enter a process of self-identification, ownership, and evolution based on group interests and ideas. They

*are not static spaces for static viewers but ever-evolving, grow-
ing, or decaying communities that build themselves, develop,
and eventually dismantle.* [2]

—Pablo Helguera

Central to the activity of public programs is the notion of audience engagement.
As artist, educator, and former director of Adult and Academic Programs at
MoMA Pablo Helguera states, we build because audiences exist. But what if a
global pandemic radically upends this understanding? Does the charge to build
and bridge social space persist despite social distancing measures? Is our motivation to convene transformed by the knowledge that intimacy and connection
now exist as threats rather than rewards of engagement? Considering how significantly COVID-19 had transformed our orientation to the work and to each
other, I invited Chayanne, David, and Lauren to reflect on what, if anything,
had changed in their approach to programming since our initial discussion
in 2018. As an outro, it felt fitting to test museums' abilities to respond to the
pandemic—and the operational challenges and direct calls for social action it
produced—in real time.

CM: The move to offer online public programming was slow yet intentional. We took
time to dream of ambitious proposals, mourn the in-person events that would never
come to be, and make and remake again our goals for what a shared space on the internet
would look like. While our programming presence was on pause, the work of championing artists of African descent lived on but as phone calls, texts, email threads, and, of
course, Zoom meetings that held space for our grief and the grief of our creative community. We took care of ourselves and each other in the best ways we knew how. This
carries a different resonance when I think of our majority-Black staff living and working
through an everyday state of emergency.

Once we made the shift to offer digital programs, we continued to center the well-
being of our audiences quite significantly in our ideation. Knowing how a program can
produce a capacity to feel joy, it was important to ensure a sense of belonging or, in
such a busy, saturated time, the sense that our guests had made the right choice in giving us their screen time. Some of this depends on what the program is about or who is
involved, but the small things count too. We can't underestimate the impact of playing
a fire playlist as people log on!

This transition has also allowed us to provide live CART captioning for all of our
online events, prioritizing the needs of audiences who are older adults, deaf or hard
of hearing, and English language learners. I'm excited about how we can expand and
include additional access services in the future so that the resources that facilitate meaningful participation of disabled communities becomes not an option but a given.

DR: Beyond the obvious challenges COVID-19 created for the sector, the sociopolitical events of 2020 made it even more obvious that art should reflect the times in which it exists. From my perspective at SAM, that meant ensuring that our programming more deeply celebrated and elevated the brilliant Black artists living and working in Seattle. What's critical to note is that the work of centering the work of Black artists was already happening and by no means a new concept; however, 2020 proved that highlighting this practice should be a no brainer.

While it may be easy for some audiences to assume that work made by Black artists will only be about police brutality and protest, it was important for me to shift that narrative to reflect the multitude of artistic experiences that Black artists are capable of creating. Rather than rushing to create new programs, I found it best to slow things down and iterate on what already exists in order to reimagine the idea of museum programming in an ever-changing landscape while centering Black voices along the way.

I truly believe that the beauty, power, and grace of Black artists exists at the helm of excellence and innovation. 2020 taught me that as an arts practitioner, it's my duty to hold steadfast to the practice of bringing the work of Black artists to the forefront.

LZ: Reflecting on our conversation, it feels like so much has changed, and yet so much is the same. We are carrying a lot of trauma and grief. Our city shuttered due to COVID-19, and in the summer of 2020, Brooklyn Museum became the backdrop for many actions in support of Black lives and liberation.

One powerful moment was the largest action for Black Trans Lives in history—organized by the Okra Project, Marsha P. Johnson Institute, For the Gworls, GLITS, and Black Trans Femmes in the Arts, as well as activists like drag performer West Dakota, who was set to perform at the museum with the collective Papi Juice pre-COVID. Other organizations such as Good Company Bike Club and Meditating for Black Lives also hosted gatherings on our steps.

It was a lesson in un-programming and sharing power. We shared resources such as space, art supplies for poster making, and microphones and PAs with community organizers and protestors. We gave out PPE [personal protective equipment], water, and snacks that we had on hand. We hired poets to read on the plaza on Juneteenth. We opened our bathrooms.

My team decided we would no longer contract NYPD for our First Saturdays. First Saturdays have long been a site of celebration and support of Black liberation and joy in our borough. Public pressure that institutions end ties with police gave momentum that made it possible for us to make this commitment.

NOTES

1. trivedi, nikhil. "Museopunks Action Recap." The Incluseum, July 7, 2018, https://incluseum.com/2018/07/07/museopunks-action-recap.

2. Helguera, Pablo. "Community." In *Education for Socially Engaged Art: A Materials and Techniques Handbook*, 22. New York: Jorge Pinto Books, 2011.

MUSEUM AS ADVOCATE

How to Decolonize Museum Practices and Drive a Systemic Call to Action

INTRO

Since 2015, I've been bouncing around the idea of building a pedagogy for *museum citizenship*. I've imagined this as a porous concept used to describe the work that lay ahead for most museums: building civic engagement and cultural belonging *within* their walls while also participating in and learning from culture produced far *beyond* them. In addition to redefining reciprocity between the museum and its various communities, museum citizenship also asks the museum to shed the veil of neutrality, adopt a political voice, and take a stand on issues faced by its fellow citizens.

Seemingly simple in its construct, I've encountered numerous challenges to mobilizing museum citizenship from concept into practice. First is that, as we discussed in previous chapters, many museums struggle to identify and serve clearly defined communities—*if a museum can't name the communities it belongs to and the communities that belong to it, how can it become an advocate for the people?* Second is the hierarchical design of museums and the proliferation of siloed work—*if a museum can't design platforms for internal collaboration that democratize access to decision-making power, how can the museum present a unified, political voice?* Third is that many museums imagine themselves the necessary epicenter of the arts-and-culture ecosystem, a perspective heavily influenced by their practices of self-aggrandizement and accumulation—*if a museum only knows an exhibitions-driven model that prioritizes the acquisition and display of objects within its walls, how can it participate in non–object-based culture and dialogue sited beyond them?*

These are only a few of the obstacles I've identified over the past few years of workshopping the idea out loud with colleagues; however, they're a good launch point for the discussion that follows. I invited four museum leaders whom I admire greatly to reflect on the political responsibility of museums. Having held primarily curatorial or senior leadership positions within their respective institutions, they each discuss their experience wielding their platform and influence to move museums from lip service toward advocacy and action.

Ryan N. Dennis of the Mississippi Museum of Art, Vashti DuBois of the Colored Girls Museum, artist Lauren Kelley (formerly of the Sugar Hill Children's Museum of Art and Storytelling), and Jasmine Wahi of the Bronx Museum share far more than a desire to curate exhibitions where communities of color see themselves reflected within the institution. They are each committed to mobilizing structural change and building an ecosystem where this is the norm, not the exception—where the work of forging equitable cultural representation belongs to *all* of us and not solely the culturally specific institutions we discussed in prior chapters. From redefining the role of the curator and the function of exhibitions to lifting the burden off artists and communities to perform political participation on behalf of a complacent museum, these leaders leverage their platforms in service of arts-led social justice.

ROUNDTABLE

RYAN N. DENNIS is the chief curator and artistic director of the Center for Art & Public Exchange (CAPE) at the Mississippi Museum of Art. Ryan previously served as the curator and programs director at Project Row Houses, where her work focused on African American contemporary art with a particular emphasis on socially engaged practices, site-specific projects, public interventions, and the development of public-facing programs for adults and youth. She is deeply interested in the intersection of art and social justice while creating equitable opportunities for artists to thrive in their work. Dennis earned her master's degree in arts and cultural management, with a focus in curatorial practice, from the Pratt Institute.

Prior to creating the Colored Girls Museum (TCGM), VASHTI DUBOIS held leadership positions at a number of organizations over the span of her 30-year career in nonprofit and arts administration. In 2015, DuBois opened TCGM to "honor the stories, experiences and history of Colored Girls throughout the African Diaspora." It is the first memoir museum of its kind, offering visitors a multidisciplinary experience in a residential space. Dubois was awarded the Arts and Business Leadership Award for Outstanding Dedication to Women and Girls of Color and for providing agency and visibility for the practices and histories of artists often excluded from the canon. DuBois is a graduate of Wesleyan University and a NAMAC Fellow.

LAUREN KELLEY is a cultural producer and visual artist based in Harlem, New York. From 2017 to 2020, Kelley served as director and chief curator of the Sugar Hill Children's Museum of Art and Storytelling, partnering with established and emerging artists to execute contemporary art exhibitions for children and families. Kelley's studio pursuits have yielded residencies with the Museum of Fine Arts Houston, Skowhegan School of Painting and Sculpture, and the Studio Museum in Harlem. Her art has been included in exhibitions at the Centre Pompidou, Paris, France; the New Museum, New York, New York; Spelman College Museum of Fine Arts, Atlanta, Georgia; USC's Fisher Museum of Art, Los Angeles, California; and the Contemporary Art Museum Houston, Houston, Texas.

JASMINE WAHI is the Holly Block Social Justice Curator at the Bronx Museum of the Arts and the founder and codirector of Project for Empty Space, a Newark, New Jersey–based, nonprofit organization that supports artists who are interested in social discourse and activism. Wahi's practice predominantly focuses on issues of femme empowerment, complicating binary structures within social discourses, and exploring multipositional cultural identities through the lens of intersectional feminism. Wahi is a visiting core critic at Yale University and a faculty member at the School of Visual Arts MFA Fine Arts department. Jasmine Wahi received her master's in art history from New York University's Institute of Fine Arts.

The following discussion took place between Ryan N. Dennis, Vashti DuBois, Lauren Kelley, Jasmine Wahi, and nico wheadon via Zoom on September 18, 2020.

nico wheadon: We're here today to discuss the museum's potential as a social change agent and your work stewarding museums from rhetoric to action, and solidarity to advocacy. Perhaps each of you can begin by riffing on how you understand *museum citizenship* and what it would take to transform museums across the board into sites for social belonging and civic engagement.

Vashti DuBois: So I'm gonna put this language of museum citizenship to the side and back into it. My relationship to museums begins with the founding of the Colored Girls Museum—a museum that celebrates the ordinary, extraordinary colored girl, through art and artifacts. My understanding of what a museum could and should be to its citizens stems from my belief that it should specifically be an advocate, a companion, a friend, and reflection of the communities that it seeks to serve.

We have these massive cathedrals that call themselves *museums*. They tell us what's important by what's there and by what's not there. They create a ritual of prayer by choreographing our movement through these spaces. And there are some things that the Colored Girls Museum, without thinking about it, perhaps lifted from that tradition. But what I'm interested in is, What can a museum do? What should it be doing?

When I think about my history, my coming to museums as a girl, I always say that it was a source of benign discomfort. On class trips to these museums as a little black girl in Brooklyn, I would unknowingly be looking really hard for myself in these cathedrals. I didn't have any language for my own absence. So I would just go home from every school trip with a headache. It was years, *years*, before I realized, oh my God, I actually don't like museums! Then, as I became a director and a theater artist, I thought, *Oh my God, I'm an artist and I don't like museums.*

The turning point was going to the Whitney to see *The Black Male Show* a million years ago. I remember speed walking through that show because I felt so exposed. There were what felt like hundreds of white people everywhere, and I just wanted to cover the art. I wanted to have private space to consider what I was looking at that felt so very personal but was just laid *so* bare. And although I was in my 30s, I still didn't have all the language for what I was feeling. I remember coming back to Philadelphia and saying to myself, long before there was a Colored Girls Museum, "I want to be able to think about what it means to have an experience like that in a way that doesn't make me feel small and naked. I'm gonna put it in a house. We've gotta put it in a house. And it's not gonna be big. And it can't hold hundreds. And the entire perspective, the entire story of what we're being asked to look at is going to shift 500 percent."

So I am not a museum citizen. These cultural institutions are the dog whistle. We all went to school with that young person in your class who was always getting into trouble and then getting everybody else into trouble by extension. But when the students said, "It's *that* person," the teacher was like, "Oh no, no, no. That person would never. . . . That person has the best clothes, is the smartest person in the class, is the funniest person in the class, is the cutest person in the class, they would *never!*" So it was never that person. But everybody knew it was that damn person.

That's how I feel about these white cultural institutions. We've looked everywhere—we're looking at the medical institutions, we're looking at the FEDs, we're looking at the police department. But I'll be good goddamn if the purveyors of anti-Blackness—if the pillars of imperialism—are not these innocuous, sexy, educational, cultural institutions that are so revered and significant that they don't even have to pay for their own existence! And if we dig deep into the history of their collections, we cannot deny that they are doing significant damage and are going unchallenged and unchecked. Nobody's asking a cultural institution, "For real, for real? What is your relationship to anti-Blackness? Why don't you talk about what you keep, what you celebrate, how you structure yourself, and how you appropriate the work of others rather than standing in the way of folks having their own institutions that tell the stories that will archive their existence on this planet? Rather than you become the owners of somebody else's story?"

NW: Wow, you just gave me chills! It's interesting, you called museums *cathedrals*, and a mentor of mine featured elsewhere in the book called them *culture palaces*. She offered that what seemingly needs to happen in this moment is that the largest among them actually need to contract in scale so that they can evaluate their relevance and audit their efficiency in delivering on their stated missions. And that the funders who cultivate this culture of expansion and unchecked power that you mention are complicit in their imperial rise.

VD: I don't doubt that. 'Cause now people are catching that kid moving. They're like, *That's the troublemaker. There he goes right there!*

Jasmine Wahi: I think you hit the nail on the head, Vashti. You drove it all the way in. I don't even know what I can add that's any more accurate than that. It resonates deeply with me as a Brown person who never saw themselves except through the lens and gaze of colonialism in the museum space and then again only in the antiquity and other other-ized space of a former colony.

NW: Jasmine, perhaps you can discuss your personal history of museums in relation to what it means to now be a social justice curator at the Bronx Museum?

JW: I have complicated thoughts about the position. I guess, personally my stance is that it's better to be late to the party than never showing up at all. I think the role of a social justice curator in the Bronx Museum is a little strange, or redundant, considering the theoretical founding mission of the institution to be a borough museum that is communities-oriented. How successfully the museum has been at that over the past 50 years has varied.

It's an endowed position that was created in memoriam of Holly Block. So it's even more complicated because it's not just a social justice curator position—it is the Holly Block Social Justice Curator position. I knew Holly very tangentially, and I know that she did great work at the museum, but to have an endowed position with a title automatically sets up a hierarchy, which is antithetical to what social justice is about, in my mind. My other fraught feelings about a social justice curator—not in the context of the Bronx Museum but in other museums adapting that position, title, or focus—is that it alleviates the responsibility of the rest of the institution to think holistically about social justice and intersectionality and essentially gives them a pass.

I think it should be the mandate of every institution to think intersectionally and to dismantle colonialism in every single show that they do, whether it's a decorative arts show or an abstraction show or a minimalist show—and in my opinion, *particularly* in a minimalist show, considering the hegemonic whiteness and maleness of that particular genre. It should be the mandate of every exhibition and every curator to consider those things. And so by having a position that's specific, it creates a dichotomy where no one else has to necessarily think about it. And I think that it's tokenizing, which is what museums historically have done.

So I have always been in the camp of *burn them down and build them back up*, even though now I work for a museum. I can't imagine what change might look like aside from just completely physically dismantling them and then starting from scratch.

Lauren Kelley: I think I'm of a different adage. I believe that there's no such thing as being all things to all people and that any institution that says it can is lying to itself. I think if everybody's clear on what their target audience and their mission is—and institutions like the Bronx Museum, the Colored Girls Museum, and Sugar Hill just get the support they need—there are options out there. 'Cause if we burn it down, whoever regains control will assert their agenda, and it still won't be an institution for *all* people. It will be whoever is at the top, and the cycle of challenges related to ensuring that certain people's voices are respected will remain a problem. So I think devoting ample space to us outliers and respecting these mission-driven spaces is a more sustainable effort and moves us toward the end goal.

JW: I think, in theory, bigger museums say that they're trying to do that, but in practice they just fall so short—optically they agree, but you don't see them putting their money where their mouth is. I think that's due to the top-down structure of museums, with boards governing all. I guess my attitude to *burn it all down* comes from a nihilistic perspective that things won't change unless we push people in power to relinquish their power. And if I'm gonna be completely honest with myself in that position, if I didn't have the experience of being a woman of color and was basically a straight, white, wealthy man, would I give up that power? Probably not. And so how do you coerce or white-knuckle-drag people out of those positions in real life rather than just in theory?

NW: As you were speaking, I was thinking of Helen Molesworth's Dear Fellow White Women initiative, which was an effort to organize white women in the art world into "a consciousness raising group to try and address [their] part in the racism that structures our society."[1] Since I'm Black and will never know the inner workings of that group, I found myself asking my friends who participated, "Did you discuss what you are ready and willing to give up?"

Lauren, I hear you. I think there is some common ground between what you and Jasmine describe—it's an acknowledgment that structural transformation is what we're after, not surface level change. Sure there are different inroads, but ultimately what needs to shift in order for change to manifest is a complete disruption and redistribution of power. And let me be clear—I'm not just calling out majority-white institutions; I'm also calling out culturally specific institutions who've thrived, in large part, due to a selective proximity to whiteness and to white privilege. Oftentimes, it's the culturally specific institutions that feel as though they have less to contribute to conversations on diversity, equity, access, and inclusion because of their historic track record in serving a particular community. But I'm like, "The diaspora is complex and spectrums of identity, vast—we all have work to do to ensure our full communities are represented!"

Ryan N. Dennis: Even culturally specific institutions take on whiteness in intense ways that need to be disrupted, called out, and reframed. Vashti, your words resonate so much with me, especially thinking about not being a citizen of the museum. I find myself as an outlier like you. I started as a curatorial assistant within a museum but was also doing a lot of volunteering work at this organization called Project Row Houses in Houston, which has always been very community-based and committed to building intimacy with folks that look like us. It's interesting to now be back in a museum that has a pretty significant vision to do racial justice work and more expansive narrative shaping around conversations of the Delta, civil rights, and activism.

The audience that I bore witness to is predominantly white, but the museum is located downtown and is literally surrounded by West Jackson and South Jackson, which are predominantly Black. The Mississippi Museum of Art serves all of Mississippi, as I'm always reminded, but I'm like, *We're in Jackson! What are we doing to find ways to connect with the folks that actually live here?* I often think about how we can build more intimate space within the museum and am always inviting folks to come here. And they're like, *Where is it? What are y'all doing? I might have gone to a movie night outside once, but I've never actually stepped foot in the door.*

So thinking about museum citizenship makes me think about place and where institutions are physically located and how they serve their hyperlocal communities. I think that's very important, and I don't think that that work is only the responsibility of the community-based arts organization, like the Laundromat Project, or Project Row Houses, or even the Underground Museum. All institutions need to be thinking more strategically and be willing to do that hard work to connect with people who haven't historically been part of the museum. And Jasmine, I agree with both you and Lauren. One day I'm like, "Burn this shit down," and the other day I'm like, "No, we need these institutions, because they offer X, Y and Z." So I don't know—I'm just so disappointed that we keep having to engage these conversations with no real work.

Vashti, I'm happy to hear you discuss how *Black Male* inspired you to think about how we develop more intimacy around our stories. I think that there is not enough care and attention paid to Black, Brown, and disabled folks, and I guess museum citizenship should be about finding ways to have more care and sensitivity. The reality is that it is not just about the objects. It's not just about the exhibition. It's not just about the hiring of individuals. It's a complete reprogramming! The reality is that we're dealing with people who live their lives in so many different ways. If individuals aren't able to do the important work on themselves, then they're bringing all their shit into the way that we engage and interact on a daily basis. I think there's not enough attention paid to that.

LK: The cycle of this conversation highlights (1) impacting the mother ships of museums and (2) building our own planets. Thelma did *Black Male*, and if she didn't then carve out the time and space to really build a mother ship in the Studio Museum in Harlem—that has now trained hundreds of museum professionals to continue to impact more museums—where would we be? I'm a product of that and of an HBCU—I could always see myself, despite how many white spaces I circulated within, because I had the Black planet of Prairie View in my life, where my parents worked. Every moment I could be in that environment, I found a counterbalance. The trying to diminish my sense of place and self didn't work because I had a very healthy, huge other planet. A reservation to exist on. I think the museum world needs reservations for people to digest the love that only a home can deliver.

VD: I'd like to touch on a couple of things that people have said. So, please know that I actually come from the school of *do that shit yourself.* I grew up in an all-Black neighborhood in Brownsville, Brooklyn. I got a scholarship to a private school when I was in seventh grade, a predominantly white school. Then I got a scholarship to a private, predominantly white university, Wesleyan University. When I grew up in Brownsville, Brooklyn, my mom owned our home. My mom was from Ahoskie, North Carolina, and one of the lessons that she imparted was that freedom for Black folks is about literacy and land. My mom wasn't just talking about reading books; she was talking about reading all the signs. You have to understand things. You have to be able to see the text that's in invisible ink, and I got that.

When I went to St. Ann's, I was appalled. I thought my mother sent me to hell, because, really, I had never seen white children outside of TV. The teachers who taught in my public school, I swear to you, I thought they floated in from the TV and then floated back out. That's how Blackity Black my neighborhood upbringing really was. And here I was in New York City, and those were my beliefs. When I got to St. Ann's, it was a complete mind shift. But here's the thing: when I was at St. Ann's, I did not think those people were better than me for one minute. I was like, *Oh, your people own your house? My mama owns her house.* I did not have a concept of not being enough, even at that predominantly white school.

There are so many complicated conversations that I think we need to be having as Black and Brown people in the world that we never get to, because we always have to explain racism or something that's in a million books and on a million websites. I want people to know my whole complicated story. I want to look at the stuff I wanna look at. I wanna get well. I don't wanna come back to this planet again. I wanna be able to evolve. What I know is, as long as we keep talking about the same shit, they gonna send me back here!

So I don't want to *burn the shit down* because I don't wanna spend my energy on it. I want us to ask ourselves the hard questions about what makes it difficult. Thelma, right? Just think about this brilliant sister. In order to build a Black cultural institution, she had to start at Whitney, right? How often do we have to go all the way around the planet to do the work we really want to do? At the Colored Girls Museum, our primary constituent is the ordinary colored girl because that's who we're representing. But a lot of the love that we expect from Black people in the know does not come, because they're waiting for white people to cosign our work.

The other thing I say about TCGM is that she is a house that decided to dress up as a museum. For our first show, she was disguised as a rooming house, a bed-and-breakfast. You know why? For her frigging protection! Because if you knew she was a Colored Girls Museum, you'd say, "Oh, that uppity bitch, let me bomb her." And we have continued to disguise her as she needs to be for whatever it is we're talking about. So really,

TCGM is a public health clinic . . . because our museums need to work at that level for us. We have to understand that our artists are our doctors, our artists are our preachers, and our artists are our natural healers.

So when you come into the Colored Girls Museum, I'm not trying to inspire you, I'm trying to infect you. I want you to get what there is to get, take that shit back to your colony, and get everybody. And I don't give a good God damn if you're Black, white, purple, or green. I actually don't care. I'm about the survival of ordinary Black and Brown women and girls. 'Cause if we don't survive, ain't none of y'all gonna survive. I know you don't believe me, but you're not gonna survive. Your survival is so tied up in us. That's my Sermon on the Mount!

JW: I started Project for Empty Space for the same reason, Vashti. And to answer your original question about museum citizenship, nico, I would say I grew up in the free museum world. I grew up in DC and spent pretty much my whole childhood in the Smithsonian, which is probably why I became interested in the arts in the first place. But I consider my citizenship in the museum to be as complicated as my citizenship as an American—as someone continuously being left out with nowhere else to go. I was 23 when I started Project for Empty Space, so I learned at a young age that if you want something done right, you've got to do it yourself. If you don't see a place where you fit in, you've got to make that space and place.

I'm sure each of you has experienced this continuous uphill battle of naysayers and people who don't want you to thrive. And I have never had the ability to camouflage well, and so it becomes so much harder when you don't acquiesce or play nice as a tactic of survival. nico, when you mentioned Helen Molesworth's white women group talking about race and decolonization, all I could think was that my experience has been that white women in leadership positions and institutional spaces aren't willing to relinquish power or even share their platform. It goes back to my pessimism of everything—how do you get people to genuinely make change if they are not actually willing to give some-thing up and instead use every tactic that they have to hold on? I don't know what the solution is!

RD: We're talking about conditioning upon conditioning. And I think this work that we are doing now, building upon previous generations, might not even become visible change during our lifetimes. No one talks about the parallels between white gatekeeping and the colonization of Black spaces or what we must endure to be seen and appreciated. I don't actually know what the next step is to decentralize that power, because that's what it actually takes. Maybe it's gathering more women and people of color to share the work that we are doing, to share the relationship building that's happening, and to share the radical advocacy work that's being done on various platforms. And maybe it needs to happen both inside and outside of institutions.

How do we reshape our narrative to start with Black and Brown people at all costs? I'm developing a new collections policy at the museum; a complete reevaluation needs to take place, and some questions I am asking are around deaccessioning and reimagin-ing the inclusion of local Black histories. The mandate of filling in the gaps is just not enough. The gaps are far too large, so I don't know if that's the approach! I think the approach is just committing to acquiring the work of artists of color, period.

So for me, it's about centering Black and Brown people, because they are always centered in my world, and trying my best way to make constellations that are not focused on whiteness, where white women or men are giving me approval to do my work. It's about finding ways to uplift our stories. If we are all operating from museums, then how can we create constellations with each other that make commitments, and cultural agreements among Black and Brown curators and cultural workers? The challenge is that there are so many people who are indoctrinated into a system that says, *You're not supposed to do that.* Some people probably think I'm not even supposed to be at the seat that I'm sitting in. "How are you a chief curator at a museum and you didn't major in art history?" Well, I'll tell you how—because I've been doing this good work, that's why. And lifting folks up. Let's focus on that.

LK: I think that the most equitable thing about our time is that there are more of us in positions where the question of, *How did you get that?* is not something we even have to pay attention to anymore. Even Peter Schjeldahl at the *New Yorker* talked about how he had no background in art history when becoming an art critic—he learned it on the fly. I think it's more common than we even understand despite, as women, being taught that we have to prove that we belong in the room. We know the underlying factor in all of what gets to stay: what gets launched is the money, and you've gotta convince somebody that their investment is not a joke.

I mean, Jasmine, your title is catchy and easy to fund right now. The tilling of the ground that I've stood on has been so flipped in terms of understanding how all these relationships and dynamics work in actuality versus in theory—being the artist on the outside of the ecosystem and then moving to the center as a potential gatekeeper and understanding the eye contact that has to happen with the board. The conversations and the culture of the development team—it's a very different reality that boils down to the funding.

JW: Yeah. I'm learning in real time all of the things I've heard rumors about over the years, and it's really terrible. I now understand the fatigue that people face who have worked in museums because the dynamics are so wild, and the level of bowing and curtsying people have to do for scraps is gross. I'm like, "Can someone give me a refund on my million-dollar education which I'll never pay off?" Because what it comes down to is subservience to get pennies, and I didn't need all of this education for that, and yet all of this education I have is the reason that I'm able to make less than six figures to basically beg.

RD: And just the bureaucracy of it all. At Project Row Houses, I worked with a level of autonomy. Because it was such a Black space, I didn't have to do the curtsying and bending backward, because that was our land. Those were our homes, built from Black folks' hands—if you're interested in being here with us, then just be here with us. Being back in a museum, it's exhausting to go through the channels to get a yes or a question answered—the defensiveness and the microaggressions are so incredible.

NW: I just want to take a beat to acknowledge the difficult emotional and physical labor that each of you has put in—not only to survive these spaces but to also *build* within them, and against the immense gravity of institutionalized oppression no less. Safe spaces to air these frustrations are just so rare, and I hope readers hear both the struggle and the triumph in the experiences you've so generously shared. I'm reminded of a comment made in an earlier roundtable by artist Jordan Casteel, who said that museums need to learn to honor that our pain is real, just like their role in producing it is real. I hear a lot of pain in these stories and hope that folks who might not share a similar experience of museums find a way to sit in this discomfort with us and learn from it.

As I listen to you discuss your work decolonizing museum practices, I can't help but wish I'd met each of you, or come across a conversation like this, earlier in my own journey—there is just so much power and wisdom in what you've shared. To those reading this that are working against the grain yet feel disillusioned or isolated in their work—you are not alone.

JW: That's so important, nico. One thing I have been thinking about is who I'm making shows for as a curator. At Project for Empty Space, it was very clear although it was never verbally articulated. At the Bronx Museum, I've decided to stop doing shows that try and convince people of our value and instead do shows for our communities that are about holding each other in communion. *How do we say that we're community-oriented or community-facing museums if our shows are not reflective of that?* And so I'm less concerned about convincing the traditional, predominantly white audience and creating shows and didactics for them and instead am making exhibitions that don't require explanation and are reflective of community. Lauren, I'm wondering if the types of politics were any different, or mitigated, when working in a museum that's oriented to children.

LK: No. I think the politics of who's on top are just the politics everywhere. I think the politics of museums are just the politics of organizing. I'm still so fresh out of the experience that I'm still processing it all. I think bringing a board together is a really hard thing to do, even when you have an amazing board, as I did. But I do think that the next iteration of my life as an administrator will be about reading the room and understanding the double-talk—what's verbalized versus what's intended. That's a decoding that I've always found myself lost in.

VD: I think we need to play around, structurally, with how we're going to exist in the world.

The nonprofit museum model is highly problematic. So if we are also going to start remaking things, we have to really be willing to evaluate where this money is gonna come from. I paid a lot of attention to Obama's campaign, and what I loved was that, yeah, they got big dollars, but you know how much money they made on 25- and 15-dollar donations?

I'm still waiting for every museum alliance that we are not involved in to challenge us as a museum so I can say, "I don't care, y'all make shit up all the time." I'm shocked. We've had folks come to the museum and ask, "What's your curatorial background? What about your collections?" And I'm happy to say, "We don't really believe in collections, we believe in people." So if we have a body of money, we're probably not gonna invest in collecting; we're gonna figure out how to push back on gentrification. So the museum really acts as a force field.

Our reimagining of what a museum is means that all of it can be reevaluated by all of us, all the time. And for those of us who are in these white spaces that we're critiquing—that's cool, just don't lose your mind there! Don't let them take your mind, and remember it's a game of steal the bacon. I always tell the sisters working here at the museum, "Listen, your job is to get other people to pay you to learn what you need to learn to live your best life."

So I admire each of you. I think it's important that you're in these spaces, creating the opportunity for crazy people like me to run around doing other shit. It's also important that we hold each other up by extending the protection, praise, and grace of all the Black institutions that continue to do the work. It important that we have our hands in all the pies and that our communities support us while we're there, because it's dangerous work. It's not for the faint of heart. This constant fighting and gaslighting and genuflecting— we all know what it's activating inside of us. Its activating a memory that we know is a problem, but we also know that this is the time to be in these spaces, pushing back. Because we were always there. And when we find ourselves back there again, it is to activate these memories of our ancestors who know their stuff is there and need their people there to care for their archive and care for their stories. I think that's critical.

RD: Can we do this every Friday morning? I need this in my life.

OUTRO

A central concern in our discussion was how to build intimacy around and care for our stories while protecting their authenticity through the processes of institutional interpretation and translation. If museums are to step more fully into their roles as cultural stewards, this is a challenge they must urgently address as they work to regain the trust and respect of communities that have been marginalized or wholly erased from the narrative for far too long. *So how might a museum achieve this?* By, as Vashti said, being an advocate, companion, friend, and mirror to their communities above all else. (In part 2, we will further unpack this orientation toward a politics of care.) This simple yet powerful proposition dares museums to become spaces of belonging and home and to exhibit the same care for their communities that they do for the objects in their holdings.

We also discussed the importance of synchronizing the work of the entire institution and promoting more symmetry between internal and external practices. This means decolonizing public-facing exhibitions while at the same time rewriting human resources and collections policies through the lens of inclusion. It means establishing frameworks for cross-departmental collaboration that dismantle silos within the museum while at the same bridging practitioners across museums through the creation of peer networks and knowledge-sharing platforms.

So in a nonprofit sector burdened by a scarcity mindset, how do we actualize this reorientation toward shared resources and accountability? In the final chapter of this section, we look at the flawed design of the nonprofit sector and consider how the funding landscape and philanthropic trends reinforce a spirit of competition over collaboration, and resource hoarding over resource sharing. And, as we did in this chapter, by unpacking the breadth and depth of the interlocking issues at hand, we open up space in which to imagine a path forward.

NOTE

1. Via a May 30, 2020, post on Helen Molesworth's Instagram account (@hmolesworth).

MUSEUM AS STAKEHOLDER

How to Retool the Funding Landscape and Invest in a Social Change Ecosystem

INTRO

In the previous chapter, we imagined the museum not only as an advocate for social justice but as a social change agent in and of itself. We discussed the internal policies, practices, and hierarchies that would need to be dismantled for the museum to more fully step into its role as an engaged cultural citizen. The more we questioned the systems that embolden museums to perpetuate practices of cultural exclusion and erasure, the closer we arrived at a shared sense of the root issue—that the nonprofit industrial complex to which most museums belong is flawed by design. From its top-heavy governance structures to its dependence on philanthropy in a highly precarious and segmented market, the nonprofit sector is ripe for a redesign.

In this final dialogue on decentralization, I invited three innovators who are actively reshaping the sector to analyze the nonprofit funding landscape and its trends, sharing strategies to move cultural institutions away from a reliance on charitable giving and toward long-term economic sustainability. Shawnda Chapman of the Ms. Foundation for Women, Ruby Lerner, formerly of Creative Capital, and Melissa Cowley Wolf of MCW Projects and Arts Funders Forum share their insights on what it means to effectively and equitably resource cultural institutions today.

CHAPTER 7

ROUNDTABLE

SHAWNDA CHAPMAN is a researcher, activist, and nonprofit professional who lives and works in Brooklyn, New York. Her work has attempted to address inequality and injustice broadly, with an acute focus on centering the needs and experiences of marginalized people. Currently, as director of the Girls of Color Initiative at the Ms. Foundation for Women, Shawnda leads and shapes efforts to address the multitude of inequities faced by girls of color by providing grantmaking, leadership development, and capacity-building resources to support their advocacy and movement building.

RUBY LERNER is the founding executive director of Creative Capital, an innovative arts foundation that adapts venture capital concepts to support individual artists. Under her 17 years of leadership, Creative Capital designed a comprehensive support system for artists that combined money with advisory support. Currently, Ruby is working as an advisor to the arts program at the Open Society Foundations, assisting in the design and implementation of the new international Soros Arts Fellowship. She is also the arts advisor to Civic Hall in New York. Ruby currently serves on the board of directors of the Andy Warhol Foundation for the Visual Arts, Eyebeam, and Light Industry.

MELISSA COWLEY WOLF is dedicated to expanding the next generation of cultural philanthropists, advocates, and audiences. As founder of MCW Projects LLC, she advises organizations on philanthropic and narrative strategies to engage new audiences and supporters, partners with rising philanthropists and collectors to achieve social impact and legacy in the culture economy, and executes cross-sector partnerships to advocate for increased support of the arts. Melissa is also the director of the Arts Funders Forum (AFF), an advocacy, media, convening, and research platform designed to increase private support for the arts and develop new models of impact-driven financial support for the cultural sector.

The following discussion took place between Shawnda Chapman, Ruby Lerner, nico wheadon, and Melissa Cowley Wolf via Zoom on January 26, 2021.

Shawnda Chapman: I'm the director of the Girls of Color Initiative at the Ms. Foundation for Women. I'm excited to do that work right now, especially given all that's happening in the world. Every day I sit down at my computer and know that the work that I do matters and that we get to push the field to do it differently. My background is not in philanthropy; it's in movement work, focused on mass incarceration and ending violence against Black girls. It's a perfect marriage of sorts to now be doing work that supports the organizing and leadership of girls of color.

Ruby Lerner: I'm Ruby Lerner, and I'm the founding director of Creative Capital, where I was for about 17 years before retiring in 2016. At this point in my life, I'm 73 and think a lot about life cycle and when to get out of the way and make space for the next generation of leadership by stepping into a different kind of role in the community. I work with a lot of younger leaders, nico included, who are incredible and are running things now.

nico wheadon: It's such a privilege to learn from you, Ruby, and you are more generous with your mentorship than anyone I've ever known! Ruby does all these amazing commencement speeches, and I just love that generations of young people get to engage Ruby's brilliance on this precipice of stepping into their power as future leaders! It's a very simple yet important way that you continually show up.

RL: I just feel lucky that people still want to talk to me! I'm really grateful to be in a position of service, especially on advisory boards. We've got to make more space for people of color, for people who are younger, to become the next generation of leaders. And if people like me just stay in our jobs forever, there's just not the space. Often, I think people are worried about losing not just money but also stature. So what can we do to create a structure that honors the contributions that people make but then moves them along gracefully?

Melissa Cowley Wolf: I'm Melissa Cowley Wolf, and I'm trying to, as I think we all are, consistently contextualize where we are in the present moment, especially as it relates to the pandemic, the economic situation, and the social justice movements that are gathering so much steam and therefore encountering resistance—and then how to apply this thinking to the cultural and philanthropic sectors. I come to this work after 15 years of institutional fundraising in visual art museums and higher education across the US. I started my consulting practice in 2017, and then in 2018 collaborated with another consulting firm to create the Arts Funders Forum. Both practices are dedicated to increasing private giving to the arts by expanding the next generation of cultural funders, audiences, philanthropists, and patrons. We conceived AFF when Donald Trump was inaugurated and threatening to abolish the NEA. The question posed was, *If public funding for the arts gets abolished, is there a mechanism to spur more private giving by galvanizing the next generation?* And we looked around, and said no. So we thought, *Well, let's start one.* I shaped my practice in response to the trends I was noticing in my institutional career as a frontline fundraiser, to help the sector pivot.

NW: Can you elaborate on what you think the current philanthropic trends are and what you'd like to see the nonprofit arts sector pivot toward?

MCW: The nonprofit sector is so stuck in their ways, and the paradigm of fundraising in which they've been operating is just not resonating with the next generation. We're seeing the largest transfer of wealth that's ever happened in the history of the country. We're seeing funding to the arts decrease as overall charitable giving in the United States increases. And we were seeing rising generations move away from the arts and toward education, public health, medicine, and environmental and social justice. In my consulting work, I advise cultural nonprofits on their narratives; one of my core beliefs is that the arts don't tell the right stories. And so before we even get to strategic planning, before we get to campaign, we're going back to mission and vision and digging in by asking, *What is it you really do?* and *What is the change you want to make in the world?* One hundred percent of the time, that's not the story they're telling.

And to go back to a point Ruby made, I agree that we don't have a system to help people move into that next phase. As we talk about the movement of folks so that we can create more space, we also need to assist in that movement. And so, Ruby, I'm curious to hear more about what you think those support structures could be and how that might work as someone that's going through that experience right now?

RL: I don't fly, so I started asking people on my train trips, a lot of whom are retired, "What was the biggest lesson you learned, and what advice would you give to somebody?" So I've been collecting information from all over the place for a long time. And I don't remember who it was, but someone said to me, "Have something that you're moving toward, so you don't get obsessed about what you left behind." I think that was some of the best advice ever. It encouraged me to put something in place at Creative Capital before I left. I was so lucky and had an amazing board, who said to me, *If you want it, we would love to serve as a kind of advisory team to bounce ideas around with about what you're thinking about doing next.* I mean, how generous is that? I was so grateful, because it forced me to articulate the things that I really was interested in. I don't think I'm currently doing a single thing that I had on that list, but that doesn't matter—what mattered was the discipline and the support. That should be a standard of nonprofit board practice.

NW: Shawnda, everything we've discussed so far underscores the importance of your work empowering Black girls to step into the full spectrum of leadership. What are some of the challenges you face in your work?

SC: Often, what I do with the Ms. Foundation is supporting girls of color in matriculating up into leadership. There is this weird paradox where, when you're a youth, you don't have any voice until you're an adult, but when you become an adult, you're expected to show up and have all the resources and know all the things. And so there's this interesting in-between period where you don't get to be seen or heard, and you don't get to have a lot of power. But then you're expected to show up and be competitive and tell people what you need.

When I think about the necessity for some folks to move out of the way, I also think that we have to have a fuller conversation about what people actually need to be able to step *into* leadership—what sort of development and access—because there are reasons that certain folks are not in executive leadership in certain spaces. There are a lot of barriers but, beyond the barriers, there's a lack of investment in the leadership of women and girls of color. And so, while they have really innovative ideas, a lot of times we set them up to fail. We need to consider our responsibility to create and strengthen that pipeline.

I also think we need to be really specific—when we say that the people who need to move out the way fear a loss of stature, what they *also* fear is the loss of power. And what does that actually mean when we start to think about shifting power? It's an uncomfortable conversation, and I think that we do the zero-sum thing where it's like, *If they have power, I have no power.*

RL: I think you're right and it's very helpful to separate power from stature. I went to a women's college and am so grateful for that opportunity. Many years ago, Jesse Jackson said on a talk show that *leadership is bred in majority situations.* And that was my experience at a women's college. Who's the editor of the yearbook? Who's the president of the class? You're seeing models of leadership all the time.

My fear about this stepping aside—and having more women of color step into these roles—is that very slowly the people with the resources, the same people who need to move aside, would stop investing in organizations as they began to lose power in leadership. It's terrifying to me that we could get great new leadership but that the people with the money would just slowly begin to abandon the organizations that are trying to undo white supremacy.

NW: I think this is where collective-impact models are such a useful framework. If *multiple* museums were to make the moves Ruby just described at once, perhaps it would be more difficult to walk back that investment, because there'd be this shared accountability.

MCW: I see us needing to do two things at once here. One, philanthropy is about power and it's not going to change until we democratize pathways to wealth creation. And two, there's the structural issue that we need to tackle and that's going to take more than just the arts sector to do. That is a massive, societal, structural change. I think people are waking up to the unmasking of white supremacy and the unmasking of the barriers to wealth creation, and that's why this moment that we're in, in terms of a social justice movement, is incredible. And now it's a matter of harnessing that within our sector.

The story we've been telling about the arts since 2000 is the Bilbao Effect, the capital-construction expansions and building of all these temples and beautiful buildings. It has created the perception that the arts are an exceedingly wealthy and exclusive sector. And then we've had what I call the Basel Effect, when Art Basel Miami Beach debuted and we saw the proliferation of art fairs. This cemented this narrative of the arts as a rich, celebrity-filled sector. It has turned off a generation that is invested in pursuing equity and justice and recalibrating power. We are long overdue to correct that story and explain how the arts are a driver of justice. For instance, how artists and arts funders help by mitigating climate change. And so, I think the legwork now is democratizing this power structure, and that's going to mean that institutions must be funded differently.

And that's what everyone is scared of, because we've now created cost disease, right? We have these inflated budgets for these temples, and there's this persistent fear that if we start to make change, we are going to lose Mr. Older (White) So-and-So and their $35 million check. There needs to be a recalibration of the work that's done in those institutions, starting with the budget. And to create space for people to come in, who can't necessarily write that check but are devoted to these issues of equity and recalibrating power and helping the institution move in a direction that is more relevant to their community.

CHAPTER 7

RL: At Creative Capital, we began to see that people had real issues around money and that they were in bad debt, which we would often find out *after* we had given them their first check, and the IRS would send us a letter saying, *If you give this person any more money, it's coming to us because they owe back taxes.* And so we realized that *all* people have issues around money—if you have money, you have issues around it; if you *don't* have money, you have issues around it too.

It took us a long time to figure out the right formula for a workshop on financial literacy, but in the end, we brought three different kinds of financial people in to work with our artists. We brought in a person who used to work with the Actor's Fund, who talked about financial health and wellness and got at people's attitudes about money. We brought in a tax and accounting person. And we brought in a third person who was a long-term financial planner who, believe it or not, was also a working jazz musician. It was great to have somebody who was an artist themselves. And we covered very basic stuff, like, you need to have enough money to pay your bills. You need to have an emergency fund. And you need to be saving for longer-term needs.

I remember one of our grantees said, "I've never heard any of this before." And then he said, "I know my parents don't know this information. My brothers and sisters, my nieces and nephews. I know they've never heard any of this before." And then he paused, and he said, "You know what? I think that's why poor people stay poor." And that's haunted me every day since. A lot of the work I'm doing now is education around financial literacy—the basics are absolutely critical. This is a gap that needs to be remedied immediately.

SC: I'll jump in, because I felt like you were preaching to the choir! I'm a year and a few months into my first job in philanthropy. Before that, it was research, policy, and movement work. And so that gives me a very unique perspective. I was in this conversation with Mariame Kaba, a wonderful organizer, where one youth was naming all the things she wanted to do with her life. And Mariame told her, "Pick the thing you're going to use to create change with." 'Cause you cannot do all the things! It sent me on this journey to locate why I'm doing the work that I do and how is it going to create change. So that informed my orientation as a researcher—I've always called myself an activist researcher. And now I call myself an activist philanthropist. This is the tool that I'm using to impact the change that I want to see done in the world and the change I'm uniquely suited to impact.

NW: Let's riff on this a bit! What are some of the tools that supported you in bridging your movement work with philanthropy?

SC: Well, there are a few tools that we have as people who work in philanthropy. One, we have the power to set the agenda. And I think that's a power that we don't talk about a lot—the ability to make demands on institutions. One of the things that we are doing right now in our current round of grant making is we're asking people to describe their board compositions and we're asking people to be very specific. Two, we have an ability to take a holistic look at what the field needs. My initiative is not quite off of the ground

120

yet, because we've spent a year doing a really aggressive landscape study and talking with organizational leaders, people who support girls, speaking directly with girls, and mapping the field and the investments to make a more definitive statement about what we think they need but, more specifically, what organizations say that they need and what girls of color say that they need. It's like philanthropic advocacy—taking that information and going out and then pressing the field. Oftentimes, we're making these processes burdensome for people, and we're not actually giving them what they need.

And three, to your point, Ruby, is capacity building. In that learning tour that we did, what we found was that people don't have financial literacy and neither do organizations, and it's causing people to fail. And they're being crushed under the weight of a lot of bureaucratic requirements, especially in places where people are simply struggling to exist, like the South. People were saying, *This is how the opposition comes for us. We're doing our work and they're telling us we didn't follow the papers, or we did something wrong.* I can't tell you how many people have submitted requests for funds that didn't know the difference between an organizational budget and audited financials. I think that just being really clear on the actual power that we each have is key—like, *I have the ability to commission research*, and *I have the ability to convene.* Melissa, I agree, we need to look at the entire ecosystem of change.

MCW: I love that. The first thing I thought of was the conversations I had this past December at the AFF Summit with artist Shaun Leonardo, about the need to create this ecosystem of change; instead of just funding specific projects or individuals, we need to create a funding community ecosystem around change. How can we better map the arts to other sectors and other causes so that we can actually focus on funding that community of change of which the arts are a part?

I love what you're doing, and how you tie that to capacity building to these larger issues versus the surgical strike of funding, which is what we've *been* doing. I was also thinking about how the general public's understanding of financial literacy is tied to their understanding of what the nonprofit structure is. I feel it's totally misunderstood from the outside, and it's completely flawed and archaic from the inside, right?

NW: I agree there is some real vocabulary building that needs to take place in order for people to shape their own understanding of, and position within, the change ecosystem. I also think it does *everyone* a disservice when we don't address the power dynamic between the grantor and the grantee and how the political agenda of philanthropy often shows up in an institution's program and communications.

MCW: Well, institutions have been put in this position where they have to respond to and build around the grant because they're so dependent on, and desperate for, that funding. And so they've really been unable to build this ecosystem of change, because they've been stuck in that surgical strike response mode.

RL: I want to share a micro example. When I was hired at Creative Capital, I'd had no experience in philanthropy at all. But I had been a grant seeker for many years in mostly grassroots organizations, like Alternate Roots, that I ran for a handful of years. At that time, I was really trying to look at two things. One was what was missing from the funding landscape in terms of support for individual artists. And the other was how to create the world that I wanted to inhabit.

There were a lot of both subtle and overt things that I tried to build into the system. And it was designed as a system; there were four parts. The first was to support the *project*, which was a very great and concrete way to start, and we did that with money. We were modeled partly on ideas from the venture capital world, so this was a big innovation in the cultural space at that time. I liked the way venture capitalists parsed money out to their businesses based on benchmarks. I think you can consider the anatomy of a project and say there are various stages in a project's life where an infusion of cash will really make a difference.

So the first was supporting the project; but pretty soon after we made a decision about what projects we were going to be supporting, we went on a journey with the artist, and this is the place where we helped people to build very specific personal and professional skills, like strategic planning. And this was so profound for people, so second was support for the *person*. There are studies that have been done that show, if you write down your goals, you are 42 percent more likely to achieve them. So we had people with their strategic-planning notebooks making their five-year goals and their ten-year goals. Another great exercise was writing your own obituary to help people imagine how, at the end of everything, they wanted people to remember them and their work. So it was personal and professional skills building that was so powerful for people that we ended up creating a national program.

The third component was building the *community*. The first part was building the community of funded artists so that people became resources to each other. And I can tell you that after decades, many of these people are still in conversation with each other. And then we did an artist retreat where we brought in people from the field that I called the *opportunity creators*. These were curators and programmers, book editors, publishers, and other funders. We asked every artist to make a presentation and end it by talking about something that they needed, besides money.

And the fourth and final component to our model was engaging the *public*. We were not a presenter or producer ourselves, so we did that by being an aggressive information broker. So project, person, community, public was our design [and] what we found was that the whole was greater than the sum of the parts.

We were not a perfect organization, but I think that somewhere along the way, I had the recognition that we needed to be a kind of permanent laboratory. It's demanding of a staff, because you have to be alert enough to see and perceive the changes that are going on around you and then respond. Since we were trying to create a generous organization, we were seeing that people were sharing information and contacts with each other. People were creating opportunities for each other that went beyond anything we might've done. We were sitting in the middle as the facilitating agency. And it was happening informally.

And one day I said to the staff, "Let's formalize and positively reinforce all these great artists who are doing this work." So we created a situation where some of our more senior artists became advisors to the new groups of artists. They would have a cohort of about five or six artists, and we paid them pretty well to continue that work as part of a two-year commitment. I think that was an example of seeing something that was going on informally, being alert enough to perceive that, and then figuring out how to more formally support it.

MCW: Wow, you've both been working to create three Ts—*trust, truth*, and *transparency*. As we think about how to shift the power, open things up, and fund things in a more equitable way, Ruby, *project, person, community, public* holds so much transparency. You're aligning people with a mentor/mentee relationship and creating that trust and an environment of truth. And for so long, both the artist funding and the artist mentoring has happened behind closed doors. One of the reasons that younger generations are rejecting systems and institutions is because of the lack of all three Ts.

SC: A major barrier to supporting youth of color is the fact that we don't trust them, especially if they are leading movements or trying to create change. Our foundation did a report recently, called Pocket Change, that really explored the lack of funding to women of color–led organizations. So they receive less funding, and when they *do* receive funding, they have to go through more hurdles. They don't often receive general operating funding. So they're getting restricted funding because we don't trust them. I feel like we don't have good measures broadly to capture the nuance there.

I'm also thinking about the fact that the trust dynamic goes both ways. Part of what I've tried to do specifically with my initiative is to prove that we can do all these things we said we could not do before. Especially in this sort of current social and political context, COVID-19 has required us to rethink all of these bureaucratic processes. Even the idea of what constitutes evidence needs to be reconsidered. As a researcher, I'm like, "Stories are evidence." Evidence is a barrier that we put in place to be able to determine who is deserving and who is undeserving. And it ties directly into that concept of trust. And like, if we really do believe that some solutions lie in communities, then we have to trust them to do the work that they say needs to be done. And we have to trust them to fail.

I have learned so much from failing. I'm a pro at this thing—so much of what I know is about what I can tell you does *not* work, and to be able to have evidence of that is super important. And I think that there are certain communities that don't get the space to creatively fail. You know, it's like you don't get the luxury of innovation and experimentation because you're always living under this microscope. And what I want to do is expand the opportunity to just be able to get out there and try something and be able to talk about it.

RL: I stopped using the failure language somewhere along the way and began to think of it more as just iterative. It's just iteration. I want a T-shirt that says, "Don't Mind Me, I'm Just Iterating."

Shawnda, you said something really important about community solutions coming from the community. That's been my orientation historically, since I've run these smaller grassroots organizations. And I can tell you that large foundations and major foundations do not generally trust solutions that come from the community. The issues around trust are huge, so how do we beat, move, or shame philanthropies into more of a trust posture? At Creative Capital, I was hired by the brilliant Art Gillies, who was the president of the Andy Warhol Foundation at the time.

And he said, "I'm not going to launch Creative Capital if we don't have at least $5 million, because you need the money to have opportunities to fail." How many people are handed a philanthropy job with that directive? How do we hold on to that spirit of experimentation as a permanent mindset? A lot of people are not hardwired to experiment, possibly fail, and then pivot. We don't talk enough about the external environment that we're operating in, where change is a constant—we're never going to have stability again. We are in a permanently dynamic situation.

MCW: I keep thinking about what you said a bit ago about how we're not taught financial literacy and we're not taught how to fail. Listening to you both talk, it's like, *We have to learn on the job.* And so much of life is like that. We're not at all given the tools, especially as women, to navigate a process of trial and error, experimentation, and failure. Everything we've seen from the last year within the cultural sector—the reactionary nature, the stress around the need to change—is all part of it.

We need to utilize our core resources, which are creativity and humanity. *How do we merge these and become more comfortable?* We need to become more comfortable now as adaptive individuals that make up institutions. *So how do we, in order to make these changes and support a creative sector for the future, recognize the role it can play in larger societal change vis-à-vis environmental justice, equity, education, and public health?*

NW: It's certainly an important question! Your talk of core resources takes me back to the prevalence of this scarcity mindset that, in my opinion, might be one of the biggest hurdles the nonprofit arts sector has yet to overcome. Given the lack of trust within and between institutions, how might we shift cultural institutions to an abundance mindset? How might we nurture more collaboration, mutual dependence, and respect?

SC: I feel like I vacillate between those various positions of scarcity and abundance every day. I've done enough research to know that there's a mismatch between the change folks want to see in the world and where they do their giving. The status quo in philanthropy is silos and asymmetric information—we're left with the idea that things just are how they are and this is all there is. I worked recently on this project called The Donors of Color Project where they took a look at high-net-worth donors of color and mapped some of their attitudes and experiences.

And one of the things that struck me from those interviews was the fact that people had really grand ideas for change. They were really committed and invested in a broad range of things, from women's issues to arts to the orchestra. But when you looked at their giving, it was like, *I gave to my alma mater.* The mismatch is they didn't actually feel equipped or knowledgeable enough to be able to direct their resources to the change they wanted to see done in the world. So they don't have access to the information that they need to have access to. But then, on the other side, *we* also don't have access to the fact that they are out here wanting to support this work!

RL: So that's another thing that we need to get clear about—where's the values match and where's the values mismatch? We funded a lot of collaborative projects at Creative Capital. And we also ended up presiding over a lot of messy divorces, and it was really harsh. And what we realized was that, in a way, the grant had been a catalyst for new and difficult conversations. And so we had the artists write contracts with each other about how they were going to work together and dissolve in an amicable way if things didn't work out.

One of the things that we encouraged artists to do around the premieres of their projects was to come together with the premiering venue and have a conversation about what the goals for the launch were. We also provided some resources to help the artists accomplish the things that the venue itself was not able to provide. So even though our money went to the artist, the venue also felt supported, and that made us a good collaborator. But it also changed the power dynamic, in a minor way, between the artist and the institution, establishing the artist as a really good partner in the enterprise.

MCW: Yeah, I think there's this connection between partnerships, collaborations, abundance, scarcity, and fear. Fear and insecurity drive the scarcity mindset, and influence or reinforce historic power dynamics. And, you know, since the protests at the Whitney in 2019, the conversation about ethical philanthropy permeated the cultural sector in a new way and brought it to the forefront.

At AFF we were curious about what it would take to shift the power and not have to be solely reliant on large funders with questionable sources of wealth. In our 2019 research study, which we conducted around the time of those protests, we surveyed the cultural sector 360 degrees: funders, leaders, artists, creatives, cultural workers, etc. We used those findings to inform the evolution of our platform. What emerged were a series of topics and recommendations for how we could move forward ethically in cultural philanthropy. And one of the biggest things that came out of that was everyone's stated need and desire to see more partnerships and collaborations—that through partnership, we can shift the power dynamic and get away from fear and insecurity. But that's going to take confidence to move in that way. And again, we're going to have to change the way we do business to achieve that, but we need to do that anyway.

One thing that fascinates me is the potential power that a democratic fund could have to shape the priorities of institutions and move power from the individual to the community. And the best way to do that is through collaboration and partnership, which I think will move us into that abundance mindset. That could really be the key to overturning it. And the key to moving out of that fear is working together.

RL: You're really talking about diffusing the power of any one person through the collective so that nobody has too much ruling authority, which I think is a really wonderful way to see it. I think we also have to talk about the power of the grassroots, and, under the Obama administration, we began to see how large groups of people coming together could really make a difference. And, obviously, there's been a lot of continued grassroots support where the average gift is like 32 dollars, right. But they're raising millions and millions of dollars. To me, that's a healthier model because otherwise we're still talking about having to suck up to rich people and rich foundations.

I mean, I really want to just be done with that. I know it's not possible, but as we talk about transitioning, I would love to see an organization that is fully funded by small donors and not one person giving millions and millions of dollars who expects their name on everything. I try, in my work with individual artists, to drive home the importance of building your own mailing lists and the power of having a direct and immediate relationship with your audience. Musician Amanda Palmer talks about her relationship at Patreon, where she has like 14,000 people who help fund her work. If 14,000 people gave any one artist a dollar a month, that'd be $14,000 a month, or $168,000 a year. And you tell me who would not be happy to have a salary like that? And that's community-powered and community-funded. And there's a line where she says, "This has changed everything about how I make my work and how I get it out into the world." The value that she places on every single one of those people is just enormous. This is, to me, another place that we need to evolve to.

It's really hard work, which is why nobody wants to do it. Obviously, it's a lot easier for somebody to write you a million-dollar check than to find a million one-dollar donors. But, when we think about health and what the components of health are, I think even if you have a *healthy* amount of money coming from grassroots support, it ironically attracts higher-level donors because they see that you have a demonstrated value to the community.

MCW: Obama, Bernie Sanders, Howard Dean—these campaigns reshaped how community was engaged in fundraising. And I think the arts sector needs to learn from how these other sectors have done it and start to model it. They re-created how we galvanize community toward political change.

SC: One of the things that we did at the Ms. Foundation was we pulled together this huge council of organizations working with girls that constituted the core of our research. We made it a point that we were going to partner directly with them and that they would be compensated for their work. Because I feel like the other thing that we tend to do is lean on folks in the grassroots to tell us what to do but act like it's a privilege for them to be able to be in conversation with us. So we're continuously extracting. My orientation is to give more than I take, *always*. When we use their expertise and don't compensate them for it, we're really replicating the structures and power dynamics we are trying to change. In my conversations with our grantees, we are recognizing them as experts.

MCW: And that's the power shift!

RL: I really feel that we have to look at how we value institutions. In this COVID-19 moment, I've been questioning, "What are our essential institutions?" Often, if you look at the path of an individual artist who has achieved "success," the path there was through these more grassroots structures in the community. And so we have to ask, *What do these institutions need?* Because—when I think about where we are—philanthropy is failing and failed.

Even before COVID-19, most organizations (and even people) that I was talking to had about two months of operating capital available. And so, it took this crisis to reveal how not great it was before. And so, we can't just say, *We've got to get back to that.* Who would want to get back to that?! We have to think about how we capitalize these entities in a more sensible and stable way. So for instance, most grants are project grants—they're not general operating grants. Now in my view, there should be a portion of that grant where the funder says (because funders have this ability) *put X percentage of this away into a self-investment fund.* Project money is not enough to sustain an organization.

Our field is littered, not just with the corpses of the failures but of the successes too. Because you would do a pilot project, prove that it works, and then the funder would say, *That's so great. Now you've got to go out and find other funders.* What would happen in the commercial world is that a lot of people would pile in with investments. We have a perverse system in our arts universe that's got to be unraveled. The perversity has got to be unraveled and revealed, and we have to help people in a generous way, help philanthropy reinvent itself.

MCW: As a leader, you've done such great work helping artists (and now institutions) really walk into that space of entrepreneur and innovator. And—and I agree with you, Ruby, that it's important to be nimble enough to see and understand that you are an agent of social change—and now we need cultural funders to see themselves as investors in these agencies of social change and investors in artists as [both] entrepreneurs and innovators who can solve global challenges. And that means we need more social enterprise. We need more impact investing. We need completely different forms of support in line with other sectors.

RL: The Design Studio for Social Intervention outside of Boston has a concept called "ideas, arrangements, and effects." When they're talking about *arrangements*, they're really talking about the day-to-day ways that we operate, often subconsciously, in our environments. And how something like racism might be at the heart of those arrangements and, therefore, produce cultural effects that might not have been intentional. And so, when the Studio works in communities, they go straight for the arrangements because they believe if you can unravel the arrangements, you can reveal the ideas, often bad ideas, that are behind those arrangements, and you can then confront them and eliminate their negative effects. I think we have a lot of "unraveling" to do in our field. I think we might finally be ready for this hard work.

OUTRO

To not only reimagine the essential forms and functions of museums but to also unravel the conditioned *ideas, arrangements, and effects* that undergird their systemization is indeed hard work. As modeled in Ruby's transparency at the onset of our discussion, it is hard work because it is highly personal work that demands each of us confront our own privilege, bias, openness to risk, and will-ingness to cede power. In sharing her experience moving aside to make space for a future generation of leaders—and in her mobilization of personal resources and professional expertise in support of cultural organizations authentically engaged in equity work—Ruby stands as an example of fierce solidarity and servant leadership in practice.

As throughout this book, a few prompts invariably invoked discussion on interrelated and compounded issues. As convenor, my commitment was to remaining open in my vision for the direction of the conversation and where its contributors might lead it. Despite our focus on reimagining the nonprofit fund-ing landscape, our analysis was wide because the issue of structural inequity and how it is upheld is far-reaching. And in our efforts to triage a crisis of economic sustainability in the sector, what emerged were tools—gleaned from our collec-tive experiences—for how to invest not only in individual cultural leaders or institutions but rather in the entire social change ecosystem.

II

CASE STUDIES
IN CULTURAL
CITIZENSHIP

8

THE HARLEM SEMESTER
How to Adapt Art History into Contemporary Curricular Tools

BACKGROUND

The curriculum of the Harlem Semester critically examines Harlem not as an inert site or abstract concept but as an intensively peopled place of complex interaction and rich history, alive today. Pairing faculty from Barnard and other colleges with Harlem-based institutions, these place-based courses teach Harlem's diverse cultural and political legacy through participatory, interdisciplinary, and multidirectional learning modules. [1]

CASE STUDY

ELIA ALBA, born in Brooklyn, is a multidisciplinary artist who works in photography, video, and sculpture. Her practice is concerned with the social and political complexity of race, representation, identity, and the collective community. She received her bachelor of arts from Hunter College in 1994 and completed the Whitney Museum Independent Study program in 2001. She has exhibited throughout the United States and abroad. She lives and works in the Bronx and is artist in residence at the Andrew Freeman Home. She is guest curator for El Museo del Barrio's current exhibition, *Estamos Bien: La Trienal 20/21.*

TINA M. CAMPT is Owen F. Walker Professor of Humanities and Modern Culture and Media at Brown University and a research associate at the Visual Identities in Art and Design Research Centre (VIAD) at the University of

Johannesburg, South Africa. Campt is a Black, feminist theorist of visual culture and contemporary art. She is the author of four books: *Other Germans: Black Germans and the Politics of Race, Gender and Memory in the Third Reich* (2004); *Image Matters: Archive, Photography and the African Diaspora in Europe* (2012); *Listening to Images* (2017); and most recently, *A Black Gaze* (2021).

CONNIE H. CHOI is the associate curator, permanent collection at the Studio Museum in Harlem, where she oversees all aspects of the museum's collections. Prior to joining the Studio Museum, she was the assistant curator of American art at the Brooklyn Museum. Choi has a PhD in art history from Columbia University, an EdM from Harvard University, and a BA in the history of art from Yale University.

LESLIE HEWITT addresses fluid notions of time. Her compositions of political, social, and personal materials build multiple histories embedded in lens-based, sculptural, architectural, and "abstract" forms. Exploring this as an artist and *not* as a historiographer, Hewitt draws parallels between the formal appearance of things and their significance to a collective "sense" of history, political consciousness in contemporary art, and everyday life. Hewitt earned a BFA from the Cooper Union for the Advancement of Science and Art, New York (2000) and an MFA in sculpture from Yale University (2004). She is associate professor of art at the Cooper Union for the Advancement of Science.

SHANTA LAWSON is a museum educator and arts and cultural leader who serves as the education director at the Studio Museum in Harlem. There she has developed and sustained education programs to serve a wide range of audiences, including students, families, youth, and adults. She is committed to exploring and developing ways in which museums are accessible spaces that inform and inspire progressive, person-centered education practice. Shanta earned her master's degree in arts and cultural management from Pratt Institute and is a board member for Arts & Minds, an organization that provides visual arts experiences for people with dementia and their caregivers.

The following discussion took place between Elia Alba, Tina M. Campt, Connie H. Choi, Leslie Hewitt, Shanta Lawson, and nico wheadon via Zoom on June 3, 2020.

nico wheadon: Tina, can you discuss the genesis of the Harlem Semester and how you arrived at the idea of siting faculty instruction and student learning beyond the walls of Barnard? Why was it important to you that Barnard and Columbia students get out of the classroom to engage Harlem, not merely as students but also as citizens?

Tina M. Campt: The idea of the Harlem Semester started with a paradox I noticed while chairing Africana studies at Barnard—that we were teaching Black studies from one of the major global capitals of the African diaspora and, at the same time, teaching within a gated campus. The fact that we were teaching from this location but we were teaching *about it* at a distance—like it was someplace in books, not literally five blocks away—didn't make any sense. Columbia University and Barnard College are in Harlem. Our students are living in this amazing community, but they had no idea what that meant. There was this sense of wanting to both go beyond the gates of Barnard to teach about our community and at the same time having the recognition that we should not be teaching "about" Harlem but instead we should let Harlem teach itself.

NW: I love that. So, you're not only shifting the lens on what it means to be a student but also what it means to be a scholar—a radical repositioning of fieldwork and expertise!

TC: Precisely. I really wanted to underline the distinction between scholars who teach *about* the place and are experts on that community, culture, or history, and the scholars *of* that community who can actually teach from within it. The great scholars of Harlem teach from a stoop, a corner, an institution, a stage, or a canvas. How could we invite students who are trying to understand the African diaspora to learn from their expertise and place that expertise on a par with that which is recognized by formal degrees? For me, it was about the exchange we could create between Harlem's institutions through partnership.

NW: And how did you initiate those exchanges? What were the early questions you asked both yourself and your potential partners?

TC: At first it had to be a series of conversations with the institutions about, *Who am I? What does Barnard have to offer?* As opposed to yet another educational institution trying to take from a community or take advantage of the scarce resources of community institutions and organizations. So then the question was, *How can we partner?* One of the early insights I had was that most of the institutions I was speaking to had either K–12 educational programs or continuing-education programs but nothing at the university level. I felt that was this was the area where students actually had so much to give to those organizations in terms of support.

NW: Leslie, can you discuss your work developing the Freestyle course as part of the Harlem Semester? As both an educator and an artist [see figure 8.1], what unique skills did you lend to the process of curricular development? And how did your syllabus resist the prescriptive canonization of art history?

Leslie Hewitt: I want to first thank you, Tina, and acknowledge your work and effort. I wish Barnard could have supported, fully. I was an artist in the art history department and experienced Tina's efforts within Africana studies before even completely aligning our understandings.

Within my classes, which were more practice based, I realized there was an opportunity to structure a course that in some ways was an enigma to the institution. Meaning that, a course like Freestyle could critically challenge and close the gap of knowledge between what students were currently studying in the context of an art history undergraduate education and the dynamism of the contemporary art world both nationally

Figure 8.1. Professor and artist Leslie Hewitt featured alongside former Barnard College and Columbia University students and Studio Museum staff. *Studio Lab,* 2016. The Studio Museum in Harlem. Photo by Argenis Apolinario.

and internationally. To me, the most important thing was that students learn, and learn collaboratively. Whenever I'm teaching a class, there's always four or five other voices that I bring into that space to problematize my approach so that the approach is not simply coming from a singular perspective. Bringing in art historians and curators of color—or art historians and curators who work closely with artists of color or who work closely with the work of artists of color in groundbreaking ways—created a space for students to begin to imagine together about what could be possible for them, for us.

NW: How did your experience of the Studio Museum's Artist-in-Residence program in 2007 inform your notions of who was necessary to invite to participate in the space?

LH: I was able to bring the Studio Museum into the rubric through my admiration and deep respect for Thelma Golden and begin to really craft a specific connection through the relationship with you, nico. By siting our mini residency at the museum, students witnessed that all the answers were not going to come from the ivory tower, and that they never did. That they had to open their eyes and see that there's this world of artists, writers, art historians, and others who are not validated equally by the institution but are still part of the critical discourse that ends up, at some point, entering that conversation.

We have to tune or teach ourselves to listen to, to be with, to experience art, and to have the meaning unfold. It was really important that the students understand that the curatorial premise of *Freestyle* allowed for that.

NW: Can you expound a bit? What art historical moment was *Freestyle* born from and why was that so central to the curriculum?

LH: The term "post–Black art" was coined in the late 1990s by Thelma Golden, curator and director of the Studio Museum in Harlem, and artist Glenn Ligon, pivoting into a dialogic on the ethos of race and art praxis. What is post-Black? Is it postrace? Is it post–Black Arts movement? If so, then what was the Black Arts movement? What did it do? Could there be a "post-Black" position without the Black Arts movement preceding it?

There were numerous critically engaged questions that developed out of the course that contribute toward destabilizing a whole host of assumptions about race, art, and culture. There were also certain themes from artists in the exhibition who grappled with notions of migration, exile, and diaspora that didn't allow for any student to rest or be passive in the class.

We really spent the first half of the class problematizing our historical playbook. I often imagined it as slowly closing the physical and psychological gap between Barnard and the rest of Harlem. And then in the spring, we walked from Barnard to the museum. It seems like such a small thing, but it was actually part of the social sculpture of the course, and those details made the experience. It created a bridge.

TC: At the same time, it was you, Leslie and nico, who embodied what the Harlem Semester could be for me. When you developed the Freestyle class, it was based on an art historical intervention that remade both [art and history] in the art world, institutionally from the position of Harlem. What does it mean to revisit that intervention now, especially because it's an intervention that Black artists and curators still continue to make and that Studio Museum is still making? The course bridged a gap that cannot be filled by the institution, art history, art historians, or art theorists—it needed this other thing that you offered, and I feel like Barnard got to benefit so much from giving you a laboratory to explore it.

NW: I think that's a great word to describe it as well. With "laboratory," you get that sense that experimentation, trial, and error are all welcomed. That there's not a singular outcome that's imagined as a result of the exercise. For me, that is part of the beauty of how it evolved over time. Elia, as a participant in that space, what was your experience of the Harlem Semester? How do your identities as artist, curator, organizer, and Studio Museum Artist-in-Residence alum [see figure 8.2] inform your understanding of the role of arts education within museums?

Elia Alba: To be honest, I was glad to participate because Leslie asked me to, and she wanted my opinion and perspective on certain things. I remember bringing up the fact that there weren't enough Black Latinos in the *Freestyle* show, but I clearly understood the institutional reckoning that Thelma was dealing with and that it had to be that way, at first. Of course, fast forward to now, and we're in a different place.

I think these kinds of spaces for education are still clearly valuable and necessary because schools are really lacking in teaching youth to understand the importance of language and structural racism. I've been thinking about that more, now that I'm curating

Figure 8.2. Artist Elia Alba featured alongside former Barnard College and Columbia University students and Studio Museum staff. *Studio Lab,* 2016. The Studio Museum in Harlem. Photo by Argenis Apolinario.

the 2020 Triennial with El Museo del Barrio—that disconnect between what students learn in school and what they do when they come into a museum.

I wish the Harlem Semester could continue and expand, because I think there is a massive gap. Even if people do museum studies, I feel they just grasp words or ideas without necessarily understanding what they're saying or doing. I'm not a historian, but I'm doing this curatorial project, and I care what it says and does.

NW: Leslie, I've heard you say you're not a scholar, and Elia, you just said you're not a historian. But the beautiful thing about the Harlem Semester is that, within this laboratory that Tina designed, you actually *are* experts because you lived through and navigated these historical moments in important ways that people can learn from.

Leslie, for me the most striking choice you made early on was to design museum staff into the space as the living embodiment of the museum's work. Shanta, you participated in our Freestyle course many times, as did members of your education team. What were some of your key takeaways, and how did you understand the importance of the Harlem Semester being sited, in part, at the Studio Museum?

Shanta Lawson: I'm thinking about roles and the opportunity that my team and I had to show up and be in dialogue with the students. There was a unique opportunity to honor and newly understand the ways we *do* show up in our roles as people with experience and expertise, even though our capacity as learners never ends. It was interesting to be in dialogue with the students about the work, present on programs, and answer questions while also showing up with all the questions I still have about that work.

I'm the education director at the Studio Museum, a title that indicates that I am leading an aspect of this institution and managing this side of work from the space of our mission and within the legacy of our 50-year history. Being in this space of asking questions about that work and being critical about what we're doing and why doesn't actually stop. I think that's why it's striking that the Harlem Semester takes place in museums and other active spaces of experimentation, questioning, dialogue and sometimes prompts really tough exchanges, because we're working those things out and interpreting them, both in real time and in hindsight.

As practitioners, I think it's important to speak these things aloud and to offer these insights to students because, so often, my team and I would walk away thinking anew about something that perhaps we'd just spoken about or questions I want to investigate further. I think it reinforces the understanding of learning and teaching as a cycle, which is really highlighted when learning takes place within communities because the power dynamic is different from traditional learning spaces. That, for me, is empowering, and it's why I love museum education so much.

NW: Exactly. I want to call Connie into the conversation to reflect on her participation in the initiative. Connie, as associate curator at the Studio Museum, how do you understand the Harlem Semester in relation to your work with the museum's permanent collection?

Connie H. Choi: I was invited to participate in my third month of working at the Studio Museum. That was pretty special, because I was still trying to figure out the institution, the collection, and the history. That session, I literally just sat there and listened. The speaker for that week was Herb Tam, from the Museum of Chinese in America. I was speechless, because I've never been in an academic situation where a curator was invited to take over for the entire session. I've gone to three universities and had never been in that space of learning from someone who had such deep expertise, history, and passion for the arts, and mission-specific arts as well.

That was a really special opportunity, and I'm glad it came so early in my time at the museum because it really helped shape how I thought about the institution and the history of the institution. It was important for me to be able to witness that early, because it did help me think about the institution's role in shaping not only an art historical narrative but in helping to shape how people saw the history.

In terms of the collection, one of the things that has always been important to the institution is supporting the art of living artists. The institution was founded as that. I think what the Harlem Semester has really done, specifically the Freestyle class, is to put that at the forefront and not talk about art history as history but as a *living* history, which I think is important because you don't often get that in the academic setting. My own academic history was always about the past—even in my contemporary classes, you didn't get that same type of grounding and thinking about artists as people. We were taught to see in terms of the artwork they're producing as opposed to their own lived experience as producers.

As nico and Shanta know, the Studio Museum did not begin with a collection. In fact, the founders of the institution were really adamant about not having a collection, because they felt it would weigh them down in terms of having to care for a specific group of objects and not give them the flexibility to be reactive and work with different types of artists. The idea of a collection was born from the artists themselves! They were the ones who gifted works from the beginning of the institution's history because they saw the importance of having their works represented in a mission-specific institution and having those works cared for in the future. Those things combined really reveal how the Studio Museum considers artists and how artists have contributed not only to the history of the institution but also to how the museum sees its own history.

NW: In your opinion, how did *Freestyle*—the museum's first F show in 2001—shift the museum's collecting priorities?

CC: In thinking about the Harlem Semester and *Freestyle*, it's important to acknowledge that these ideas are cyclical and in conversation with each other. That particular moment was important because there was the James Van Der Zee exhibition the year before, another demonstration of how Harlem has always been grounded within the institution's exhibition history and the collection. And the *Harlem Postcards* series started the year after, in 2002. Again, this idea of grounding Harlem as central to the institutional mission. This idea that we're not just a studio museum but that we are the Studio Museum in Harlem and thinking critically about Harlem as our context.

Freestyle marked a big institutional change: Lowery Stokes Sims came on as director, and Thelma Golden came on as chief curator and deputy director the year before the exhibition opened. They both had experience working at the museum before and came back committed to the idea that individual moments don't exist in and of themselves. This commitment to combining the contemporary with historic is something that has always existed within the institution's history. This juxtaposition of contemporary and historical exhibitions is something that I'd love to hear Shanta reflect on in terms of how she and her team approach educational programming.

SL: It's funny—we're walking back in time here talking about what was happening in 2001, and I got to the Studio Museum in 2002. I've been around for a while and have really enjoyed the dynamic with the flow of exhibitions—each puts the education department in a position to discuss what collections are, why they're important, how we look at artworks together to build meaning, and what we can learn about an institution from its collection. The conversational space of the Studio Museum encourages open discussion and debate about what living, practicing artists are making and presenting, and why.

The Harlem Semester encourages us to think progressively about modes of learning that can take place within the museum space. Providing direct access to artists and staff is so essential, as is dialogue with communities of learners. That's how we approach what can and should be unique about programming these exhibitions. The word "dynamic" is in our mission, and a dynamic conversation is not two-way or binary or hierarchical but instead can be a conversation and dialogue that moves—conversations between students, learners, visitors, the artwork, and/or the artist, the educator, or, in this case a professor. The Harlem Semester exemplifies that aspect of the Studio Museum's mission and what it can look like through this kind of innovative programming and exchange.

NW: As you were talking, you reminded me of some unexpected outcomes of the Harlem Semester that I think are important to name. First, by sharing dedicated time and space with fellow staff—and across all departments and levels of leadership—the museum was able to dismantle the departmental silos that often hinder authentic collaboration. The platform's open environment produced new understandings about shared values and interests, and the profound mutual respect for each other's work that it engendered was transformative. So thank you for that, Tina and Leslie.

Second, we found a way to celebrate Harlem as both a cultural anchor rooted in a deep sense of place *and* a mythical construct comprised of endless perceptions and projections. I'm still shocked that, for so long, Barnard and Columbia leadership advised students to take the downtown 1 train followed by the uptown 2 train to get to the Studio Museum, instead of walking 15 minutes down the cultural mecca that is 125th Street. I'm glad that the program helped to reorient students to their surroundings in healthy ways that replaced fear with learning.

CC: This reminds me of a friend of mine who did undergraduate at Columbia and opted to go into a dorm that was on 110th Street. The university gave her a free monthly MetroCard because it was trying to encourage people to live outside of the boundaries of the campus, which was literally four blocks away. The idea that the university was encouraging students to separate themselves from the neighborhood that they lived in is really upsetting. My friend took it because she was out and about all the time, but the fact that the university had to bribe students to live below 116th Street is crazy and something that I think goes to both your experiences, Tina and Leslie, in terms of the battles you had to fight in order to bridge that gulf.

TC: The irony is that so many Harlem institutions are built atop the history of 125th Street, a former canal that ran river to river from the Hudson to the East River. Thelma Golden talks about this often—that in order to build, you literally had to go around this canal and other prehistoric formations that have structured Harlem geographically. These formations affected the relationship between the Studio Museum, the National Black Theater, and the building on 5th Avenue where both were hatched. That building cultivated and nurtured all sorts of different institutions throughout Harlem!

I remember so fondly the culminating Harlem Semester events, where everyone came together from all the classes and it was a whole network of cultural workers and community members, and I remember equally fondly our walking tours that kept expanding the community to include folks on the street. I say that to say something about what it meant to do this in Harlem. Harlem was a place that teaches us what community means and how people collaborate, not just on a one-off basis but through the mutual enrichment of different organizations. We know that Harlem is a community, but in do-ing the Harlem Semester, one of the things I came to understand at a profound level is the networks of care and support that make a community, not just among neighbors but among artists of various different forms.

LH: Harlem is a cosmopolitan center with all of these stories that live in its architecture but also in the people. My family was there in the 1920s—I don't speak about it often because it's so far back, but it's there. These stories are always entangled in ways that are important for us to remember. It was very important for me to dislodge this notion of "poor" means "Black," "poor" means "Brown," or "poor" means "other." It was re-ally important for me to help us collectively imagine that art has this intrinsic value that doesn't only circulate as a commodity and that all kinds of depth and aesthetic value can come from a community that you have to train yourself to see, if you were trained previ-ously to unsee or to devalue it.

SL: That's so interesting. I'm struck by that idea—that the benefits of being nearby and within walking distance allowed you to break down barriers, real and perceived, and make space for people to be curious in a different way. Making space for curiosity is important for any kind of transformative learning experience.

TC: Something that strikes me as well is what both of you said about the family connec-tion and daring to be curious in proximity. The Harlem Semester was that for me. My parents met at Chock Full o'Nuts on 125th Street in the late 1950s, but I didn't grow up in New York; I grew up in the suburbs of DC. Although I spent much of my life in and around New York City, it was always in Brooklyn, where I live to this day. Working at Barnard was my opportunity to be curious about that very close personal history. The most exhilarating part of my entire professional career was shuttling back and forth to meetings along 125th Street for the Harlem Semester!

I would go into the back rooms and back offices of the Apollo and go from there to the Studio Museum and from there to the National Black Theater and from there to the Schomburg Center. The physical transit back and forth to different places—and the fact that our students were doing that with people who were the living legacies of these institutions—is different from learning about what the Schomburg is, or what the Apollo is, from a book. It's different because it's an embodied social experience that I think is a huge luxury for the students to have. I'm grateful to know that every student who took one of those classes thought of it as an incredible gift. That is the gift that Harlem, as a physical space and social formation, doesn't offer everyone—it was this collaboration that made it happen.

NW: And that embodied experience becomes a form of muscle memory that they carry with them as they step out into the world and effect change. Tina, I don't know how one replicates the Harlem Semester or if that even necessarily makes sense. But since the collaboration imprinted upon us all so deeply, let's discuss its essential DNA that must be present in any future iteration.

TC: I was trained as an oral historian, so the first thing I always do is to set up a situation where you listen. The first step was to introduce the idea of the Harlem Semester to the people I hoped to work with and listen to what they had to say. If they say, "Yes, but what are you going to do for me?," take that seriously. Or if they say, "I don't trust you," take that seriously. Or if they say, "This is what I need," take that seriously too.

All of this was about trust, because the only way you can do a collaboration with a community or an institution is if you have a baseline of trust. I can tell you there was not a baseline of trust between Columbia/Barnard and Harlem institutions because we had just ripped up the entire landscape and people know who you are when you walk into the room. We don't live in a vacuum—as academics, artists, or community leaders, we are not outside of the politics of our community and must be aware of the politics—specifically, the inequities that we are complicit in. That to me is really the most important thing about any kind of replication of this project or any collaboration, really, because it is very rare that we come together on equal footing to identify and address those inequities upfront.

NW: And what's the second step?

TC: The second step was what Leslie said about valuing the work of those who are not in the privileged position of being recognized as experts. Even within Barnard, the most wonderful collaborators that we had were the professors of practice, like Karen Fairbanks, who is the head of architecture. Garnet Cadigan, who led our Harlem Walking Tours, is not technically an academic—he's a journalist, community worker, and activist. Again, what are their contributions, and how do we value them? Because they're enacting the very question you're asking about, nico. It's the question of how to teach beyond a traditional academic institution and transform institutions that don't necessarily identify as educational institutions. It's about valuing the knowledge that all sorts of people have and bring to the table.

EA: In my work, I wanted to create our own table and not continue to ask for a seat at the table of others. That was part of the impetus for the Supper Club, an art—and later book—project that brought together over 50 contemporary artists of color from the United States, mostly from New York, through portraiture, food, and conversation [see figure 8.3]. It was rewarding, and it was something that I was doing quietly, even though many knew about it and wondered where their invitation was!

NW: Those dinners really mobilized the creative community to connect in new and critical ways. You should know that this book's use of the roundtable format was in part inspired by the dynamism and intimacy of that sacred space that you created, Elia!

EA: Thanks! When I started out, there was always this sense that BIPOC wanted to be a part of the table white folks built. But I don't think they want us at their table, so we have to make our own table and invite our allies, because I'm not about shutting the door completely—I don't think that works either.

The Harlem Semester fills the gap, because I think there's a disconnect when people graduate from school and the lived experience is not there, and they enter the next

Figure 8.3.   Elia Alba, second Supper Club dinner, Brooklyn, October 3, 2012. Attended by Lorraine O'Grady, Kalup Linzy, Saya Woolfalk, Shaun Leonardo, Rachelle Mozman, Wanda Raimundi-Ortiz, Derrick Adams, Dahlia Elsayed, Brendan Fernandes, Deana Lawson, and Carlos Sandoval de Leon, as well as Alison Weisberg, of Recess. Photo courtesy Elia Alba.

chapter with all these assumptions. I started to notice that because, during my work on the Triennial at El Museo and through working with institutions on this project, I saw that disconnect even among folks of color, because, sure, they're folks of color, but they don't identify with the vendor on the street. Privilege is a reality we must all confront, and it seems like the Harlem Semester helped students confront that.

NW: What other connections do you see between your dinners and the Harlem Semester?

EA: People and institutions keep asking me to do more dinners, especially after the book came out. I even had an art fair that wanted me to sell tickets and create a space of unity—I told them they could only sell tickets to Black and Brown people, to which they said, "Well, we can't do that." So I said, "Then I can't do a dinner!" Tina, you created this platform much like I created my platform, and I think it's time to pass on the baton. Let's expand to other places so people can keep on going, and carry the work forward. I think the Harlem Semester should find its way into many academic circles beyond New York.

TC: That was the plan! The reason that it was called the Harlem Semester is because all these universities have semesters abroad or off campus—some universities have a New York semester, a DC semester, so I thought, *Why don't we have a Harlem Semester?*

My question was, what would it be like if Harlem was an immersive, semester-long experience? The other plan was to bring in other universities to collaborate, so we'd have a whole cohort of people who are doing these kinds of collaborative classes. It doesn't have to be replicated; it just has to be considered anew beyond the limitations of Barnard. It was always supposed to be open and something that traveled and grew and transformed.

NW: I hear you; however, in the way I understand it, you can't teach the Harlem Semester outside of Harlem, right?

TC: No, you can't.

CC: I was thinking, Leslie, of what you did so beautifully at Artspace in New Haven when we were there. There aren't many students at Yale who actually leave campus. The idea of creating a program that structures that and does it in a way that's safe so students feel that they can step outside of the boundaries of the campus is something that they will take with them. I think this is something we struggle with in the museum world too. I know that Shanta has to think about this all the time, trying to help students and learners bridge the divide.

NW: So, Leslie, it seems like you have a history bridging these gaps! It's interesting that you talked about the framing of the Freestyle course as a curatorial framework. I don't think I've ever acknowledged that before, but it's so true. Connie, can you talk about your permanent collection exhibition *Their Own Harlems* and how your curatorial premise for the show might map onto this discussion of the site-specificity of Harlem?

CC: A lot happened in 2017, which was my first year at the Studio Museum, including the centennial of Jacob Lawrence's birth. Given that the museum had celebrated Romare Bearden's centennial a few years earlier, we took the opportunity to create a small exhibition around Lawrence that explored his relationship to Harlem. The exhibition originally emerged from considering the urban landscape and how that inspired Lawrence growing up in Harlem.

The title for the exhibition was taken from Lawrence's Archives of American Art oral history interview in which he discussed how Harlem continued to inspire him even after he left the neighborhood. He encouraged everyone to find their own Harlems, which I thought was really beautiful and poetic but also really spot on in terms of understanding Harlem not only as a physical site but, as we were saying earlier, an emotion, noun, adjective, or place of continued and collective memory.

NW: What a call to action! As we wrap up here, how do lessons from the Harlem Semester continue to impact our approaches to institutional collaboration and arts education? How might museums begin to develop a pedagogy for what Connie so poignantly termed "living history"?

EA: When I think of Harlem, I don't think of it as just a place. It's way more than that. Harlem is a state of mind, and there should be books written about Harlem in all manner of ways, because it's much more than just a place for so many people.

CHAPTER 8

LH: As an artist, I think it's so important that we don't look away. We are in a constant state of witnessing without action, which is its own form of violence and trauma. The Studio Museum created a space of neutrality, of diplomacy—a space to think about borders, since they immediately create a dichotomy. Upholding certain borders can limit students' educational possibilities no matter where you are studying. The opportunity to see, understand, and think critically about difference is essential to education.

And in the spirit of radical love and healing, I'm also reminded of Deepa Iyer's *Mapping Our Social Change Roles in Times of Crisis*. It's an incredible resource and very inspirational for identifying the myriad ways that social change happens. The Harlem Semester opened a new way to perceive the landscape.

CC: There are these neighborhoods, like Harlem, that exist throughout the States and around the world. We need to find those locations and embed ourselves in them and be inspired by them in order to continue to create the history we want for ourselves and to create those memories. The Harlem Semester teaches us how important a site is, but also how important the memory and the experience of the site is, and how those memories and experiences are continuing to evolve.

SL: I will enjoy revisiting this idea of letting Harlem teach itself. That is so fun. I'm just going to sit on that and enjoy my memory of the wave that has happened over the years. nico, one of your last questions was the central element here—if someone wants to replicate this and is thinking about progressive and radical methods, I think what Leslie described, in terms of allowing things in the curriculum to be a bit undefined as you map out a plan, is key. Letting Harlem teach itself fills in the gaps with all the participants and players that make the initiative unique. That is so site specific, and that is so Harlem.

NOTE

1. "The Harlem Semester." Barnard Center for Research on Women, https://bcrw .barnard.edu/projects/harlemsemester.

144

9

FIND ART HERE

How to Mold Static Museum Collections into Educational Access Initiatives

BACKGROUND

*F*ind Art Here is the Studio Museum in Harlem's initiative to bring its permanent collection into schools, libraries, and service centers in Harlem. In addition to providing high-quality reproductions of artworks, the Studio Museum will collaborate with each location to offer public programs and education initiatives, including collection-based curriculum materials anchored in art education and visual literacy.[1]

CASE STUDY

JORDAN CASTEEL has rooted her practice in community engagement, painting from her own photographs of people she encounters. Posing her subjects within their natural environments, her nearly life-size portraits and cropped compositions chronicle personal observations of the human experience. Casteel is an assistant professor of painting in the Department of Arts, Culture, and Media at Rutgers University–Newark. The artist lives and works in New York.

CONNIE H. CHOI is the associate curator, permanent collection at the Studio Museum in Harlem, where she oversees all aspects of the museum's collections. Prior to joining the Studio Museum, she was the assistant curator of American art at the Brooklyn Museum. Choi has a PhD in art history from Columbia University, an EdM from Harvard University, and a BA in the history of art from Yale University.

DR. DAWN BROOKS DECOSTA began her service of teaching 27 years ago, has worked as a teacher in Harlem for the New York City Department of Education for 16 years, and has served as principal of Thurgood Marshall Academy Lower School (TMALS) for the past 9 years. TMALS was created in a collaboration between the Abyssinian Development Corporation, New Visions for Public Schools, and the Department of Education and is located in Harlem. DeCosta holds an EdD in educational leadership, Teachers College, Columbia University; an MS in fine art education, Queens College; and a BS in Education, St. John's University.

SHANTA LAWSON is a museum educator and arts and cultural leader who serves as the education director at the Studio Museum in Harlem. There she has developed and sustained education programs to serve a wide range of audiences, including students, families, youth, and adults. She is committed to exploring and developing ways in which museums are accessible spaces that inform and inspire progressive, person-centered education practice. Shanta earned her master's degree in arts and cultural management from Pratt Institute, and is a board member for Arts & Minds, an organization that provides visual arts experiences for people with dementia and their caregivers.

KYLE WILLIAMS is the director of the Andrews-Humphrey Family Foundation, which oversees the Benny Andrews Estate, a collection of the artist's artworks, writings, and documents, located in his former Brooklyn studio.

The following discussion took place between Jordan Casteel, Connie H. Choi, Dr. Dawn Brooks DeCosta, Shanta Lawson, nico wheadon, and Kyle Williams via Zoom on June 12, 2020.

nico wheadon: Shanta, can you begin by discussing the genesis of Find Art Here? Where within the museum was the conversation about activating the museum's permanent collection taking place? Who were some of your early collaborators beyond the museum, and what role did they play in bringing this project to fruition?

Shanta Lawson: Thank you for bringing us together for a conversation about this initiative, nico. This project is easily one of my favorites since joining the Studio Museum, and I say that earnestly as someone who has been here for a very long time. In early conversations around the construction of our new facility, Find Art Here emerged as we were thinking about ways to deepen the museum's engagement with our neighborhood and working to develop new approaches to providing our Harlem neighbors with access to works from the permanent collection. The question of the day became, *What is the Studio Museum in Harlem without the Studio Museum?* Thinking about the physical space, this became a creative solution to that question.

Early on, this started as a conversation between the Curatorial, Education, and the Public Programs & Community Engagement departments. We birthed the idea of Find Art Here through brainstorming sessions around coffee, and my colleagues in Curatorial sparked this dialogue by introducing the possibility of being able to produce high-quality reproductions of artworks from the museum's permanent collection. From there, we further developed the idea and vision for what it might look like to foster connections with artists and artworks beyond the museum's walls. It really deepened the way every department in the museum thought about collaboration. That's not to say it wasn't happening already, but this felt like a new level where we thought together about a project that would deepen connections with our neighbors.

This was, for most of us, the first time being part of an institution that was undergoing major construction that required us to think differently about everything. We were really interested in exploring how placing artworks in schools, libraries, and other community spaces might shift or enhance people's relationship with the artwork and the artist, and also their sense of ownership of the work. It's striking to claim something, like, *This is mine, I own this, and I own my experience with it.*

After some ideating and incubating early on among ourselves in the museum, we initiated conversations with some of our existing school and community partners such as Thurgood Marshall Academy Lower School, with whom we've had a long-standing relationship. We've built a level of trust over the years and wanted to collaborate on shaping what this initiative would look like, understanding how it might mutually benefit our students, teachers, families, and other community members.

NW: I'm struck by the fact that this is one of your favorite initiatives during your nearly 20-year tenure at the museum—that's huge! From where I sit, what was so powerful about this initiative was how directly and deeply it responded to a clearly articulated need: access. How did you and your team assess which works would live in which schools?

SL: We launched Find Art Here with an invitation for each space, school, or community center to consider an essential framing question: How might artworks in the Studio Museum's permanent collection invite us to connect to our communities and investigate the world around us? Understanding that the activity and engagement with these works would look different in each space, we wanted to make it a very open-ended invitation with no formal deliverables.

Each site was offered at least a dozen works of arts to choose from. We encouraged an inclusive process in which the whole school community could vote on which work would be installed in their space. For some spaces, it was a collective of teachers or staff that came together to make that decision. And in other schools, students, parents, and perhaps the PTA had a say. It looked different depending on the space and what they needed, and every space ended up getting their top pick! Following the installation, each site had an opening reception in which museum staff, school staff, and community members came together to toast, celebrate, and welcome this work into their space. By now, some sites have been living with their artworks for a solid two years.

I can't move forward without thanking you, nico. As then-leader of the Public Programs & Community Engagement team, you helped us to develop the name Find Art Here. How do you name something where art is on location without being cheesy or sounding like a film crew showing up somewhere? There were all these thoughts and ideas around what to call it, and you were the one who found the words, so I just wanted to say that, too, was part of the process—we even had to talk about what to call this.

NW: You're welcome, and thank you for engaging me and my team in the exercise! It reminded us of the power of language to cultivate a sense of belonging. It also felt particularly important to acknowledge, honor, and name the creativity that preexists in these spaces beyond the museum—that we were not bringing a value that wasn't already present.

Dawn, I would love to pass it over to you to talk through your lived experience of Find Art Here and how Jordan's work became number one on Thurgood Marshall Academy Lower School's list. Could you share your experience of the project and how you're continuing to learn from having the work installed in your school? [See figure 9.1.]

Figure 9.1. Studio Museum in Harlem and Thurgood Marshall Academy Lower School, 2018. Photo by Jennifer Harley, courtesy The Studio Museum in Harlem.

Dawn Brooks DeCosta: Like Shanta was saying, we have a relationship with the Studio Museum that has spanned many years, and it's a relationship that we have regardless of money. It's just love, and sometimes we have money, sometimes we don't, but we make it happen whenever we can—I don't think there's really been a year that we haven't figured it out some way! Our students, parents, and families are very familiar with being at the museum and engaging with the museum through a committed, high-quality relationship. So we wanted to create an experience where we could still have that connection even though the physical space that typically brought us together was under construction.

We've done a lot of things like having events at other locations, but of course it's not the same as being at the museum that we've become very familiar with. When this opportunity came up to have a piece of work at the school, I was really excited about that. My background is visual arts and that's what my undergraduate degree is in, so the arts are a part of who we are at Thurgood Marshall, and it's really important to us to make sure that we engage students in all of their gifts and talents, giving them positive self-concepts. Like, *if I'm an artist, if I'm a dancer, if I'm a mathematician, I have something at this school that I look forward to and love. Now I'll address the areas that I have difficulties with because I already feel self-esteem because people are honoring my gifts and talents.*

We like to look at the arts as part of our holistic experience and the learning environment of the classrooms. We always want to engage the students through our art on the walls, which is different from Find Art Here in a couple of ways. It's different because of the quality of the piece, number one; with this initiative, the art looks like the original, and the kids notice the difference. On top of that, the reason that Jordan was our first choice is because Jordan has created a relationship with our children. She has become a part of the school, so I wanted the students to see a reflection of someone that they knew. We study so many artists who have passed on, and of course we want to be respectful of the history and what brought us to this moment, but at the same time we want to show the kids that you can do this now, today! What's been interesting is having the kids, families, and teachers pass the work and say, *I know where that is! I think I know that man!* It's familiar and beautiful, and we have placed it in a location that gets a lot of traffic.

We're in an old Catholic school building, so space is a challenge for us, but it's in this beautiful alcove with the perfect lighting. We created a sacred space, this calming corner that's right there, so either you can pass this work or you can sit there with it and enjoy it. It's in the perfect location for everybody to see it every day and engage with it however they like—it feels like we have the museum in the school.

When we did the opening, we had wine and cheese, we did the tour, they got the introduction to the piece, and they went in groups. We celebrated just like we would do at the museum, and it's wonderful to have that feeling inside of the school.

NW: Jordan, it seems like every time we're in a conversation, the first theme that arises is relationship building. I think that's such a beautiful testament to who you are as a person and how your values continually show up in your work.

Jordan Casteel: It's unbelievable! When you're describing these relationships that build over time and the importance of that, it often starts with a simple engagement that can manifest into something else—a beautiful, ongoing relationship.

NW: What was your first impression when invited to participate in this initiative [see figure 9.2]? How did outreach around this particular project differ from the countless other times you've been invited to engage the Studio Museum?

Figure 9.2. Studio Museum in Harlem and Thurgood Marshall Academy Lower School, 2018. Photo by Jennifer Harley, courtesy The Studio Museum in Harlem.

JC: When I first found out about it, I was really excited because it felt like the perfect opportunity to bring together my love for art and my love for the Harlem community. My passion has always been about getting behind the curtain and getting to know the people who are the lifeblood of an institution. I've been raised to believe that and watch that manifest itself in various ways.

For example, showing up at Studio Museum, there was Thelma Golden, who was the boss and was intimidating when I met her initially, and I basically melted. But I also melted when I met Shanta, Connie, and you, nico, as I moved through the hallways of the museum. There is a relationship and trust that I have with the Studio Museum to begin with. Obviously that mutually beneficial relationship means the Studio Museum is going to think of me as somebody who is passionate about the community, is still living in Harlem, and is perhaps making work about Harlem.

I think when they first reached out about this project, I'd been thinking for a while about how art moves through the commercial art world, and the work begins to feel more and more distant from the people it originated with. I went to art school because I wanted to teach and was passionate about education and young people and recognized the power of art to support young people in envisioning themselves in the world. It was a no-brainer, obviously, but because I'm in the commercial art world, there were nuances to be worked out with the gallery that made it more difficult but not impossible. I went to the gallery and asked all these questions because protecting myself as a Black artist and a young person is important. The Studio Museum is one of those institutions that's like, *We're going to make this work!*

I remember the language saying, *You were chosen,* but I don't think I realized that there were multiple people to choose from and that they chose me. Hearing you, Dawn, describe all the thoughts that went into it produces a whole other level of feeling connected. I remember the day I went to visit Thurgood Marshall and spoke to a class—it's literally on the other side of my block; we're neighbors. I got off the train maybe two weeks later, and this little girl ran up to me holding her mom's hand and was like, "I just met you, you're the artist. I just wanted to say it's so great meeting you! Mom, this is who I was telling you about!"

It reminded me of why this work is important—that building those actual relationships is as important to me as making the paintings that tell these stories. Paintings allow for me to tell stories, that's what I have decided in recent years. That's all it is. I love telling the story of how I met someone and that they recognized Kevin the Kite Man. That they have genuinely seen that man flying a kite in front of Adam Clayton Powell. That's just what it is.

NW: As you say that, I'm reminded that even people—like Kevin, James, Mike, and the other men you painted during your residency who are fixtures on the Harlem streetscape—can become institutions in and of themselves. Can you describe a key difference in your experience of exhibiting *Kevin the Kiteman* at TMALS and exhibiting that same work at the Studio Museum? Does the portrait take on a different meaning in this new context?

JC: The way I thought about it was that the students are little people, so the scale is probably the same as a big person standing in front of a big painting. In reality, it's probably been shrunk down to their size. That's a good thing, as it's not as overwhelming—it's a thing that they can approach and feel familiarity with that is not as intimidating as museums can feel.

Studio Museum is one of the few institutions where everyone seems to feel at ease there. People are always trying to figure out how they exist in institutional spaces, and little kids in particular have a hard time figuring out what their boundaries are because, within those spaces, they're not supposed to touch this, make too much noise, or cross some invisible line. So I love the idea that my work is in their 'hood, in their hallway, and that they get to choose how to engage with and own it. But I also love that they might have that same recognition at the Studio Museum, and be like, *Yeah, that's mine, I owned that; that's part of my story.*

Of course, as a painter, the actual lusciousness of the paint is lost in the reproduction, and that always makes me sad, but that's not what this is. It's about creating a vision of oneself and the potential for oneself to build on that curiosity by asking questions. *Can I do that? There's a young Black woman who lives in my neighborhood who painted this; that's cool. Yeah, I know that guy.* So all the rest of it just falls aside.

NW: Remember when Kevin showed up to the museum opening reception with his own PA system? It was such a powerful and beautiful moment and one where the museum really had to reckon with its own prescriptions for public engagement.

Connie, as associate curator, permanent collection, what are your thoughts about how Find Art Here embodies important institutional gestures within the community? Did you consider the initiative a project or a permanent shift in how the museum was thinking about its permanent collection and the public's access to it?

Connie H. Choi: I entered the project after it had already been thought through and crystalized as an initiative for inHarlem. I come from a museum education background and, because of that, had worked directly with two elementary schools through museum education departments. So I had that experience of bringing art to spaces and class-rooms that are different from museum walls. In thinking about this project, what initially struck me was the idea that we would be entering spaces and meeting people where they were as opposed to asking them to come into a space that they might not be comfortable being in. I think that's what we struggle with every day with museum work. We're here to open up that space and bring art to people and try to meet them where they are.

For me, that was the most important aspect of this project. What I love about work-ing with Shanta and the rest of the education team is collaborating and figuring out how to make that possible. I think that collaboration impacted the entire curatorial team in terms of thinking through what our collection means in this moment that we are closed. What does it mean that we have a collection of now over 2,500 works, most of which are not accessible to the public and many of which have never been seen by the public before? What does it mean for a museum to do that not only for the public that it's serv-ing but also for the artists whom it is serving too? How do we increase access to the arts and not just the favorites or the ones we're used to seeing but to everything, to all of the works?

The artwork that I always think of is by Stephanie Weaver, which had basically been buried in our collection. She had been an artist-in-residence, and her work hadn't been photographed, so no one really knew what it looked like. We only have about 30 percent of our collection digitized, so what does it mean that the museum can't easily access a vi-sual understanding of its full collection? Find Art Here just opened up all those avenues of inquiry in terms of forcing us to go and look deeply at the collection and find works that might make sense for the organizations that we were working with. It forced us to look and consider what these lost gems were.

It became important, too, in terms of thinking ahead into the future and our new building: What are the works that haven't been shown or could take on a different life or that have different meanings based on what audiences are looking at them? How are we interpreting them in this new space? I'm not sure if all of that was going through our heads at the time we were talking through what Find Art Here could be, but it's definitely crystallized in the moments since then, because it opened up a lot of questions that we need to answer while also providing a lot of answers to things we hadn't really considered before. Like, *What does access look like in this moment? What is the institu-*

tion's responsibility to create access to art? Find Art Here empowered us to digitize works from the collection and add those to our website, which has in turn increased access to our collection. From there, we're adding scholarship and extended labels for works that never had such texts before.

This was one of my first projects when I started at the museum three and a half years ago. Everyone was like, *Here is a project you're doing because we're closing.* I think it forced me to learn the institution and its history and how to work with the different departments at the institution in a way that perhaps I wouldn't have had to do right away. I would've been able to pick and choose whether or not I wanted to enter into certain types of discussions and spaces. It also forced me to learn about the collection in a different way. Find Art Here and *Black Reflections* brought different ideas and understandings of the collection together in a very different way than it would've been if I had just focused on the collection without having to worry about programming it at all. Now I'm thinking about the audiences that education is working with or planning to work with. Now I'm thinking about audiences that were outside of Harlem at these different venues for *Black Reflections*. It opened up more problems but in a good way.

NW: Well, let's unpack that a bit, since I think the way you moved through the challenges is something others can learn from. What surprises or obstacles did you discover in the process of digitizing the collection, securing reproduction rights, and actually reproducing and installing these artworks in spaces like schools, community centers, and libraries? So many of us within the museum field are trained for a specific context—to shift the nexus of museum practice out of the galleries and into these dynamic community spaces must have been both jarring and rewarding.

CC: Luckily, we were so closely collaborating with Education that some of the responsibility fell on them, which was great for me! Quite frankly, we had no idea what we were doing. Those first emails that we sent out to galleries and artists were very vague because we didn't know how we were going to reproduce the works, what they were going to be printed on, or what size they were going to be. It was just putting out a feeler to see whether or not an artist, their representative, or their estate would be open to the idea because, as a curator and an art historian, for me there's a lot of trepidation in that. What does it mean to reproduce an artist's work at such a high quality that the potential for it being confused with the real work could actually be a thing? What does it mean to potentially put a "fake" out in the world?

There's a reason why all of the works are scaled down or up, so the dimensions are very different from what the original work is. There's a reason why we went overboard and bought stamps that said "This is a reproduction" and put them all over around the edges of the canvas and stuck labels on the back of stretchers. We were just trying to ensure that we were protecting the artists that we serve and also not knowing how to do that necessarily—this was the first time that we had ever embarked on this, and there were not many institutions that had done it! We talked to one other organization that did, but they were doing something very different.

We learned by asking questions of people and getting feedback from galleries, many of whom responded and were initially suspicious of the intent of the project, and whether or not it would protect the artist which, as Jordan said, are real and valid questions. In terms of rights and reproductions, most of the living artists who were working with galleries graciously gave their permission and didn't really ask for any assurances. I think the museum's reputation as an artist-centric institution certainly helped.

We had a timeline: school starts in September, so it all had to be settled in September, but at the very last minute, when we were about to send off the high-resolution files to be printed, we found out that those photographs that we took were not actually high resolution enough to be reproduced at the quality that we wanted. That's why the project ended up being stalled for a little bit, because we had to go back and rephotograph all of those works, and we were about to leave the building at that point. It was a mad rush and highly stressful but also an interesting process to go through.

NW: Kyle, we spoke a bit about the life of collections and archives, and the importance of imagining an accessible home for these cultural artifacts beyond the archival or digital space. As director and archivist at the Andrews-Humphrey Family Foundation, how do you work to make Andrews's archive accessible, and why is that work so important? Who are your key collaborators in activating and animating the collection? And what excited you most about having Andrews's legacy present in P.S. 79 Dr. Horan School in this particular way?

Kyle Williams: The Benny Andrews Estate is a nonprofit foundation with an educational mission. When we were first invited to reproduce his work, we understood that it would go in a public school. It seemed like a huge opportunity to us. As an initiative, it definitely falls under the scope of our mission, and it is also where my personal interests lie. I've worked with middle school and high school populations for a long time. And Benny Andrews himself, during the later stages of life, did a lot of children's book illustrations. Throughout his career, he found opportunities to bring young people into the studio. We were completely thrilled to do it!

I think the thing that was most exciting about it, that I didn't really expect, was the way that the Find Art Here initiative built the relationship between our foundation and the school. During the reception, we got to meet the principal of that school, who's totally incredible, and we got to meet a lot of the students. The entire school is a special-needs population. It was a really fantastic and exciting experience to meet them and their incredible faculty there. I thought the reception might be the last time we'd get to see this great installation. However, we stayed in touch with the education department at the Studio Museum, and Jennifer Harley, school & community partnerships coordinator, followed up with me and invited me to come and participate in the art classes. I got to sit in on those classes and talked a little bit about Benny Andrews, but mostly I was just excited to be a part of the moment and meet the students there. That also expanded our relationship with the Studio Museum because, from there, our foundation conducted regular visits.

I should say the Benny Andrews Estate has an archive of Andrews's writings, photographs, and archival objects, like his paints and paintbrushes, and also about 1,300 artworks. Most of that is stored in our headquarters, which is his former studio. When you come into the studio, it's now repurposed as an archival storage space, but you can definitely still tell that it was once a working studio. It has paint all over the walls, and it still feels very much like you're entering someone's studio. We first did a visit with some of the Studio Museum's educational staff and later the curatorial department. We followed that up, then, with another visit that Jennifer helped me coordinate with the teaching artists at the Horan School, and a few other teaching artists came to see what we were doing there—this was right before the COVID-19 pandemic hit. The next thing that we were planning was bringing a field trip of those students to the Benny Andrews Estate, which I am still very excited about and we'll definitely make happen whenever we can all be outside again.

SL: Kyle, somewhere in between there, didn't some of our interns and fellows come to visit you too?

KW: Yes. I was so thrilled to build a relationship with not just the Horan School but also with the Studio Museum! I would say our unofficial strategy of trying to tell Andrews's story is to bring in as many young artists and young educators as possible. When I say "young," I mean like me—people who are at the beginning or middle of their careers who are still kind of searching and are hungry for what their touchstones are going to be in terms of engaging with all sorts of discourse in history.

I hope that by bringing in different artists and educators, they'll get hooked and have a memorable and visceral experience learning about this artist. Bringing in the young, professional program of interns and curatorial fellows is like my dream come true in terms of who I'm trying to bring into our foundation to make sure that Andrews's story is told and discussed.

What was also really exciting about the Find Art Here initiative was that I'm always trying to make sure that Andrews is not only seen in a historical context. I'm an artist and a painter, and I really love the idea that Andrews's work is going to be in a conversation with people who are actually making paintings, not just someone who's studying the arts movements of the mid-20th century. Both are important, because Andrews was also an activist and was really socially engaged in the '60s and '70s. I sometimes worry that he'll fall into one silo of being historically significant but not someone that comes up in your undergrad painting class. I think the large majority of artists included in Find Art Here are working artists who are still making work in New York. I know it's not exclusively that, but that's something that's really important to me personally and to the mission of the foundation.

CC: Shanta, do you want to talk about why the Horan School chose Benny's work? I think that's relevant to what Kyle was just talking about.

SL: Absolutely. We were talking about *Composition (Study for Trash)*, and I was present when the school had the debate and dialogue about which work they would choose.

They were passionate about that work, because they felt strongly that it would provide a platform for some really needed social, political, and cultural conversations. Some of the figures and representations within the work—including a Statue of Liberty figure sitting atop a globe surrounded by people of African descent in different gestures of motion, strain, and strife—provided a catalyst for conversations that they wanted their students to have. They felt it was very much a timeless representation of the issues that they were grappling with. It became an interesting merger of a historical moment, current questions, and contemporary conversations. So that was very squarely in their reasoning for picking that work.

KW: That's awesome. That's really, really heartening.

NW: Something I've observed elsewhere in the field is that, often, many of these rich community partnerships emerge when museums are undergoing radical transformation—this can take the form of a shift in leadership, a capital campaign, a scandal, or a redesign or expansion of physical space. I'm wondering if there is a way to consider projects like Find Art Here as precipitators of institutional change rather than responses to it. I've heard from Dawn, as I've heard from Kyle, that this collaboration with the museum has greatly impacted their organizations and the communities they serve. So how do we encourage museum leadership across the field to see this way of working as the new status quo?

CC: I mean, it's an investment, right? It's investment in time, staff, and financial resources. You really need to have an institution that is willing to put in that effort, to really dig deep. At the Studio Museum, Find Art Here is not something that we're imagining is going to go away once the building is up. That's why these reproductions were seen as permanent gifts and not things that were on loan, because our education team has invested in each of these locations through long-term relationships.

It's about implanting ourselves deeper into our different communities and investing in our audiences in a different way. Everything that has been going on in the world in the last few weeks has brought up all of the controversies that have come as the result of museum solidarity statements—there's a difference between making a statement and taking action. There's a difference between saying that you agree with a particular point of view and actually doing something to enact change.

What has always impressed me about this initiative is the way that we, as an institution, have decided and committed to dive deep, because there was a way we could have done this that would have checked all the boxes yet skimmed the surface in terms of getting the collection out there. The impact we've been able to have is in large part due to Shanta and the education team really taking this on, really thinking and committing and seeing it as an opportunity but also an investment.

NW: Exactly, because it's not just an investment of financial resources, as Dawn said earlier, but it's also an investment of professional attention and care. It's an investment in the relationship.

SL: Part of it is also getting on board with the idea that the museum is more than a museum building. Of course, it is physical in terms of the experiences that we build around the collection and exhibitions. But it's also more than just a building, right? What we think about as museum experiences can take shape in different locations and spaces and can be informed by those environments—it's a commitment to that. Museum experiences can extend beyond what we think of as a visit to see a work of art. This has flipped it on its head and I think demonstrated a way in which we're shaking up this idea of "the museum visitor."

Early on in my time, I can remember family visits with the museum cultural ambassadors and the grandparents club from Thurgood Marshall Academy Lower School and all the fun family gatherings we had in the museum. One of my favorite games to play in the galleries was called something like "museum make-believe," and the idea was that families had an opportunity to explore the galleries on their own and pick a work of art they would take home. They were asked to imagine that they could take it right off the wall and bring it home, so then they began to think about where it would go. We'd ask questions like *Why did you pick that? What spoke to you about that work? Why are you curious about that work? Where would it go in your home and why?* Experiences with art can and should be intimate, personal, and meaningful to each of us and can perhaps break apart the traditional ways that we invite people to engage our collections.

JC: I can't help but listen and think about the power of education, especially in moments like this. I think that the education aspect should bleed into every aspect of an institution and that it should be on the front of everybody's minds, from the president of the museum to the person at the front desk. That it's about that holistic approach to education and not just about putting it in a corner and saying, *You go teach the kids over there.* Museums house collections and study collections and spend time with collections but to what end and for whom? Who deserves that knowledge that we seek as being so valuable?

I just keep hearing the connections between the things you were saying and thinking that it's crazy that museums are furloughing education department staff left and right in response to COVID-19. But these are the moments [when] we're reminded where the essential workers and the essential work of a museum is based—it's education! Museum education builds narratives around the collection and draws people in. That's how you keep people connected and nurture mutually beneficial relationships. *I'm going to give you my 20 dollars for entrance to gain access to something, but what I have to offer is just as valuable as what you give in return.*

SL: I love that, Jordan. I'm glad to hear that reflection from you, because I think this has all been an exercise in understanding what it means to create experiences in which our students and our neighbors are authentically part of their own learning experience, and that their embodied expertise is just as valuable.

JC: I joke with my students on the first day of class, saying, "I'm walking in as your professor, but I'm going to tell you right now that you hold the knowledge. My job is to

CHAPTER 9

point you to it within you. I am no keeper of knowledge, and I'll be the first to tell you that Google is my best friend. I know very little, more than you're capable of acknowledging. My job is to point you back to the things you already know about the world and that the value lies within you."

The value doesn't lie in the collection; it lies in the way people relate to that collection. Those are two different ways of thinking. So it comes down to the way that the institution perceives themselves in the power structure: *This is what we're giving* rather than *This is theirs to begin with.*

DD: I just want to say that the relationship that we had with the museum was important in the initiative because, as a school, we have lots of initiatives. We almost have initiative overload! If there's not a committed relationship, it's hard to manage all of the different pieces, but because there was already a mutual respect between us and the museum, we understood how important this was, and we were able to honor all of the needs and requests as a school.

Also, even though this was something that we wanted to do, there were certain requirements on our part to make sure that the art would be in a certain location, that it would be safe, that there would be time to install it, and that we would take care of it. And so I think that in terms of Find Art Here, the thoughtfulness behind it and the trust between the institutions is what really made it more than just an initiative. Defining who the partners are is really important, and so is thoughtfulness on both sides in making sure that both institutions see the initiative as being equally important and of the same priority. If it's not a priority, then it doesn't get the respect that it deserves.

NW: Dawn, I'm curious what you've learned from the students' and teachers' interpretations of Jordan's work?

DD: They've had so much engagement with Jordan and her work. The Studio Museum is always really thoughtful about which artists we engage with and how that connects to our curriculum. Our teachers still reference and include Jordan's work, even though they may be teaching about something else. When we teach about community, we can bring her work back in. It becomes part of the curriculum.

I think that the kids became very familiar with not just *Kevin the Kiteman* but other works of hers because she was there with them and they got to see, learn, talk to, and engage with her as a human being. Jordan's work was a huge part of second grade for them, and now that they are in fourth grade, they still remember everything about their time with her!

NW: Thanks, Dawn. OK, everyone, any parting thoughts before we adjourn?

JC: Thanks for creating a space for this. I left our first roundtable thinking we can change the world, and I'm so ready. I think there's often a sense that we're fighting in isolation, we're fighting our own institutions, our own schools, my own studio, or whatever our careers are. To be reminded that, in actuality, we're fighting these systems and creating and envisioning a future *together* is just so brilliant.

SL: I just want to share that I was smiling when Kyle was talking because, of all the things you recounted, you didn't mention that you were the subject of a figure drawing class at the Horan School! You were just observing, and I know that they will not have an opportunity to meet Benny Andrews in the same way that our community got to meet and engage with Jordan, but they will remember a man who came to their class and was representing Benny Andrews. I wasn't there, but I did see the drawing. Maybe just one more moment of connection that I think is really special and emblematic of the community that we built around this initiative. I look forward to the ways that it just continues to evolve.

NOTE

1. https://studiomuseum.org/find-art-here.

10

ARTIST GRANTS INITIATIVE

How to Redirect Resources to Shape Future Relationships

BACKGROUND

Staff from both the Visual Arts and the Public Engagement, Learning & Impact departments at the Walker Art Center discuss a 2020 initiative where $120,000 was diverted from the museum's acquisition fund to be redistributed to BIPOC artists as emergency funds.

CASE STUDY

NISA MACKIE is the head of the Public Engagement, Learning & Impact department at Walker Art Center. At the Walker, Mackie has been responsible for developing strategies to expand inclusion and equitable access to the institution, stimulate curiosity and critical thinking within museum audiences, and strengthen the museum's civic role as a resource and leader. Mackie earned her BA in creative arts administration from Macquarie University and her MA in art theory and sculpture performance and installation from the University of New South Wales.

ALEXANDRA NICOME is a Minneapolis-based arts administrator. She was recently a fellow and curatorial assistant at the Walker Art Center and has interned at the National Museum of African Art, Allen Memorial Art Museum, and the Minneapolis Institute of Art.

VICTORIA SUNG is associate curator in the Visual Arts department at the Walker Art Center, Minneapolis, where she works with artists to create exhibitions, publications, and public programs. Recent and upcoming projects include solo shows with Laure Prouvost, Siah Armajani, Theaster Gates, Rayyane Tabet, Shen Xin, and Pacita Abad.

This conversation took place on February 3, 2021, and was subsequently edited for length and readability.

Nisa Mackie: We're here to talk about a specific project, but I have a feeling the conversation might lead elsewhere too. To start, can you share the nuts and bolts of this artist grant project and how it came about?

Victoria Sung: We were three months into the pandemic when the murder of George Floyd set off a wave of reckoning around police brutality and racial injustice across the country. As the Walker reckoned with its own history of white privilege and lack of racial diversity among its board, leadership, and staff, community members (and many staff members) called on the institution to start thinking differently about its responsibility to the local communities it serves. There were conversations in all corners of the museum about how it could put its resources to use. Suggestions were raised that the Walker become a food relief shelter, that our art-transporting vans be dispatched to ferry protesters, or that we help preserve the murals being painted on boarded-up windows. As arts professionals, we were attuned to the suffering of artists who had been furloughed, laid off, or had participated in the creation of murals and other forms of protest art. Ultimately, we felt we could make the largest difference by directly supporting artists in our communities.

Alexandra Nicome: The artist grant initiative was structured to reach beyond the Walker's familiar network. We understood the limits of our engagement and wanted to connect with a true diversity of artists in our community—that is, in place of whatever definition of "diverse" we came up with as an institution. We hoped to reach the widest possible network of folks who might benefit from financial assistance, which meant rethinking how we structure our external partnerships. We wanted to build a grant structure that would subvert any biases, value systems, or other barriers that have limited the Walker's community work in the past.

To do this, Walker staff reached out to 10 Minnesota-based organizations that directly support artists in their communities. These organizations were selected to represent the diversity of folks who live in the Twin Cities and range of disciplines that the Walker engages (i.e., moving image work, visual art, performance art, and social practice work).

We asked these 10 organizations to each nominate two artists. We felt it was important to compensate the organizations for their time and recognize their expertise, so distributed $2,000 to the partners and $5,000 to each selected artist. The eligibility requirements and selection criteria were intentionally left open to interpretation so that each organization could use to funds to meet the specific needs of their community.

NM: How has the process unfolded so far?

AN: Museum work involves a good deal of paperwork and a lot of approvals; anything involving "immediacy" or "urgency" undermines that bureaucratic structure. I think our attempt to devise a thoughtful and responsive grant initiative—within the rigid nonprofit structure—was instructive for everyone on the Walker team. We wanted to act quickly, expedite procedures, and release aid swiftly, but we also wanted to be thoughtful about how we engaged our partners and the artists. It was definitely trial and error, but I think the team came up with a good strategy. We did things with speed but tried to focus that momentum inward, hoping to create a positive experience for our partners in which they had ample time to make their decisions.

VS: We're still very much in the early stages of things. I want to make sure that we're careful not to tout this effort as something that's been successful, because I don't think we're anywhere close to that yet.

NM: It's really like a very initial step. . . .

VS: I see the grant initiative as signaling our interest in reengaging with local communities, and now we really have to do the work. The grants themselves are in a sense a gesture—a good-faith gesture, but that's all that it is. I'm not trying to discount the financial need—artists in our communities were certainly hurting, and this idea came out of a desire to alleviate that need—but I worry about how we talk about the work, because it's too easy to describe in a way that positions it as having been successful in reaching out to communities and partnering with local organizations. That feels slightly disingenuous to me.

NM: I actually think that's one of the problems with the way that museums talk about the cultural work they do. Whether working directly with artists on projects or when looking at the work that Alexandra and I do in the education space, there is a tendency to present things as fait accompli, as successful. The fact is, the relational piece, particularly when working with a local community, is always ongoing and recursive. Folks with different working styles come and go at the museum, the people we work with change or come in and out of focus for the institution–often on the basis of projects. And so we have a storied history–it's never wholly one thing or the other. Some of it is good, and some of it is bad. I don't want to present this project as something where the Walker is patting themselves on the back, because the Walker, like many institutions, has a really long way to go.

AN: Outside the museum walls, we encountered a challenging lack of trust. Trust eroded and trust eschewed—we were faced with damaged, neglected, and compromised relationships. Organizations were wary of being instrumentalized, weary of one-off contacts with the Walker. I think an important approach we took was to not become defensive. As an institution with relative money, power, and connections, we recognized that it was not our place to decide how potential partners should respond to us.

NM: As this is a good-faith gesture to the community, as you were saying, Vicky, it's also a good-faith gesture to the staff. Many staff, I think, have been wanting to see change internally too. That's why I think the cross-functional workgroup was a really interesting model, because it brings a distributed accountability and an opportunity to both give and get feedback to and from different departments. Do you both want to talk a little bit about that process of working together? Particularly, how did the different vantages of different departments emerge in the conversation as the initiative was developed?

VS: I feel like this working group was an early prototype of the cross-departmental efforts that are now being replicated across the organization. It was a way for a group of us to workshop what that could look like and how that could translate into different initiatives that we're now looking to spearhead institutionally. Museums are notorious for siloed departments. It was really nice to create space every two weeks just to meet with a group of colleagues from different departments and recognize that we are all trying to move in the same direction toward the same goal. That's been a positive side product of this project–that it's not just the work that we're doing together externally but also internally. I think we're learning how to work together in a more collaborative, productive way.

AN: I think what was also interesting about that space is that because it was a new initiative that we were building as we went, nobody had a sense of individual ownership or expertise. We all came to the table knowing that we were trying to learn and create something new together and stumble through it with each other. That created a more level playing field, and a very convivial atmosphere. I think it was in part because of the new nature of what we were working on. It allowed us to think a little more flexibly too.

NM: That's a really interesting point. I have seen that the Walker and many other institutions right now are trying to reimagine what exhibition or major project planning should look like so that different voices (internal and external) can be heard at the right times. I think because those long-standing processes are so baked into the system of the institution, everybody brings a particular role or attitude or vantage that they have to perform in those meeting structures. It sounds like within the workgroup you had for the artist grants, precisely because of the new challenge that you shared, all of that could fall away. . . .

AN: . . . also because we knew we were in the position of needing to build trust with external partners. I'm thinking about institutions and defensive behaviors as a symptom of white supremacy and then also thinking about trust, and what it means to build trust, while recognizing that as representatives of the Walker, we can, in some ways, embody and present that defensive behavior. It's really off-putting for our partners. I think that that's something we were thinking about and trying to work through: how to build trust in an authentic way.

NM: Was there space held for working through some of that? Because, in the past, the Walker has had some really challenging relationships with local community partners. The Walker has a long history with some very successful projects and some total failures in terms of partnerships with our local community. Was there a processing space in your group for those conversations?

VS: Yes. Each of us served as point person for one or two of the community partners. At each meeting, we would come back to the group and talk about the nature of our conversations. The responses spanned the full spectrum. Like you're saying, Nisa, there were organizations with whom we've had long-standing relationships, where we've built that relationship of trust, that signed on immediately. There were other organizations that asked to have multiple conversations in order to understand what the Walker's motives were. Then there were some partners who just flat out said no.

One of the conversations that stood out to me was when one of the community organizations asked someone on our team, "We go to Walker events; do you come to ours?" The answer to that question was no. I just thought that was interesting, as obvious as it may seem, and should inform how we all engage with the wider Twin Cities arts community. We can't just bring organizations on board when we're looking to start an initiative, but we have to meet them where they are too. How do we engage with their programming, their events? Do we understand what they want out of a relationship, if they want one? We need to ensure we are building reciprocal relationships.

AN: I feel like that was another thing. There are lots of documents that came out of this group. I think that one of them was about trying to set up a calendar with community events and then be intentional about attending them.

VS: I'm sure this is true across many of the different departments, but I think we see one of the roles of visual arts as being present in the community, whether that is exhibition openings or artist studio visits. Obviously, all of this has been harder in the last year, given the pandemic, but we are trying to keep up with virtual studio visits and online talks. Alexandra, as you were saying, I think we're cognizant of the fact that the work we're doing with this initiative is and has to be part of a much larger institutional commitment where we are centering community in much of what we're doing. Not just via giving artists grants but by actually showing up.

NM: I think the work that the group has done with the grants does, as you say, Vicky, dovetail with this broader institutional impetus to rethink the relationship between the Walker and its local community. One of the things that has been raised in some of these conversations is this idea of a global/local tension. I'm wondering if you have any thoughts on reconciling the internationality of the Walker with an accountability—and a need for care—for the local community and the artists within it?

VS: I don't necessarily see a divide between the global and local. I feel like when we set up the global/local dichotomy, it automatically imposes a certain hierarchy with global connoting one thing and local connoting another. This is a conversation that I have heard time and time again at the Walker and at other institutions, but I don't see the two paradigms as being oppositional to one another. I think there's a way we can do both. The work we're doing right now in reimagining artist residencies at the Walker is a good example of how we might put global and local artist communities in direct dialogue. But again, so much of the work that we need to do—whether it's at a global or a local level—is about building long-standing relationships of trust. I feel like all the work that we're doing, essentially, boils down to that same question: How are we building relationships of trust?

NM: In some ways it's an impossible question to answer, because it automatically sets up these presuppositions that don't necessarily need to exist but we reinscribe it into our conversations at the institution again and again. I was just chatting to Alexandra about some strategic-planning sessions that I've been facilitating with gallery attendants and visitor-experience staff, and some of those staff raised this idea of global/local being coded language. "Global" meaning an international set, and "local" meaning people who are less professional, less rigorous, or folks with a lesser understanding of contemporary art. I wonder if it's just a crutch that the institution has because it's hard to think noncategorically. Is there anything you wanted to add to that, Alexandra?

AN: Maybe the tension is just built in—I'm just thinking about what it means to build a building for contemporary art on stolen Indigenous lands in a city that has struggled with redlining and racial covenants and restrictive geographies . . . just in the way that the city was constructed and has been built up and cordoned off over many decades. It lives in the land, this divide between the local and the global, or the low and high art, or Indigenous, Black, and Brown, and the West. They were literally built in opposition to one another. Even just thinking about how people who live in Near North Minneapolis, which is super close to the Walker Art Center, don't necessarily feel connected to the work that's being done at the Walker.

   In that sense, just thinking extemporaneously about it, I wonder if it's just this inescapable tension. Working at the Walker, it felt part of my responsibility to hold that tension, to hold space for it and to talk about it.

VS: I agree with what you're saying Alexandra, and I'm wondering if maybe we need to pose the question slightly differently. Maybe the question is not about setting up this dichotomy between global and local but expanding or adding nuance to our understanding of the local. As you said, Minneapolis is one of the most racially segregated cities in the entire country, and many of the social ills we're seeing today are a direct result of histories of redlining, unequal access to education, health care, government services, and job opportunities. The question is, When we talk about our local audience, who are we talking about?

   In the '90s, there was an effort to focus engagement on the residents who live in the immediate neighborhoods around the Walker. That was one way of defining the Walker's local community. *But when we talk about "the local" today, what do we mean?* Because if we're talking about Greater Minneapolis, we're not serving all of our local communities. Earlier today, during one of our all-staff meetings, we saw a presentation about the demographic makeup of Minneapolis versus that of the board. I think they said something along the lines of, *40 percent of Minneapolis residents identify as BIPOC,* and in contrast, the percentage of the board makeup is around 15 percent.

NM: Which is basically the same as the staff. . . .

VS: Right. To me, that's an interesting question. When we talk about serving our local communities, who are we talking about? How do we add more nuance to what we think about when we refer to "the local"?

NM: It's such a challenging, foundational, or existential question. One of the things you were saying, Alexandra, made me think that we are all talking now about the ways in which the foundations of museums and collecting practices are linked to colonial violence. Then you're also talking about the specific geography of Minneapolis and the Walker in relation to redlining and dispossession: these things are related. Then to layer on top of that, there is the function of the art market and its influence on the way that we collect that has systemically marginalized people of color. For an institution to hold all of those things and then think about how to incorporate a sensitivity and responsiveness to all of those dynamics into the practice of a museum practitioner. . . . It's a lot!

There was this op-ed by Yesomi Umolu last year, which was about how in museum institutions, care is oriented toward the museum patron. That is, museums have had a notion of a museum public that has not served them [the museums] very well and also reinforced the oppression of BIPOC folks both inside and outside of the institution. I would add that, particularly in contemporary art institutions, when we think about who deserves our care, or who is the subject of care, it's usually the artist first and foremost. Yet there are so many other stakeholders, including the public and the staff.

The Public Engagement, Learning & Impact team at Walker often thinks a lot about their work as care work. It's highly facilitative and responsive to the needs of others first and foremost. We talk a lot about the emotional labor that is done by that group because not only are they trying to facilitate different areas of the organization or outside of the organization, whether it's curatorial or local artists or specific nonprofits that we're working with, but they're also having to respond to whatever people are bringing to that space. I think that's particularly challenging for their externally facing work.

Every museum that I speak with is currently trying to figure out how to have the right people in the room at the right time, and I think so much of the work of the institution is about making sure that we are facilitating pluralistic conversation at the right time so that we can feed into how that shows up within the institution.

It sounds really simple at the outset, but it's actually so challenging. By nature, it actually operates inversely to some of what you were describing, Vicky. As a visual arts curator, you're working to build relationships with artists, and some of that relationship building has to happen in a more insular private space in order to engender that trust. I'm invested in how we create a public space for more voices that can be brought into closer proximity with curatorial—I think that will invariably allow us to build trust in other spaces outside of the museum.

VS: As a contemporary art center, the Walker really does center living artists. I think that's actually quite different from other, say, encyclopedic museums, where it's more about collecting and working with objects. Of course, we do that work here, too, but we're always thinking about how we can follow the ways artists work and having that inform our practices.

In general, I think a large part of my practice is about centering human relationships, whether with artists, internally with other colleagues, or externally with community partners. And because my interest in the museum field came out of my experiences as a visitor growing up, I always circle back to the visitor experience, because that's how I fell in love with the museum space.

It's about trying to hold space for all of those different relationships and seeing how they can be in conversation with one another. Again, at the end of the day, I think a curatorial practice, or the practice of so many different museum practitioners, is about building relationships. It's those one-on-one relationships. There's no easy way around it. There are no shortcuts; you have to build real, genuine, reciprocal relationships. And I think that's where many museums are finding themselves in trouble right now: there's a desire to build relationships with communities, local communities, global communities, but there's no way around individuals doing the work to build those relationships.

AN: That makes a lot of sense to me, centering relationships. As you were talking, because this is sort of tangential, I was thinking that I feel like contemporary art institutions are actually at a particular disadvantage in this era because they have a responsibility to the contemporary moment. The moment we're living in asks museums and people to take a position. Museums are used to being able to refuse that position, even when they present political work, like the Walker. I'm thinking about Ron Athey and others. I don't think that those culture wars are the same as what's happening right now. Like, either way, the way that arts institutions are being forced into a position is becoming untenable.

This is kind of ridiculous of me, but I was just watching a National Geographic documentary about earthquakes. There's a friction zone, and tension builds up, and when that friction can't be held anymore, it breaks. It feels like that is happening right now. To build relationships with people—and to acknowledge people and their wholeness—you have to acknowledge something about the relationship with the institution that isn't working. I'm not really sure how to position myself in relationship to that crisis because I'm invested in museums and I want to see what happens on the other side of that.

NM: What both of you are saying made me think about this educational term that we use a lot within our youth programming. The term is "community of practice," which refers to a group of people who share, explicitly or implicitly, a common understanding around mutual goals. I think when we talk about museums trying to forge relationships with marginalized communities, or also identity-based communities, I think the ultimate question is, Do these groups actually share mutual goals? Can they be a community of practice?

It's an open question. and if the museum is to put a stake in the ground, how can it adapt its thinking, truly, around what its goals are? I think that would create more of a mutuality with these various groups and communities that we purport to be pivoting toward. I guess that's the problem with the reification space of the museum. We've done a really good job of presenting ideas, but we haven't necessarily had to structurally rethink our purpose.

To circle back to the grants, one of the interesting things about this project is that museums—as our director, Mary Ceruti, said—are based on an acquisitive violence and so what does it mean to test a more distributive model? At first you might question, why start with such a seemingly transactional exchange, but then on the other hand, it's like,

Well, of course, it needs to start that way because museums have been extracting for a really long time. If you were to speculate beyond the gesture that Vicky mentioned at the beginning of the conversation. . . . What lies ahead for the Walker? Or what do you *hope* might lie ahead for the Walker?

AN: I'm really excited to see all of the projects and initiatives that the Walker's working on in a few years. I feel invigorated, especially by the artist grant projects and what it means for building relationships with artists and organizations around the Twin Cities and helping to build and participate in that network. I feel like I'm having a crisis of my own beliefs right now, but I'm invested in that crisis and just going to work through it. For now, I'm really glad to be helping artists with administrative stuff. I feel like even that feels like an act of care, just to help someone fill out some paperwork.

VS: Your point about how we bring in as many inputs as possible is something that I'm interested in, not just in terms of planning a program or an exhibition but to ask, more broadly, how we make decisions as an organization. I think this question about whether or not we're bringing in as many inputs as possible, asking the opinions of those who might not normally be considered in a certain decision-making process, starts internally. Ultimately, I think how we engage with our communities will be reflective of how we engage with one another within the museum. I'm hopeful for how all of this can happen, because I think we have a group of people at the Walker who are invested in the future of the institution, believe in its dual mission of supporting both artists and audiences, and want to model a way forward for working differently.

DESIGNING MOTHERHOOD

How to Midwife Equity Inside and Outside of Museums

BACKGROUND

*D*esigning Motherhood (DM) is a first-of-its-kind consideration of the arc *of human reproduction through the lens of design and spanning the last century. It is a flexible constellation that includes a book (MIT Press), two exhibitions that took place in Philadelphia in 2021 (at the Mütter Museum and at the Center for Architecture and Design), a series of public programs, and a design curriculum intervention. It started life as an Instagram account (@designing motherhood) when no institutions at which we worked would take it on as a project. In 2019, a few years into this project, we met and fell in love with the team at Maternity Care Coalition of Philadelphia, a direct-service organization that has served pregnant people and their young infants for the past 40 years through doula and lactation support, policy advocacy, and other means.*

CASE STUDY

JULIANA ROWEN BARTON, PhD, is a historian and curator whose research centers on the intersections of race, gender, and design. Through her work, she strives to make a more equitable museum experience and to reframe perspectives on familiar objects and spaces. She has worked on exhibitions and programming at the Center for Craft, Philadelphia Museum of Art, Center for Architecture, and Museum of Modern Art.

Hailing from Scotland, MICHELLE MILLAR FISHER has worked as an educator, curator, and historian in universities and museums including the Museum of Modern Art, the Philadelphia Museum of Art, the Guggenheim, and the MFA Boston, where she is currently the Wornick Curator of Contemporary Decorative Arts. Her work focuses on the intersections of people, power, design, and craft. She has coauthored many books, essays, and exhibitions, including *Design and Violence* and *Items: Is Fashion Modern?*

ZOË GREGGS is an artist and a nonprofit administrator who works as an executive assistant at the Maternity Care Coalition. She is a project curator specializing in community engagement for the Designing Motherhood project.

GABRIELLA NELSON is a mother and city planner, possessing a strong interest at the confluence of urban development and public health. She currently works as the associate director of policy for the Maternity Care Coalition, advocating for the best policies and practices regarding maternal–child health and early learning. She believes the city is for everyone, especially for those who want to stay after bearing decades of disinvestment and devastation. Gabriella identifies as a problem-solver, an inquisitive thinker, and a creative whose experiences and opinions are deeply rooted in her womanhood, motherhood, and Blackness.

AMBER WINICK is a mother and design historian. She holds an MA in design history, decorative arts, and material culture from the Bard Graduate Center (BGC) and a BA in child development and anthropology from Sarah Lawrence College. She has received two Fulbrights and has lived and researched maternal- and child-related designs, policies, and practices around the world. She has expertise in the designed systems, environments, and objects that empower (and disempower) us, particularly around birth, family leave, caregiving, schools, and early childhood.

The following conversation happened as part of a Designing Motherhood team meeting over Zoom on March 4, 2021. Participating in the discussion were Juliana Rowen Barton, Michelle Millar Fisher, Zoë Greggs, Gabriella Nelson, and Amber Winick (figure 11.1), just five of the many people who make up the cross-institutional team for this project. Find out more about all the project collaborators at designingmotherhood.org.

Michelle Millar Fisher: So the first question we ask ourselves is, How does the Designing Motherhood project define diversity, accessibility, equity, and inclusion? What institutional or organizational structures exist around these goals, and what have we self-defined around these goals?

Amber Winick: I think it's interesting to think about how the project started as a small kernel of a collaboration between us [Michelle and Amber] and how when the project

Figure 11.1. The Designing Motherhood curatorial team, from top left going clockwise: Amber Winick, Michelle Millar Fisher, Zoë Greggs, Juliana Rowen Barton, and Gabriella Nelson. Image courtesy Michelle Millar Fisher.

expanded, its goals expanded the further that we went. The more that we intentionally embraced, made space for, and wanted to include different perspectives, and wanted different voices within the team and within the pages of the book and in the exhibition, the more the core tenets of diversity and equity became embedded.

MMF: We should be really transparent that we did not define DEAI [or diversity, equity, accessibility, and inclusion] in our primary funding application. We thought about these ideas from the beginning of the project but not within the rubric of DEAI, as it may be spoken about in the museum context in which I work, or in a nonprofit context in terms of climate assessment or anything like that.

AW: It was more organic. Our goals were definitely coming from a really authentic, heart-centered place.

Juliana Rowen Barton: Yes, I was going to say that in some way I don't think about DEAI with this project. I think about DEAI as a very institutional and corporate language for talking about diversity, equity, inclusion, and access. In a lot of ways, that infrastructure isn't applicable to us, because we have defined our own relationship to institutions and haven't had to be beholden to the sometimes-conservative values that come along with traditional DEAI. I think Designing Motherhood takes a more strongly anti-racist viewpoint than the somewhat milquetoast language of DEAI these days and is more firmly working to be actively anti-racist, both before the events of summer 2020 and George Floyd's killing and all that came after it. I think that language was always part of the project, though it became more articulated after.

I would also say that of "diversity, accessibility, equity and inclusion," *equity* seems to be the driving force behind Designing Motherhood in my mind, and that the other descriptors fall in line based on our definition of equity in this project. I hate that these terms have become bland, but I think equity is the least bland and feels the most true and resonant to this project.

Zoë Greggs: I also completely agree that diversity, accessibility, equity, and inclusion has just been so watered down and really whitewashed at this point that it doesn't really feel like it means anything to me anymore. And I think another issue that I see arise a lot is that terms like diversity and inclusion are used without understanding or conversation around white supremacist structures. So even if there is a diverse body of worker bees, that doesn't mean that they occupy a liberatory workplace in any way or that employment structures are trying to fight the status quo or that anyone is really trying to undo white supremacy at all. It has just become about co-opting or changing the faces and the looks of our oppressors to make them more diversified and therefore more palatable.

And I think the great thing that Designing Motherhood has done is that we are thinking beyond this rationale. If you have a group of people who truly believe in a more equitable future and really believe in collaboration and community, then that shows up automatically. That's something that is not forced. So if you have to force diversity and force inclusion—you have to force implicit-bias training, blah, blah, blah—rarely the end product of that is people who are invested in liberation of any kind. But they're more invested in appearing like they're invested in liberation. We're not perfect. There are definitely parts of the project that can be expanded and more accessible and include more folks, of course.

MMF: When I was listening to what you were saying, Zoë and Juliana, a few things sprung to mind. The first is that this project could only actually happen outside of institutional structures. I think it would have died and withered if it had to adhere to the types of DEAI conversations that I see happening in museums that I think others are experiencing within other types of nonprofit or cultural organizations. Second, I agree with you, Juliana: I think equity is at the heart of DM, and that points to the centrality of our very favorite Shine Theory and the notion of reciprocity, of credit and voice that is deeply historically rooted in feminist and explicitly anti-racist thoughts and actions and is also—crucially—part of popular culture rather than management culture.[1] Our team is small enough that we can be nimble, and when ideas come up, we are not reactive to them, as I see many other institutions being. We can be *responsive*, but in thoughtful ways rather than putting out a statement of any kind. I don't think we feel like we need to say something; instead, our position is one of listening and really seeking out and amplifying the experiences and expertise of others.

And third, Zoë, you're absolutely right in your comment about worker bees. The culture that we've built ourselves on the Designing Motherhood project is in progress and is an imperfect science. It is something that requires daily vigilance, and it is a culture where the folks who are working are part of the decision-making and part of the communicating about the project. And therefore it is a culture based around staff and the internal systems it takes to create a workplace, not just about representing externally through programs or a diverse participant roster.

JRB: You know, I love "responsive" versus "reactive." It seems like such a small difference, like a semantic difference, but I do think they are very different. I think about the Designing Motherhood team's discussion around what to post in response to specific instances of police brutality against and murder of Black people, like Walter Wallace in Philadelphia, where our project is based, and the relationship to motherhood in that story. And our recent Instagram post amplifying our amazing publicist for DM, Sarah Brown McLeod, who told her personal story of anti-Asian racism. These are not forced into our project. It is a testament to not just the kind of structure that we've created but to the fact that, as our colleague Gabriela Nelson has said, all of these things *are* motherhood, and so it's not forced for us to find a way to express solidarity or empathy or other kind of expressions of justice and inclusion in our work; it comes naturally. Speaking of Gabriella. . . .

Gabriella Nelson: I was reflecting on our last meeting with the amazing Community Advisors [four expert MCC direct service staff—doula Tekara Gainey, lactation expert Porsche Holland, early childhood expert Sabrina Taylor, and culturally appropriate–care expert Adrianne Edwards] where we talked about participating in certain systems but still being critical of them. I think that is one of the things that we have been doing really, really well. And not just in the anti-racist spaces and practices we aim to embody but within the oppressive systems that exist under the command of capitalism. There isn't enough dialogue in the DEIJ [diversity, equity, inclusion, and justice] space about capitalism as it relates to racism; you cannot isolate racism from capitalism and vice versa. Within this project, we aim to rebel against certain capitalistic ideologies, whether it is through the honoring of a healthy work-life-play balance, sharing of space and media exposure, or compensating people appropriately for their time and thought leadership. Because we are delicate and purposeful with the way we honor each other at Designing Motherhood, we have the autonomy to define and allow for the evolution of our project ecology.

MMF: I agree. I think part of that comes out in recognizing care work as *work*, which comes into the family leave discussions that we've had. I'm proud that our project has put money aside for childcare, for example, for program participants. That we will have a maternity leave on staff and will support a maternity leave cover so that leave can be taken, and that person's work will still be covered equitably. We are, however, still doing this project on a shoestring nonprofit budget, and so no one has health care or paid leave of any kind through DM, a mirror of the wider inequitable microcosm in the US.

AW: We don't shy away from making that visible. Like, Gabriella, you can be making lunch for baby August as we have a meeting. And meetings can be scheduled around nap times, bath times, personal time—things like that. I mean, these are things that aren't welcome within institutions and other more standard work environments, where motherhood and other forms of care work are erased and invisible.

MMF: Care work is demeaned, it is not given value, it is seen as something that takes away from a job rather than adds to it. On our project, it's seen as a form of expertise to have this understanding of the ways in which care is part of the designed systems of everyday life. I really feel like if there was a reorientation of understanding how important care work is as part of the design of everyday life, we might have a very different Department of Architecture and Design at MoMA or different design collections or different designs out there in the world.

JRB: The idea that institutions can't do that—that's false in my mind. They can; they just don't. They aren't built for or by people who grapple with those realities. There's a radical reckoning that needs to happen. I'm reading *Invisible Women: Data Bias in a World Designed for Men* by Caroline Criado Perez, and it's a good route into the root cause of some of these issues.

ZG: What are the opportunities and challenges of our project as they relate to creating an inclusive team and an inclusive project?

GN: One of my biggest challenges has been working with institutions where there is a constant display of power struggle between divisions of labor. Within our team, there is no competition for control. Yes, we have the creators of Designing Motherhood, thank y'all for the blueprint and foresight. However, we all purposefully and proactively share space through collaboration, direct communication, and an honest appreciation for individual expertise. Inviting people and institutions that exist under hegemonic structures to trust that the spaces we've created are safe, honest, and fair has been a complicated effort. We've experienced moments of skepticism and mistrust from staff when trying to describe the nature of this project. In response, we set aside time for more intimate, one-to-one conversations about the project where everyone has spoken candidly. Sometimes, the sincerity of things can get lost in translation when they are communicated from a bird's-eye view. We've learned that communicating things from a worm's-eye view can help us gain more context and meet people where they are.

ZG: I wanted to build on what Gabriella was saying. I think something that is often not talked about when you're trying to create a team—and there are people with very different social locations on it—is that no matter how many Instagram posts are made and how many inclusive-looking ads we see on TV, there's still a very, very large population of people that will push back on those initiatives. And I think that something that I have seen with this project in particular is us wanting to push past the ceiling that we've been given, push past that bubble, and watching some of the outside reactions of discomfort. And discomfort tied to white supremacy and capitalism, discomfort of watching other people take up space, and the immediate reaction to want to tear that down. I think that is the darker side of creating an inclusive team, and it's something that's also not talked about.

JRB: Also, in the category of challenges, I don't think the outside world is ready to respond to what we've created with respect to an inclusive team and an inclusive project. They're not prepared for nuance. I know some of us have been parts of teams where the standard is not to give everyone credit or to show the broadness of the team. Media and press is one example. But there are many others in which there just isn't an infrastructure beyond our own team to understand or to recognize the kind of work that we're doing. And I really hope that this project can help push some of those boundaries.

MMF: I think that speaks to the *process* of this project being way more important than the end product in many ways. And it pains me to say that thinking about the book, because the book really took blood, sweat, and tears! But the process of coming through making our culture as a team is I think the best thing that has come out of this project. That brings us to another question: How might you have approached equity differently on the project if you could start it again from the beginning?

JRB: I think I'd be interested to hear from Michelle and Amber, having worked on this for the longest. You two were the ones who brought us in in various ways.

MMF: I can think of a number of things. The first is, there's a lot of really nice, middle-class white ladies in the design history world, topped with a thin layer of white men in positions of decision-making power. In the US, it's often very expensive to get an education, period, not just in design history. It's a specialized area that isn't often shared in schools. I hope that will change; Designing Motherhood is also a curriculum project. But as a field, it's not particularly accessible right now, whether in architecture or in design. And so it's a personal responsibility: working in the field to work actively toward the system being different in terms of the diversity of thought and participation.

AW: I second what you're saying. Institutions that train design historians have such a long way to go. For me personally, I feel like it's been an interesting experience. And I'm speaking from my own social location here, but when we started this project, I was pregnant with my now three-and-a-half-year-old. At the time, I was just so excited about the idea and eager to prove myself and not fall behind just because I had just given birth. As a result, I found myself struggling to stay up on emails and keep up with writing just a week or two after giving birth. And now I'm pregnant again. And I really will hold that space this time. I will take the time that I need to fully heal and connect with my baby. And the maternity leave replacement that we are hiring will not only benefit my family, and me as an individual, but will set an important standard for the time that *should* be afforded during postpartum and will also ensure that the larger team will be supported and won't be overworked or scrambling to figure it out without me.

ZG: I think that equity of care extends into everybody. I mean, Gabriella, you're feeding your baby, August, just now; many people are doing lots of different care work at home during a pandemic. And I feel very strongly that very different structures of equity and access to work need to be engendered in our social locations in the US and in general to allow all different types of people to have the conversations they want in the workplaces that they want to be in.

JRB: I was listening to this podcast about the trials and tribulations of Condé Nast and *Bon Appetit*. One of the interviews with a Black editorial staff member described how he had spent so much time thinking about how he could integrate into an institution like Condé Nast—but the institution spent zero time thinking about how he could be a part of them. I think that everyone can always be more conscious of what it means to work with people of different backgrounds, whether that is racial, socioeconomic, or otherwise. And I think parenthood and caregiving is another one of those. Institutions do not think about how to integrate necessary caregiving into the workplace in this way. *We* didn't always either. I think that's a really valuable lesson to take away from that mode of thinking.

GN: The question about what we would have done differently is really hard for me. I think I'm so used to toxic work environments that when I experience anything a step above that current environment, it's like, *I don't need to change anything. I'm just happy to be here.* DM has set a new standard, so it's a very hard question to answer. And I think that needs to be considered. When you're just trying to survive through a project or workplace, you're not always thinking about what policies you could put in place to make it better or how you could make a difference. Many times you feel like you have no ownership over the things you work on. So you're not even thinking that you would have a say in making things different. You're just trying to get through to the next job or to the next project. Questions like this are really hard to answer, because sometimes you don't feel like you have the time and space to think critically in that way, because you just want to move forward. And this is a product of capitalism, right. The idea is to keep workers working so hard and in demoralized spaces so that we never get the chance to imagine what a revolution, rebellion, or even a better project looks like.

MMF: I keep thinking about our team culture and the way it requires constant tending like an infant. We're doing it right within the resources that we have, which are not limitless.

AW: I just want to fantasize for a minute, because I realized that we're talking about this all in the context of COVID and Zoom and work structures that have just been forced into that scenario. Imagine if Designing Motherhood was a physical workplace and how beautiful that would be. I mean, not only aesthetically, of course, but a beautiful culture and place for us to build space to go outside and see the sunshine or nurse or visit with your child if that's what's going on for you.

JRB: I'm going to take up Gabriella's point—DM's workscape is a space that is not only *not* toxic but it has encouraged us to be vulnerable with each other in ways that are so healthy for the rest of our lives and that are not typical in workplace environments. We have been able to acknowledge when we're overwhelmed, when we need help. That's so rare. The capitalist structure and system is such that you just suck it up and keep going. And if you're not productive, then you're not worthy or valuable. And that's *not* the dynamic that we have set up here. I know it's something I will take with me in future work relationships and personal relationships.

ZG: I just keep coming back to the word *humanity* because I think that's just been infused across the entire project. We're not afraid of being human with one another, or showing vulnerability.

AW: Some of you know about the respectful, caregiving philosophy that I try to practice that comes from the work of Magda Gerber and Emmi Pikler, and a core tenet is to honor a child as a full and complete human being. And make space for whatever experience or emotion comes up, and allow and support feelings as they play themselves out. And how productive it is to make space and view this all as a healthy part of being alive. It's interesting to recognize that we as adults obviously need that, too, and can make workplace environments that are more productive because they are healthy and respectful. Just like we need to show that kind of respect to our children, we need to show it to each other, to ourselves.

GN: What I learned from this project, which I hope to carry with me in other projects, is to just allow people to be their full selves. This project taps into almost every part of who I am or who I want to be. It taps into my role as a city planner, mom, policy advocate, and creative. It encourages an interdisciplinary way of allowing people to be all of themselves. We focus on the synergy and interplay between team members instead of focusing solely on the deliverables. And that is a big reason why we have been able to work in harmony. Designing Motherhood is the first time in my professional career where I've experienced an honest and mutually benefiting relationship with white women. I'm not a fan of the word "ally," but this project has taught me what camaraderie can look like across class and race. I've never worked with white women that so enthusiastically give up space for this Black mama to shine. Redistribution of power is always at play. That's where the real change happens, not just in a project or a workplace but in the world. And now that I've experienced it, I will always demand it. I will carry that with me forever.

JRB: All of this goes back to the idea of humanity, treating people as humans. People forget that there are people laboring behind the books that you read or the exhibitions or the programs you see. We work to show other people that it is *work*, and I think that that is so important and has great ramifications for work culture.

NOTE

1. Writers, friends, and cultural theorists Aminatou Sow and Ann Friedman coined the term on their podcast *Call Your Girlfriend* with the simple tagline, "I don't shine if you don't shine." Shine Theory is a practice of long-term, mutual investment in each other. It is listening to one another with openness, enacting solidarity with each other in our daily work, and a practice of everyday kindness given and reciprocated. It's colleagues amplifying someone's good idea at a meeting table; it is delighting in someone else's success rather than seeing it as less of the pie for you. It's the kind of thing that sounds easy, but it takes work. You may already be a devotee or an unknowing practitioner.

III

PERSPECTIVES
ON PRAXIS

ON DEFINING AND BUILDING EQUITY AS A FIELD
Nicole Ivy

INTERVIEW

NICOLE IVY is a historical thinker and professional futurist who is passionate about the arts and social change. Her professional and scholarly interests include strategic foresight, public history, visual culture, and inclusive change management. She earned her BA in English from the University of Florida and her joint PhD in African American studies and American studies from Yale University. She also works widely in the museum field, having begun her museum practice as an Institute of Museum and Library Services (IMLS) Curatorial Fellow at the African American Museum in Philadelphia. She has held several inaugural positions at the American Alliance of Museums, including serving as its first director of inclusion. She is an assistant professor of American studies at George Washington University.

The following discussion took place between Nicole Ivy and nico wheadon via email between spring 2018 and spring 2021.

NW: Nicole, I was so impressed by your presentation at the Associations of African American Museum's 2017 conference, "PRESENCE. POWER. PERSISTENCE: Advancing the History and Possibility of Museum Activism." At the time, you were working at AAM as the director of inclusion and presented on your working group's initial work building vocabulary for what would ultimately become *Facing Change: Insights from AAM's Diversity, Equity, Accessibility, and Inclusion Working Group.*

I remember being so blown away by the depth of your research, the intention and care with which you delivered your findings, and the universal relevance of the shared tools and vocabularies that it yielded. Who were your collaborators on that initiative, and what were some of the challenges associated with translating your findings into a national resource guide?

NI: Thank you, nico, for these kind words and for the invitation to think with you and the other culture workers convened in this amazing project. The *Facing Change* report came out of the American Alliance of Museums' DEAI working group co-led by Laura Lott and Dr. Johnnetta Cole in 2018. This working group convened 18 museum professionals from across the country to identify the most pressing challenges to, and also leading practices and future visions for, promoting equity in the museum field.

The group was composed of people with a range of perspectives and experiences in the field: there were independent museum professionals, participants from other museum associations, and representatives from a diversity of museum types—from the Smithsonian system, from art museums, from children's museums, and from science centers. I was honored to spend six months with so many brilliant, committed people.

Throughout the entire process, we were keenly aware that we were part of a significant moment in a longer history of changemaking. Dr. Cole, specifically, kept us accountable by not only reminding us of the stakes of the field's inequality but also by connecting our working group to the history and future of the field. Our biggest breakthroughs—and our most heated debates—stemmed from the weight of that connection. We wanted to do the most effective work we could do, in solidarity with the organizing efforts of museum colleagues and also with leaders in equity-building in the public and private sectors.

NW: How did you feel presenting on diversity, equity, access, and inclusion to a majority Black audience? What were some of your thoughts leading up to the dissemination of the report?

NI: I was extremely nervous about presenting on this work at the Association of African American Museums' (AAAM) annual conference in 2017. The DEAI working group and the *Facing Change* report remains an effort that I am immensely proud of, but I wasn't sure how applicable that work would be to museums dedicated to interpreting the cultural heritage of historically marginalized communities—and to Black museums, specifically.

Diversity and inclusion strategies are typically targeted toward power: toward hierarchical institutions and the people who control decision-making and resource allocation within them. To put it another way, much of organizational equity work is focused on creating structural pathways for predominantly white or male or straight-identified or wealthy leadership to meaningfully incorporate the wisdom of people with different lived experiences. It seems to me that significantly less attention is paid to supporting the institution-building work happening at the intersection of communities of color, queer folx, working-class leaders, and underfunded organizations. While I recognize and encourage the kinds of transformative strides museums are taking to reverse decades of practiced inequality, I am also keenly aware that this engagement can sometimes look like the privileged organizing the privileged.

Presenting on DEAI to a standing-room-only conference room filled with so many respected Black museum professionals made me hyperaware of that discrepancy. I wondered whether a discourse so convincingly pitched toward the mainstream would be of any use to people who had built an entire field in the wake and shadow of anti-Black racism.

What I found was an important valence in the DEAI conversation. A senior Black woman museum professional said to me after the talk was done that it was important that the field had defined the terms of equity for itself. She pointed out that funders were using language that felt, at best, borrowed—and, at worst, imposed—from outside sectors to frame museum inclusion. Using the working group's definitions helped the field define its terms from the inside out. This kind of self-determination was not something I'd considered as part of the value of DEAI work to Black institutions or to people of color working in the museum field.

NW: These are such important revelations! Most recently, I was fortunate enough to collaborate with you in your role as a consultant, hired to lead the Studio Museum in Harlem through a series of workshops and readiness assessments that would prepare a cross-departmental cohort to launch a DEAI Working Group in 2019. You were the perfect person to shepherd our group through understanding what it means for a culturally specific institution to be engaged in DEAI work and how our efforts might feed into a national movement. Can you describe how this project fit within your broader practice, and what about it excited you?

NI: I learned so much from my work with the Studio Museum in Harlem. Importantly, I got a chance to see in practice a vision of equity where the term "diversity" isn't simply a euphemism for "nonwhite" or a heuristic for "those folx over there." Even before signing on, I had been inspired by a case study done by the team at Ithaka S+R in partnership with the Andrew W. Mellon Foundation and the Association of Art Museum Directors published in 2015. One of the key findings of that report was that the Studio Museum in Harlem is an institution that is consistently working within a necessarily expanded understanding of diversity. The report held that, although the museum locates itself as a space promoting the work of artists of African descent, the full scope of these artists' bodies of work disrupts any simplified meaning of the term. The report maintains that "rather than dismissing diversity concerns as a non-issue, leaders and staff at the museum have developed a more nuanced view of the term." This nuance is a distinction that makes all the difference. In my work there, I witnessed teams successfully grappling with questions of ethnicity and nationality inside of a demographic that would traditionally be coded as Black in the typical census-taking language—and no other questions asked. Right from the start, I was presented with an institution that refused the kind of flattening that diversity and inclusion initiatives tend to suffer from.

Ultimately, thinking DEAI outside of the context of predominantly white institutions allows for us to develop a vision of equity that does not take white supremacy as its starting point. That context opens up space for imagining that is not tied to reaction to harm but to the potential for world making. My interest, always, is in how we might live together more justly.

NW: I think this call for equitable cohabitation is a great prompt to deepen our discussion of organizational work culture. In your opinion, how can institutions build equity that is both internal and external facing? And how does your work in strategic planning and board training help to stabilize institutional transformation?

NI: Redressing and unmaking institutional racism requires work that is both top-down and bottom-up, simultaneously. It requires the kind of evaluation that is not sexy, that is sober-minded, and that is willing to look at the bottom line in clear and unvarnished ways. I've found that strategic planning and board training are both absolutely essential to making lasting change in the field.

For one notable example, we need only think on how many museums issued statements affirming that Black life is important—that Black life *matters*—in the wake of the nationwide protests against the killing of George Floyd this past summer of 2020. As a collective statement of intention, these pronouncements were right and good. Many of these were deeply moving. However, as far-reaching acts of organizational change, they remain insufficient. I've heard stories of staff persons of color in predominantly white institutions being deputized to draft their museum's public statements of solidarity—on top of their other assigned work—only to have those drafts belittled and wordsmithed to the point of ineffectiveness.

Public statements serve a critical function. They signal momentum to the field and to visitors too. But they do not reduce the gender-pay gap. They do not replace longitudinal surveys of trends in hiring and promotion. They do not help leaders assess the diversity of vendor relationships or corporate partnerships. They do not help boards prioritize inclusive art-collecting strategies or culturally responsive growth. Only the difficult work of evaluation, benchmarking, collaboration, and power-sharing can accomplish lasting positive change in our nation's museums.

We are seeing a trend toward this kind of deep culture change. I've witnessed thoughtful board chairs throughout the country push for museum leadership that reflects the nation's diversity of thought and experience. But I've also witnessed boards so reluctant to change that when marginalized people finally join their ranks, they run after serving a single term. I think we're witnessing a relative increase in the gender and racial diversity of new curatorial and leadership appointments currently. However, it's still difficult to get a full sense of how many brilliant, promising professionals have left the field altogether because of lack of availability of meaningful opportunities that make use of their gifts at a living wage. There is still much more strategic and structural work to be done.

NW: And that work, in my experience of it, is slow, arduous, and often dangerous work for cultural workers that look like you and me. In 2019, at "A Museum for the People:

Fifty Years Later," Kinshasha Holman Conwill—a hero of mine—offered a vision for *resilience training* to support those already deeply engaged in DEAI work. In your imagination, what might a *resilience training* look like?

NI: I like the sound of *resilience training*. I've been trained in resilience from birth—both intentionally and unintentionally. I'm the Florida-born daughter of two Black, Mississippian parents. According to family lore on my father's side—what we might properly call a paternal oral history—I have an ancestor who survived a 19th-century journey to Mississippi from Virginia by holding onto his donkey's tail as he crossed a raging river. The account handed down to me holds that my grandfather's (great) uncle was given the donkey at the close of the Civil War as a commendation for his service in the Union Army. The donkey could swim, my ancestor could not. My father's father still has the Civil War–era rifle; it's part of our family's material culture.

This story's absurdity is part of how I've come to know myself: as improbable, as connected to a lineage of unlikely and extremely self-willed folk who believe enough in futurity to brave the whirlwind on a donkey's tail. I am responsible to that kind of care-taking people, who've preserved both the impossible story around the object and the object itself.

The term *resilience training* calls up the organizing work pioneered by activists in the long Black freedom struggle, including the nonviolence trainings done by the Congress of Racial Equality (CORE), the Southern Christian Leadership Conference (SCLC), and the Council of Federated Organizations (COFO) during the 20th-century civil rights movement in the US.

I believe that Black museum work is processual. It is connected to African diasporic practices of resistance and freedom seeking that predate even the century-long effort to create the National Museum of African American History and Culture. If the Black cultural heritage that we are working to collect, preserve, interpret, and expand persists in deep time—beyond anti-Blackness, beyond heteronormativity, beyond patriarchy—then we ought to at least be inspired toward resilience in our time.

NW: I just love you so much! And what about the future? What does it mean to be a futurist and educator in a field that is often change averse and obsessed with the weight of its own historical accumulation? How do you balance looking forward and looking back? And what do you think the future for culturally specific museums looks like?

NI: Being a futurist and an educator is a difficult balancing act, but I believe that the charge of cultural custodianship requires it. Cultural work is an honor and an inheritance that demands all my best efforts. Museums are junctures between the past and the future. As institutions imbued with public trust, museums actually carry a mandate to be relevant and responsive in the present. Museums, and tax-exempt US museums most especially, are charged with thinking beyond the five-year strategic-planning timeline. They must look beyond the boom-and-bust cycles of commercial markets while also maintaining viable business practices in any given moment. The aversion to change that you mention actually butts up against the real-time pressures that museums navigate in a world increasingly marked by uncertainty. That is to say, while some departments in a given museum might be more concerned with historical preservation and past narratives, other departments in that same institution will concurrently be concerned with future audiences, year-to-date revenue, and other pressing present issues. Museums avoid looking forward and backward at their own peril, and so do I.

I think the concept of Sankofa best captures what you describe here. The idea of Sankofa originates with the Akan-speaking peoples of Ghana and is expressed in English-language translations as "Go back and fetch it." This principle is typically symbolized in Ghanaian iconology through the image of a bird whose body faces forward while its backward-facing head carries an egg in its mouth. Sankofa as both an image and a maxim elegantly figures the past, present, and future in a unified relationship. The bird depicted in the Adinkra symbol is always delicately balanced; although it faces forward and backward at once, it appears sturdy, sure.

Like the Sankofa bird, culturally specific museums are spectacularly adept at going back to go forward. They are charged with interpreting the stories of communities undergoing change all the time. The features of a given culture are never sedimented. Even though we might view a culture's artifacts across centuries, we can be sure that those cultures can and do change. People manage loss, growth, and also survival in the face of what futurists typically call "wildcard events." Even the specifics of culture in what we name as "culturally specific" museums change over time. I think the most savvy leadership in these institutions recognize this and build change into their institutional visions. So many of the museums in this country that we now name as culturally specific emerged from the determined actions of a cluster of people who wanted to preserve their own heritage, even as their communities were under threat of death in the 19th and 20th centuries. If those founders could be both educators and strategic thinkers, then it is incumbent on we who live in their legacy to do the same.

13

ON NUANCING DIVERSITY AND DIASPORA WITHIN BLACK MUSEUMS

Ariana A. Curtis

INTERVIEW

ARIANA A. CURTIS, PhD, is the director of content for "Our Shared Future: Reckoning with Our Racial Past." In this role, she leads the development of themes and issues that educate about systemic racism and its impact on our communities. She is also the first curator of Latinx studies at the Smithsonian National Museum of African American History and Culture, where she leads research and collections related to US Latinx, US Afro-Latinx, African American and Latinx, African diaspora, and African American migrations to and engagement with Latin America. Ariana is a Fulbright Scholar with a doctorate in anthropology from American University, an MA in public anthropology from American University, and a BA from Duke University.

The following discussion took place between Ariana A. Curtis, PhD, and nico wheadon via email between spring 2018 and spring 2021.

NW: Ariana, we first met in Miami when we were on a panel together discussing "Black Diversity in Black U.S. Museums." At the time, I was at the Studio Museum in Harlem, and you and fellow curator Michelle Wilkinson were at the National Museum of African American History and Culture. As the panel convener, can you discuss your motivations behind staging this conversation as part of the 2017 Museums Association of the Caribbean Conference, "Beyond Boundaries: Transcending Geographies, Disciplines, and Identities"?

AC: Blackness transcends boundaries. Black identity in the United States is generally not thought of or presented as multicultural and multiethnic. Blackness is often flattened. I am always surprised by the number of people that are unaware that in the era of the transatlantic slave trade, the majority of kidnapped Africans did not come to the US but rather were taken to other parts of the Americas. We talk about the African diaspora as though the United States is not part of it. The US is connected to the movement and exchange of global Blackness as both sender and receiver of people and cultures.

I think the Studio Museum in Harlem has been leading by example for decades, showing how renowned and respected Black institutions can articulate and cultivate a diverse Black diasporic narrative. I think the National Museum of African American History and Culture learned from the Studio Museum's example. For our institutions, and each of us as cultural workers and as panelists, the term Black reached beyond a US-bound African Americanness. I wanted to engage with the non-US diasporic audience at the Museum Association of the Caribbean (MAC) to talk explicitly about the reality of diasporic Blackness in the US and what that has and can look like in US Black museum spaces.

Since each of us, in different ways, engage with the Caribbean and the Caribbean diaspora in our work, I thought the MAC conference in Miami would be a great space and audience to discuss the work through Black lenses. Generations of *legal* segregation make Black history in the United States different but not unique. Presenting at the MAC conference also gave an opportunity to unpack and challenge the US context we often take for granted. Knowing the people and scholars that we all are, while we each had something to teach, we also wanted to learn from and engage with Caribbean-based cultural workers whose national histories and museum contexts are different from our own.

NW: And why in particular did you invite me and Michelle to participate? What did you imagine we'd each offer to a conversation on diversity and diaspora within Black museums?

AC: I had actually fangirled Michelle Wilkinson since her time at the Reginald F. Lewis Museum. I had met her years back through the Mellon Mays Undergraduate Fellowship (MMUF) network. She was my inspiration to diverge from academia and attempt this curatorial career path. Her teaching and curatorial work has always included African American, Puerto Rican and other Caribbean experiences, and the African diaspora in general. I reached out to her when she joined the staff at the National Museum of African American History and Culture (NMAAHC) in 2014. I was working at the Anacostia Community Museum (ACM) at the time. And I reached out again, of course, when I joined the NMAAHC staff in 2017. Before I joined the staff, Michelle was doing the Latinx-inclusive work at NMAAHC and much more.

You and I connected through Chayanne Marcano, who is also part of the MMUF network. She interned at ACM while I worked there. When you and I met in early 2017, I had just left ACM for the NMAAHC. During our conversation, I was moved by how you incorporated art, artists' voices, collections, contemporary issues, justice, and a strong sense of place in your programming in service of this collective diasporic Black narrative. Exhibitions and programs are both public-facing work, and they should work in tandem, but they are not the same. I love the thoughtfulness behind *how* you work.

NW: Well, I'm so fortunate that you reached out because I learned so much from you and Michelle—and through my research in preparation for the talk—that helped reorient my department's programmatic approach to serving Black diasporic community at the museum. In your discussion prompts, I heard a strong call for Black museums to be more inclusive in how they consider diversity within diaspora, and use this expanded consciousness to arrive at more authentic representation in their collections, exhibitions, and programs.

I spoke about the Studio Museum's mission and how it has evolved over the past 50 years through articulated nuances that acknowledge the complexities of global citizenship, especially in the realm of arts and culture where Blackness has been unabashedly commodified, traded, and consumed. Can you expound on what the source of our institutional blind spots might be, particularly when it comes to codifying Black identity, othering our own, or placing a selective filter on how we interpret our collective history?

AC: Black immigration history and the evolution of identity labels describing Black people can be institutional blind spots in Black museums. Black is not a synonym for African American. They should not be used interchangeably. The assumption that if someone is "Black," then they are African American no longer holds. Black Americans are increasingly more diverse. According to 2016 American Community Survey data, 1 in 10 Black Americans is foreign born.[1] This distance lessens when we expand to second-generation immigrants and beyond. Black identities include many things like immigration status, nationality, and ethnic identities.

For the Latinx-specific curatorial work that I do, language matters. It can feel like othering when Latinidad is separated from Blackness. Commonplace phrases like "Black and Latinx" perpetuate the whitening of Latinidad by separating Black from Latinx. Latinidad can be Black. Afro-Latinidad is often an afterthought or filtered out, if considered at all.

NW: Can you talk a bit about being hired as the first curator for Latino Studies at the Anacostia Community Museum? What was your relationship to the rest of the Smithsonian?

AC: I started at the Smithsonian in 2013 at the Anacostia Community Museum as curator for Latino studies. I had no idea at the time I was hired, but I was hired through the Latino Curatorial Initiative. The Initiative is one of the multipronged institutional responses to a 1994 report titled *Willful Neglect* which, after studying the Smithsonian's governance, personnel policies, collections, programs, and budget allocations, concluded that that "the [Smithsonian] institution almost entirely excludes and ignores Latinos in nearly every aspect of its operations."[2] One outcome of the report was the 1997 creation of what is now the Smithsonian Latino Center. And almost 20 years later, the Latino Curatorial Initiative hired a cohort of curators, including me, at multiple Smithsonian museums in 2013.

Formally, we met as a group and each gave updates to Smithsonian administration, not just metrics but the actual, *How is this going for you? Do you feel supported? What success are you enjoying? What challenges are you having?* They created a safe and honest group space for us, with actual accountability and action steps to handle issues as they arose. They truly listened to what we had to say. Many of us were "the first" and the only in our respective museums. Institutionally, leadership wanted the initiative and each curator to be successful. This cluster hire and larger support network that included high-level decision makers is frankly why I am still working at the Smithsonian.

NW: So despite the lack of transparency around the formation of the Latino Cultural Initiative, your participation in it was important to your professional journey. Without this community of support and professional practice, how might your path have diverged?

AC: I leaned on that network often during my years at Anacostia, and it is not an exaggeration to say without it, I would have left the Smithsonian. I wrote in *The Public Historian*[3] about some of the difficulties, including my first day on the job when a colleague asked me, "What do Spanish people have to do with the rest of us?" Although the Anacostia Museum was founded during the Black museum movement and has always focused on (Black) DC, in my immediate workplace, there was no vision from museum leadership about how Latino studies or I would integrate with the existing work of the museum. I had to create and articulate that path myself, which is an uncomfortable position to be in as a peer and subordinate.

I was bolstered by the larger support of the Smithsonian. I give a lot of credit to Richard Kurin, then undersecretary for museums and research, Joanne Flores, head of special projects, and Eduardo Díaz, director of the Smithsonian Latino Center, the office that administers the funds through which we were all hired, for convening us regularly in those first years. Through these formal meetings and then informally, we got to know each other's lives, families, and research. We shared resources and acted as both cheerleaders and sounding boards. I felt supported by this network.

I say all of this within this conversation about DEAI because being hired in an institutionally supported cohort was a professional life jacket. Too often we read about DEAI positions where a nonwhite person is dropped into an institution without support or mechanisms to address the toxicity, hold anyone accountable, or enact change.[4] That was my situation at Anacostia: I was one person in a newly created, nonleadership position, without the power to change exclusionary institutional processes that hindered my ability to do my job. I got along with my colleagues, and I know they wanted to see me—to see us—succeed. It was not a likeability issue. I did not have access to resources—financial or human—to fully support the work I was hired to do.

NW: What surprised you most, and what could the museum have done differently to support you?

AC: I did not anticipate needing to fight for resources, accountability, structure, and equity in a Black museum setting. I also knew it was site-specific, since the others in my cohort did not have these same issues. It was emotionally difficult and professionally surprising how narrow the definition of "African American" was. This reality reminded me of the Toni Morrison quote, "Definitions belong to the definers, not the defined."[5] As a curator, I define, shape, and interpret. I needed to define, shape, and interpret broader understandings of African American, Black, and community.

Although I leaned on my cohort for many things, I was the only Black person hired in that cohort. Not only did they not have the same institutional struggles I was having, they did not share the professional or personal racial context. As an anthropologist who is both African American and Afro-Latina, this was not just about accurate representation and fighting institutional erasure. It was also very personal. In order to be successful in "doing" Latinx studies at ACM, I felt that the museum needed to first acknowledge, or at least understand, why diverse Black stories are relevant to our collective work and to our community. I did not want my work to be seen as separate from the museum's work. I wanted it to be understood as *our* work, collectively, moving forward. I needed clear messaging and support from museum leadership. Instead, I was left to make an argument and implementation plan for my integration into this museum on my own.

NW: What was your response?

AC: My response was layered. I knew that the Studio Museum in Harlem had long been doing this kind of inclusive work in the art world and I could uphold them as a model. But it seemed easy for people to attribute that deliberate, inclusive Blackness to NY's diversity or to the art world. The real reason is because that is who we are as Black Americans. Stuart Hall writes about people using identity labels as they become historically available.[6] That is true for personal identification, exhibition scripts, and even museum cataloging.

Black multiculturalism has always existed but was masked by racially general terms like "colored," "negro," and even "Black." "African American" came into popular usage in the 1980s. The term now articulates a US-based lineage and history, a US-based Blackness as opposed to other identity labels like Afro-Caribbean or Afro-Latinx. ACM's collection was predominantly Black, with Black being understood (erroneously) as African American only. Given this evolution of identity terms and the demographics of the nation's capital—literally people from all over the world live here—I wasn't convinced that our collection was African American only. I wanted to take a step back and say, "Let's look and see what we actually have in our collection."

It was educational for my colleagues but also empowering for me to pull artists, objects, images, and stories from the ACM permanent collection, which was "African American" focused, that were immigrant and/or Latinx related, to demonstrate that Anacostia was always doing this work. Therefore, my work was an extension of existing research, not a new thread. I started with programming to showcase relevant themes and build a network of collaborators. I curated and developed exhibitions using previously unshown ACM collections, framed through new lenses. I made new acquisitions and curated exhibitions with new, but related, content.

This framework also offered an institutional foundation for solidarity with other Black museums, like the Studio Museum. It also offered me the opportunity to reach out to like-minded Black museum professionals like you and Michelle Wilkinson to talk explicitly about doing this work and purposefully unpacking the terms Black or African

American within US Black museum spaces with a diasporic museum audience that included non–African American, Black museum professionals.

Race as a social construction means Blackness is not static. Articulating this reality was important for ACM because it had served as Smithsonian's de facto African American museum before the NMAAHC was legislated. My first mentor and supervisor, the late Portia James, shared this vision. She was the curator of the landmark 1994 exhibition *Black Mosaic: Community, Race, and Ethnicity among Black Immigrants in Washington, D.C.* Highlighting diverse Blackness at ACM, recognizing demographic change, and reinterpreting existing collections provided a fresh processual framework for the whole museum, not just my place in it.

NW: Who have been some of your mentors along the way, especially as you made the transition from ACM to NMAAHC? And how does your new role as director of content for "Our Shared Future: Reckoning with Our Racial Past," sit in relation to NMAAHC's broader mission?

AC: Portia James, the woman who hired me, for sure. She was important to me. She passed away in 2015. Talking about the Studio Museum, I have to also acknowledge the great Kinshasha Holman Conwill, who is a mentor and friend. I had the pleasure of collaborating with Deborah Mack, associate director at NMAAHC, on a diaspora project while I worked at ACM. That project actually set the foundation for the MAC panel. Dr. Mack has advised, championed, and mentored me since very early in my Smithsonian career. E. Carmen Ramos, deputy chief curator at the Smithsonian American Art Museum, was the first Latino curatorial initiative hire in 2010. I definitely looked up to her, and, in part from the larger Latinx scholar gatherings, we developed a close relationship. Adding Michelle Wilkinson to this list, I have deliberated with these women before any of my professional moves, including the move from ACM to NMAAHC and from NMAAHC to the Smithsonian Castle. They have and continue to affirm and mentor me. I would be remiss to not add Lonnie Bunch to this list, who was integral in my move from ACM as well as inviting me to this new role in the Smithsonian's race initiative.

Given the difficult experience I had at the Anacostia Community Museum, I wanted to talk about the Latinx curatorial position at NMAAHC before committing to it. This is professional work, but it would be naïve to say it is not also very personal. I had a very moving and powerful conversation with Lonnie Bunch, the founding museum director, before I joined the staff. I asked why he wanted this position and what my role would be. We were completely in sync that this role would be much more than Afro-Latinx studies, although it is rooted there. Latinx studies as a field marginalizes Blackness. Lonnie and I agreed that NMAAHC is a place to explore all of the complicated histories and relationships between African American and Latinx cultures and identities. As such, my work centers Blackness, but I have five interlocking areas of responsibility: Latinx, Afro-Latinx, African diaspora (mainly Latin America), African American and Latinx, and African Americanness and Latin America. I wrote a collecting plan to detail each area. We created an award-winning Latinx collections portal that publicly displays what this looks like in our collection.[7] Lonnie and Kinshasha's leadership and support were critical, but honestly the embrace from and collaboration with my colleagues has been superlative.

In the summer of 2020, I received an email [and] then a phone call from Lonnie, now the secretary of the Smithsonian, inviting me to help lead a new Smithsonian-wide initiative about race and racism. It was a tough decision. I love my curatorial work—my colleagues, the intellectual models, the collecting and cataloging, the community engagement, the audience engagement. I consulted with my team of mentors referenced above, as well as the then interim director of NMAAHC and former director of the National Museum of American History, Spencer Crew. Spencer is amazing. He really helped me acknowledge this as the huge opportunity it is: to work across the whole institution, build new relationships, center racial justice, share intellectual authority, amplify good work being done both inside and outside of the Smithsonian, and actively create spaces for change in our field. This is *how* we work at NMAAHC, and we can make these institutional processes for all of SI.

Again, linking this to DEAI, these are deliberate choices with broad institutional impact. In a question posed to me in a 2020 interview about this initiative, I connected my career to institutional choices. I said, "I know I'm lucky to have the Smithsonian career that I have, from a personal and professional standpoint, as a Black Latina scholar and as a curator. I am lucky in the timing. Previously, spaces like the Smithsonian were not available to someone like me. I know that a series of institutional commitments made my career possible. I have benefited from the Latino Curatorial Initiative and the building of the National Museum of African American History and Culture. I understand how institutional commitments can be life-changing at an individual level. I get excited imagining the transformative impact of a long-term commitment like this and its legacy on the Smithsonian, the museum field, for our visitors and for future museum professionals."[8] I think about the people that have mentored me, and I think we share this vision: always thinking of ourselves as part of a collective, of our own opportunities with respect to the ability to create opportunities for others. Spencer reminded me that our training, perspectives, and approaches to the work can shift paradigms far beyond the walls and networks of Black museums. I currently have an opportunity to help do just that.

NW: I appreciate your nuanced approach to bridging curatorial work with museum practices more broadly. How does NMAAHC's decision to create and fund such an intersectional and inclusive curatorial role—and its associated research and scholarship—factor into the larger movement toward decolonizing museums?

AC: The very first object donated to the NMAAHC collection was a boat seat from Esmeraldas, Ecuador, one of the first maroon settlements in the Americas. Multiple people proudly shared that collections factoid with me long before I ever dreamed of joining the staff. At the time, I did not interpret that factoid as foreshadow for my own curatorial work but rather as a seat at the proverbial table of Black diasporic representation. NMAAHC is expanding public definitions about what an "African American" experience means and the diversity that *is* Black American identity. This inclusive reality sets a didactic and emotional tone for the audiences, the staff, the collection, the programming, and the museum field.

Curatorial is one of the whitest museum professions.[9] It is rare that a research area focuses on a "nonwhite" group[10] in a nonwhite museum context. But that's what I do. I have so much respect for people like Lonnie Bunch and Dr. Deborah Mack, among many others, who felt this position was important and advocated for its creation. I think I am the only curator for Latinx studies at an African American museum. That is powerful. Whiteness is not guiding this intellectual production.

In that way, I believe we are helping shift paradigms and create new precedents for how we tell American history. It is powerful that my position is curatorial, not an education or outreach position with the goal of increasing Latinx visitorship. It is a permanent curatorial position. This is a statement that Latinx history and culture is fundamental to the intellectual and material foundation that we are building. It represents an institutional decision about diversity and inclusion, how this collection will grow, and who this museum will represent as its permanent institutional identity. It is not based on demographic shifts or exhibition themes but rather the belief that Latinx history and culture can be and should be understood through the lenses of African American history and culture at a national level.

NW: You are so right about the importance of the permanency of this work. It strikes me that your work is also highly collaborative and community oriented, which are two words rarely used to describe curatorial work. What other stigmas and stereotypes are we up against as we continue to advance diasporic diversity across the work of the entire museum?

AC: Most museums are not Black museums. Blackness is a "diversifying" element to predominantly white museum structures, meaning whiteness remains central for them. During our panel, not only did each of us engage with the Caribbean but we approached our work with Blackness at the center and spoke about visible Black diversity, not Blackness as diversity. I think our work exemplifies another Toni Morrison quote: "I stood at the border, stood at the edge and claimed it as central. I claimed it as central, and let the rest of the world move over to where I was."[11] That is how we structured our panel, with diverse Blackness at the center rather than the margin. Through those lenses, conversations about diversity, equity, access, and inclusion look quite different. Now we are talking about geographic diversity, national identity, ethnicity, intraracial tension, immigration, identity labels, language and dialect, hair, literature, urban settlement, music, and any possible human issue but with Blackness at the center. We work at institutions where Blackness is not singular. It is not flat. It is complex and multifaceted. It is the thing, not the contrast. Our work reflects the communities to which we belong and with which we engage. Those are important models to represent while admitting we have room to grow.

Talking about audiences, social media comments in response to my work let me know that Latinidad is not necessarily what people want to see in an African American

Museum, and it is not necessarily where Latinxs want to be represented. I do my job anyway, with the full support of leadership and my colleagues from all departments, and much of our audience. I feel deeply respected, affirmed, challenged, and enriched from working in museum spaces full of Black museum professionals, Black collections, diverse Black stories, inclusive public histories, and multilayered stories about women. NMAAHC is part of a PWI [predominantly white institution]. Having that museum as my home base fortifies me to actively participate in institutional service, like directing content for this Smithsonian-wide race initiative.

NMAAHC is helping push the Smithsonian and hopefully the whole museum field forward in a progressive and inclusive direction. The popularity of this museum shows that people are hungry for alternative perspectives of our shared history. I am personally proud to be a part of that and proud that Latinx art, history, and culture are a part of that. Now that Lonnie Bunch is the secretary for the Smithsonian, I think we will see a higher standard for what qualifies as diversity, inclusion, and have more profound measures of impact.

Institutionally speaking, the National Museum of African American History and Culture understands and presents Black American identity as multicultural. I appreciate that many of my curatorial colleagues at NMAAHC honor the diversity of Black Americans by calling out various ethnic and cultural heritages and experiences throughout the museum—Shirley Chisholm as the daughter of immigrants, Geoffrey Holder's Trinidadian influence on the costume design for *The Wiz*, or Celia Cruz as Black American music. I love that Black people, including but not limited to Black Americans, see NMAAHC as a space of representation.

NW: Me too. OK, a final prompt—what can the Black museum of the future learn from our work today?

AC: NMAAHC is the newest African American museum, soon to be supplanted by even newer institutions. Part of the power of Black museums is that we create our own frameworks and help people understand the power of that self-articulation. We define ourselves and decide how we show ourselves to the world. It is proactive. I love how open and honest you were about the evolution of the Studio Museum's mission during our panel. I think it is an example of a Black museum responding to the world around it. Culture is not static. Demographics change. Identity labels evolve. Movements shift and splinter. New movements take shape. Black museums must include all of this.

Instead of being more "inclusive" per se, I think Black museums in the US can be more intentional in how and where we articulate our diversity. I don't think institutions do enough to present Black people, history, and culture as multidimensional, multicultural, multiethnic, and global. This is important not only for how society as a whole sees and understands Black history, but also for how we, as Black people, understand ourselves.

NOTES

1. Anderson, Monica, and Gustavo López. "Key Facts about Black Immigrants in the US." Pew Research Center, May 30, 2020, https://www.pewresearch.org/fact-tank/2018/01/24/key-facts-about-black-immigrants-in-the-u-s.

2. Yzaguirre, Raul, and Mari Carmen Aponte. *Willful Neglect: The Smithsonian Institution and U.S. Latinos.* Smithsonian Institution, May 1994, https://siarchives.si.edu/sites/default/files/forum-pdfs/Willful_Neglect_The_Smithsonian_Institution%20and_US_Latinos.pdf.

3. Curtis, Ariana A. "Afro-Latinidad in the Smithsonian's African American Museum Spaces." *Public Historian* 40, no. 3 (August 1, 2018): 278–91, https://doi.org/10.1525/tph.2018.40.3.278.

4. See Asare, Janice Gassam. "Why Chief Diversity Officers Often Fail." *Forbes*, April 27, 2019, https://www.forbes.com/sites/janicegassam/2019/04/27/why-chief-diversity-officers-often-fail; Hall, Diane M., and Howard C. Stevenson. "Double Jeopardy: Being African-American and Doing Diversity in Independent Schools." *Teachers College Record*, Columbia University, 2006, https://www.tcrecord.org/books/PrintContent.asp?ContentID=12715; McGirt, Ellen. "Chief Diversity Officers Are Set Up to Fail." *Fortune*, December 19, 2019, https://fortune.com/2019/03/04/chief-diversity-officers-are-set-up-to-fail; Owusu, Nadia. "Hiring a Chief Diversity Officer Won't Fix Your Racist Company Culture." Catapult, January 22, 2021, https://catapult.co/stories/women-of-color-chief-diversity-officers-cannot-fix-racist-company-culture-nadia-owusu#disqus.

5. Morrison, Toni. *Beloved: A Novel.* New York: Knopf Publishing, 1987.

6. Hall, Stuart. "Cultural Identity and Diaspora." In *Identity: Community, Culture, and Difference*, edited by Jonathan Rutherford, 222–37. London: Lawrence and Wishart, 1990.

7. In April 2021, NMAAHC's Latinx Collections Portal tied for the Best Online Resource Award from the Association of Art Museum Curators.

8. "Healing A Nation." Smithsonian Institution, November 2020, https://www.si.edu/support/impact/healing-nation.

9. Westermann, Mariët, Roger Schonfeld, and Liam Sweeney. *Art Museum Staff Demographic Survey 2018.* New York: Ithaka S+R, January 28, 2019, https://mellon.org/media/filer_public/e5/a3/e5a373f3-697e-41e3-8f17-051587468755/sr-mellon-report-art-museum-staff-demographic-survey-01282019.pdf.

10. Latinx is not a race. Some Latinx people are, in fact, white. But generally, it is considered an identity "of color."

11. Director, Gary Deans; producers, Alan Hall, Jana Wendt; a co-production between Beyond Productions and the Australian Broadcasting Corporation. *Toni Morrison Uncensored.* Princeton, NJ: Films for the Humanities & Sciences, 1998.

14

ON SHAPING RESILIENT ARTS-AND-CULTURE ORGANIZATIONS

DéLana R. A. Dameron

INTERVIEW

Poet and writer DÉLANA R. A. DAMERON is the founder and chief architect of Red Olive Creative Consulting, a boutique firm whose work since 2013 includes supporting arts-and-culture organizations and resourcing their missions. Red Olive supports the cultivation of creative cultural communities across the United States through various programs and services and since 2017 has been collaborating to shape the future of Black art through her Black Art Futures Fund. She is the author of two books of poetry: *How God Ends Us* and *Weary Kingdom*, both from University of South Carolina Press.

The following interview took place between DéLana R. A. Dameron and nico wheadon via email between fall 2020 and spring 2021.

nico wheadon: I'm excited to discuss with you what resilience looks like for the arts-and-culture sector and the role you and your team at Red Olive Consulting play in shaping cultural organizations with sustainability in mind. But first, what are some of the structural challenges faced by cultural nonprofits?

DéLana R. A. Dameron: I have been embracing folks who are considering alternative or hybrid models of organization. What I mean is, if we accept that everything has a type of cost and that cost manifests itself in different ways, then that might free us up to imagine different structures.

As a consultant in service to not-for-profit entities, I have chosen to keep my business for-profit, an LLC, to be exact. This means that I absolutely maintain ownership over what I say and what I want to do. And the "cost" of that is I must pay taxes on my income, although I have mechanisms in place, such as a fiscal sponsor, to leverage for tax-deductibility purposes. It means that there are extra hoops, more fees even, some things might be harder to figure out or take longer to execute, and I might not have access to the *ability to apply for some grants*. But I will not become a 501(c)(3). The cost for that, in my opinion, is much higher than the checks I write to the IRS on a quarterly basis.

I have had the privilege of being at the beginning and germinal stages of so many artistic enterprises, it's truly an honor. Almost always there comes a moment when the founder considers—and usually they use language like "professionalize"—changing their entity structure. Almost always the knee-jerk response is to become a not-for-profit entity. When I ask why, the response is generally some combination of "I pay so much in taxes" or "I want to be able to apply for grants." If that is their *why*—and their priority for choosing their business structure—then they have traded, I think, ownership, right?

You must have a board, and how you engage the board is important if you choose this structure. That board's main legal responsibility to the 501(c)(3) is to hire and fire the executive director and to make sure the entity is not doing anything illegal. All the other requirements of the board are, as I say, "manmade." Anything we complain about a board doing or not doing for the organization, or doing too much of, is a direct response of the rules and bylaws set by people of the organizing entity. But here's the thing: *they can be changed*. The only thing that can't change is that they must exist. And they have the power to fire you. Get that: they can fire you from the thing you've created—that you created because you didn't want to pay the cost of ownership: paying taxes. Not-for-profit organizations live and die by this collective of individuals, truly.

NW: This default behavior of opting into hierarchy for (1) presumed access to resources and (2) a false sense of protection from the woes of capitalism is wild to me. Especially when the organization choosing this nonprofit structure—which relies so heavily on philanthropy that is historically rich and white—is oriented toward serving low-income Black and Brown communities. How does Black Art Futures Fund empower Black arts organizations to protect their mission while also building the capital to both sustain and grow?

DD: One of the things that I preach–and practice–is that no matter how small your operation, *be a small ship with big sails*. I think this is an extension of how I live my life. I'm super short. At one point, I had a complex about that, mostly when I was younger. But then I got older, and that meant that I either continued to only take up the space that I physically occupied or I could puff out my chest a bit and stand taller and use my musician lungs to project my voice. So when I am working with an organization, I constantly remind them that somehow along the way, we've let the power differentials get twisted. We think that "in order to get X we have to give up Y," and that's just not true. It *is* true for some donors, and I argue, that's not *your* donor.

I also say, "Don't let the [funding] tail wag the dog." This is the business that I'm in: translation. It's also like what it means to be a Black woman in America: constantly code switching, translating one thing in one context to be useful in another context. By not letting the funding tail wag the dog, we can enter into any situation knowing what we need and how to leverage those with resources to meet that need without giving up any creative, programmatic, or organizational power. Those who are truly philanthropic are here for the ride of what you already have going. Being in alignment with what you're up to—vibing, as the kids say—is the gift! Truly. That's the exchange. Those who are there for personal or organizational gain and leverage funding for it are not after what you're up to. Don't align yourself with those folks.

Another way to say that is to sever the feedback loop between who is giving the money and who is making the decisions about what to do with the money. That's something that was very intentional in the creation of Black Art Futures Fund. I want to reiterate it though: we tie so closely (think: board give/gets) what folks give to what the organization does, and the only way to protect any of it is to sever that relationship. Give to give. Let the experts expert.

NW: For me, this raises the question of who's in the feedback loop in the first place. Recently, I've heard a lot of Black founders of nascent nonprofits say, *We need Black celebrities and athletes to support Black institutions*, which is a complicated position in that it presumes a cultural affinity that may or may not actually exist. In your opinion, what does sustainable investment in Black arts-and-culture organizations look like, and who is making that repeat investment long-term?

DD: I'll be very happy for the day when we relinquish the idea that just because someone has capital, they are going to be interested in what we're up to. My process and practice for resource development is pretty simple: *find your people* and *find the people who will let you do the thing you do.* They are not always the same person or type of people.

Right now, a lot of the rhetoric is that they *should* be the same person (see the folks who are like, *I want the community to be financially invested in X organization—it's for them!*), but I disagree. Especially when it comes to Black folks. So much of what Black institutions have created has come out of a lack in a field, right? Folks created Black performing arts programs because the white performing arts institutions didn't showcase Black talent. The arts music program for Black youth to learn professional methodologies and be exposed to professional-level talent was created because budget cuts slashed the arts programming in the already under-funded schools. The Black museum interested in showcasing everyday peoples, putting them in dialogue with a larger local history, and developing an artist fellowship program for Black emerging artists was created due to a lack in institutional representation. Those are the folks who are the direct recipients or direct audiences of these institutions. I think.

One of the things the last few years has given us, publicly, is a conversation about the generational wealth gap of Black Americans, specifically, and diaspora Black folks broadly in America up against white wealth. We use celebrity and Black exceptionalism to ignore the larger conversation about Black wealth, which is why I'm not necessarily answering your question directly, but I think I am. My argument about not pressuring "the community" to also "invest in" these institutions financially is, *How do we ask Black folks to pay for, or correct, the very systems white folks put us in?*

If we accept all the research and findings that have come out pre-COVID—that for every 10 dollars a white household has, a Black household has only 1—how does that fund the institutions? If these institutions buy into the not-for-profit model as their organizing structure—which does *not* mean the institution cannot pay its staff or run a surplus, however, *does* mean they are reliant on philanthropy, which is driven explicitly by a community's access to discretionary income—how does that fund the institutions?

So I don't know. Asking celebrities to fill that gap is still a quick-fix measure to me, and it goes against my earlier point about finding your people. Beyoncé giving me a $5,000 grant is *great*. I should think about how to stretch that (boy, do Black folks often know how to do this pretty well). To me though, what's more powerful is 50 folks giving $10 a month for as long as they love the work we do. That's $6,000 a year of income I can count on, and you know, those folks might bring other folks to my events and might encourage other folks to give their $10 a month or connect us to their employer, who has greater resources. But at the center of it is my *work*, right? The institution. At the center of it is this thing I'm offering to the world and inviting people to help continue to make it possible for the long term.

NW: I love this so much. I often find myself reminding people that institutions are not entities in and of themselves—they are merely containers for their people and platforms for their people's work! In your opinion, how could a reorientation toward people and process offer visions for new philanthropic structures or partnerships?

DD: Of the 3.5 years that Black Art Futures Fund has been in existence, we've partnered with only one philanthropic funding entity (actually a collaborative funding opportunity) for the work we've been doing. And because I often renegotiate terms of engagement that almost always bear in my project's favor, that means I disappear from folks' funding list. So it goes. And yet, I'm excited to think about what that has asked me to do, think about, and create despite not having access to swift movements of resources in the ways in which I've seen it move for some of my Red Olive clients, when I was a development director, and even a board chair, of an institution. In the past year, I've been interested in investigating small businesses who want to be philanthropic and ally themselves with Black cultural and artistic production.

NW: I agree that the past year has produced a new public consciousness around the relationship between funding structure and organizational sustainability. One of my mentors recently said that, in the language of COVID-19, we are seeing an emergent dichotomy between *essential* and *nonessential* institutions. Which do you deem essential and why? And, given BAFF's funding priorities and the values you've espoused in this conversation, how do we fund and protect Black innovation in an ecosystem ripe with Black cultural and intellectual parasitism?

DD: I am of the belief that small and community-based Black arts organizations are the Gardens of Eden for all American culture. That is, there is no American culture without the spaces that nurtured Black artistic talent on a local and small level, trained them up, or allowed them to take risks. In my Maslow's cultural hierarchy of needs, there is a small and community-based Black arts organization at the foundation of the pyramid. We'd have almost nothing else without them.

Black folks have a tradition of "making a way out of no way," and I truly believe we'll continue to produce, even without a budget. For so many years, we've been under-funded and deemed nonessential. Sure, we have the markers of Black exceptionalism (Smithsonian, Studio Museum, etc.) that make us believe that Black institutions are all right, but the wider swath could certainly use more resources.

There was an article from DeVos that came out in 2015 about the state of Black and Latino organizations. Certainly, there were critiques, and I have several, but one of the pieces of the conversation that gets glossed over is this mapping that happened regarding funding for "diversity." White institutions, with their oversized budgets, could attract Black talent and pay them rates that small and community-based Black institutions *could never*. They could also come with, you know, collectors, and other highly sought-after resources and networks. *But where did that artist that gets the full-museum retrospective cut their teeth?* So then the institution is like, *You can come be our season opener or closer*, and the artist, used to much larger budgets, either has to consider pro bono, doing it at a loss, not being able to get their "market value," or turning down the opportunity altogether.

I had this conversation with my mentor, Shay Wafer, in my podcast *Deep in the Work*. She was the executive director at 651 ARTS in downtown Brooklyn, in the shadow of Brooklyn Academy of Music and the emerging Downtown Brooklyn Cultural District, of which, 651, with their presenting African diasporan art since 1988 in the same area, certainly contributed to (see my cultural hierarchy of needs). 651 has been "getting a new building" for some time now, closing in on a decade, and I'll let folks think about the absurdity of how many other cultural spaces—Center for Fiction, Theater for a New Audience, all of the BAMS, etc.— have popped up in the in-between.

In our conversation, Shay mentioned how she and a former 651 ARTS executive director lamented about the situation and tried to find a way to "sell" their contribution and came up with the idea that maybe that institution was a "research and development arm" for the field. Imagine that? They knew and could trace the artists we know and love today from their stages to the world stages, and the only way they felt they could get major philanthropic dollars was to say, *OK we're a feeder school for the white institutions*. In some ways, that is the unspoken agreement that has been made, right? Small and community-based Black arts institutions *take the risk* and develop the talent, and white institutions leverage *already developed and nurtured Black artistic and cultural* talent for their own sustainability and future. Meanwhile, the organizations I'm deeply invested in, suffer.

I don't like to use COVID as a before-and-after for Black institutions because the decisions about essential and nonessential have always been made in philanthropy. It's how we got here. Even in the "course corrections," which happened post whatever folks want to call June 2020, there are still decisions being made about how and who and where and how much. It wasn't COVID. Before 2020, there were small and community-based Black arts organizations insisting on their organizational cultural and artistic excellence without the deep investments from philanthropy, which, absolutely, means that for a lot of them, they will "make do." For those who are chosen and have been the recipients of resources, many of them have been more flush with cash than in the history of their organizations. Much of that had to do with their ratio of grants that they already had or were in the pipeline to receive.

In the field, to "rely too heavily on grants" was seen as a threat in the "before" times. For many small and community-based organizations who could get them, and for whom even the small grants made up the bulk of any revenue they had, they were still mostly restricted in their use. *Here's a $10,000 grant, and only 20 percent can be used on overhead.* So many of these organizations had a budget that was something like 90 percent of those types of grants, right, and then overnight in June 2020, they all turned to general operating support. And all of a sudden, some of my clients could do things like buy health insurance for their staff members, hire grant writers, hire administrative and operational staff, and think about a future, because the money could be used however they needed. Isn't that something?

⑮

ON MOVING FROM GATEKEEPING TO DISTRIBUTED LEADERSHIP

Sandra Jackson-Dumont

INTERVIEW

Curator, author, educator, administrator, and public advocate for reimagining the role of art museums in society, SANDRA JACKSON-DUMONT has served since January 2020 as director and chief executive officer of the new Lucas Museum of Narrative Art—a 300,000-square-foot building and 11-acre park currently under construction in Los Angeles's Exposition Park. She has held positions at the Studio Museum in Harlem, the Whitney Museum of American Art, the Seattle Art Museum, and the Metropolitan Museum of Art.

The following interview took place between Sandra Jackson-Dumont and nico wheadon via email between August 2020 and May 2021.

nico wheadon: Sandra, you've had such a prolific career that I don't even know where to start. Perhaps we can begin by discussing your origin story in museums. Why and how did you land in the field, and what formative experiences helped shape your early interest in museum practice?

Sandra Jackson-Dumont: I landed in museums because I see them as custodians of histories, past, present, and future through objects, people, experiences, and ideas. I've always been interested in how and why certain perspectives and stories are chronicled in our social and cultural archives. I was most interested in the histories that are not shared. My hope is that museums can serve as sites for nuanced narratives to reveal the often-complex contours of realities, imaginations, and aspirations.

I was very much invested in becoming someone who contributes to these houses of legacy, where the creation of history meets everyday existence. The places where intellectual rigor meets personal style—that's what I love about places like the Studio Museum!

There, I encountered Black people who were invested in dynamically compelling people engaged in creating thinking communities [and] buoying environments that foster self-ideation and self-determination where the past, present, and future can coexist.

NW: In your love for the culture and the style of the Studio Museum, I also see an appreciation for the collective and complex expression of Blackness.

SJD: That's right. What's radical about a place like the Studio Museum is that *education, aesthetics, history,* and *community* are intertwined. What the Studio Museum, El Museo del Barrio, and the Caribbean Cultural Center of the African Diaspora brought to the table was a genuine connection between what the community members were doing and what was going on with art and what was transpiring inside the spaces. The cultural workers in those spaces practiced elevating artists as integral parts of community welfare. It is imperative that community partners and community members serve as critical collaborators and not solely distant audiences consuming content. The collective and complex expression of Blackness you refer to is also central to content creation and authorship. This highly reflexive model presented by these institutions at their inceptions is one that most museums are just now grappling with.

NW: Exactly—a synergy between the culture of the institution and the broader culture in which it's situated, and the fact that the cultural production that transpires beyond the institution is *just* as important as that which transpires within it. It reminds me of an earlier roundtable in which we discussed the Harlem Semester, created by Professor Tina M. Campt, as a platform for repositioning scholarship as a daily practice—one that's *as* embodied by the street vendors on 125th Street and the performers on Adam Clayton Powell Boulevard as it is the work of the museum.

SJD: I've been on what I call the "practitioners as scholars" soapbox for some time. I am interested in the redefinition of what constitutes scholarship in the same ways that I feel it is crucial for us to expand and interrogate the "canon" of any discipline as they are often invested in an economy of intellectual oppression and the politics of respectability.

We need good writers, we need good makers, we need good organizers, we need good curators, we need . . . we need . . . fill in the blank. And we need to lift up all of that good work and shine a light on it wherever it is. It is truly tragic when a few select voices are lifted up while the remaining balance are not supported.

NW: Agreed. Can you discuss a few memorable experiences from your time in the Studio Museum's education department? What are some of the unsexy things—or the behind-the-veil, under-the-carpet lessons—that could be useful to somebody reading this book and considering a professional life in museums? So often, we hear about the shiny case study, yet I know from firsthand experience that there are these unshiny things underneath the surface of the work that are really important to talk about and learn from.

SJD: I think there is a difference between having an opportunity and really *using* the maximum potential of an opportunity. I think the less-than-glamorous things that I've done to substantiate this work are akin to something my mother would ask me to do to help family and friends. She would say, "Go on over there and see Ms. Jean—she's not well. Take her some soup and visit with her for a while. You know she's a private person so don't mention it to anyone." In that example, one understands that there is nothing beneath you, so to whom much is given much is required. Also, there may be no public acknowledgement. How does this Ms. Jean example translate into our cultural worker/ institutional space? Well . . . there is a great deal of work that no one sees or even realizes is happening. And that's the thing—you don't *want* anybody to see that stuff! It's what I call the shadow economy. It's the foundational work. It's working and participating when you don't have the mic. It's not work that is done to get something in return. It's the manifestation of the institution's human capacity binding itself to issues and ideas of concern that it cares about.

Let's see memorable experiences . . . when I found out Ossie Davis was a Studio Museum member, I somehow got his number—which was completely inappropriate—and called his house. As soon as he answered the phone, I hung up, because I was terrified. I gathered myself and called him back. When he picked up, he said, "Did you just hang up on me?" I couldn't lie, so I just played coy and giggled. We went on to have a full conversation where I invited him to read Zora Neale Hurston's "Now You're Cookin' with Gas." Betye Saar actually selected the text as we were having the program to celebrate a series of serigraphs she had created, one of which was for the great piece of literature.

I shared with him the modest honorarium, and he said all he needed was a car service to pick him up from his home and take him back. He simply would not take our money. I was told that I needed to get him out of the museum really quickly after the reading. Well, the night of the reading, he simply would not leave. He first wanted to thank Betye Saar for making a beautiful work of art—she honored him with a framed print. He also wanted to see the exhibition that was on view, which was Whitfield Lovell's *Whispers from the Walls*. But . . . first and foremost, he wanted to spend leisure time talking to the people. This is my constant experience with program participants.

Speaking of Whitfield Lovell . . . during that show, we took classes of small children from Harlem's first public pre-K to Whitfield's studio. They were probably three and four years old. They each brought objects that held personal significance with them to the visit. This was so transformative for them and for all of us. Whitfield had open shelving in his studio kitchen. The kids asked if the canned food was art. I recall him being so excited by their perspectives on what they saw as art. Their little eyes and minds were so wide open and spongelike.

NW: You say you don't want anybody to see that stuff, but "that stuff" is *you*! It's an expression of your grace and expertise, and even the invisible labor that you pour into your work is always super palpable. OK, so you took these formative experiences with you to the Seattle Art Museum in 2006. What was at the top of your agenda when you arrived?

SJD: When I arrived in Seattle, I wanted to explore ways to program across a city. I also wanted to ignite or what I called *curate* a city. The Seattle Art Museum is one museum in three locations. There are many wonderful experiences I had in Seattle. There are two I will mention here. When I moved to the Pacific Northwest, Washington was ranked 40-something out of the 50 states in public education. I was curious about the role the arts could play in lifting up education in the city. People were already doing some really good work, but our program took off like wildfire. It ended up integrating into this citywide initiative—a network of the cultural institutions, cultural leaders, and the Department of Education. It ensured that people were in the work together, and that everyone had skin in the game.

We also launched a program called REMIX, which was essentially a heavily curated cultural experience that catalyzed the art-and-cultural scene of the city. There were performances, art making for grown folks, artists' interventions and highly opinionated gallery talks by influencers, curators, educators, artists, etc. It formed a scene that was rich with critical content, a covert curriculum and an opportunity for creatives, community members, and cultural producers alike.

NW: It strikes me that, wherever you go, you take with you a commitment to collaborative process and to creative problem-solving. I imagine there being a bit of culture shock going from Friday nights with Ossie at the Studio Museum in Harlem to developing citywide educational programming in Seattle, to rolling out museum-wide initiatives at a museum as large as the MET. How did you experience these shifts on a personal level, and how did the field understand your professional transitions at the time?

SJD: There are times when I felt a little piece of my heart break every time someone would say, *You're at the MET now, you just don't understand.* There are certain assumptions people make about other people without knowing the contours of their personal or professional existence. One of the painful things is the assumption that, as the platform gets bigger, as you gain access to certain things, people feel emboldened to say and do things that under other circumstances, they wouldn't. In the public space, you take the hits and in the private space, you heal. That's the hard part.

I've always believed that to whom much is given, much is required. A great institution like the MET has infrastructure and resources in place. We felt it was our duty to hold ourselves accountable and contribute to that ecosystem.

The unsexiness is the messiness, the paying attention to the interstitial stuff, the recognizing when we're not ready for something and figuring out what it takes to get us ready, the getting people to fall in love with good process and good practice, and the making sure that we don't let perfect be the enemy of progress. It's doing all that and reconciling with the fact that there is a level of anonymity that lives in the work that we do.

NW: "In Love with Good Process" is about to be a T-shirt! And I feel you on a few levels; the anonymity is something I'm still learning to reconcile. As someone who's ghostwritten, ghost-curated, and ghost-founded so much in my career, my default has been to just process it as a side effect of working in a hierarchical field, where work exists on a spectrum of visibility.

SJD: Yeah, one of the challenging things about that though, nico—and I'll just say it—is that's not OK! We end up having these historical moments where no one knows who actually did the work. Some of us are not used to experiencing the pleasure of acknowledgment. It's so deep that we don't want to steal any light that we absolutely don't need. Now that's a discussion. For all that is well known about the *Harlem on My Mind* exhibition that took place at the MET, there is an entire historical conversation and body of work that isn't attributed to the right time or individuals.

I gave a lecture at Duke University once, and when Rick Powell was introducing me, he said, "When I was a fellow at the MET . . . ," and I was like, "You were a fellow at the MET?!" I went back home and asked my team who oversaw fellowships about it, and they said, "There are no records of him having been a fellow." They did a little more digging and found that there was this one program . . . and that program was literally a precursor to someone like me entering the field, which was basically to develop public intellectuals, professionals who specialize in scholarship breaking out of the academy and meeting the public where they are without dumbing it down.

Their fellows were intersectional and interdisciplinary and cross-sector in their approach. They included Marta Vega, Rick Powell, Romare Bearden, and Linda Goode Bryant. These folks presented complex ideas, histories, and issues in ways that were magnetic. Outside of the participants, I found one person who knew this fellowship existed. The person at the institution who designed that fellowship was a genius.

NW: Wow, I don't think I even knew that full history. So, you've touched on process—or a lack thereof—a few times. As the new director and CEO of the Lucas Museum of Narrative Art in LA, what does *good process* embody there? In *A Note for Now*—your first public correspondence in the role—you stated, "We have the opportunity to implement inclusive hiring policies, acquisition protocols, and cultural norms at the onset rather than retrofitting entrenched practices." I was struck by that as someone who believes that DEAI is a daily practice that must be seeded within the very foundations of our institutions and not merely veiled atop an ailing structure. Can you discuss your plans for hiring, acquisitions, and culture making at the Lucas?

SJD: I feel I've always approached these things through the lens of equity. And I really mean *equity*, as opposed to equality—like, *We're going to do 10 for this group, 10 for this group, and 10 for this group*. Well, the ramifications of just adding 10 in this moment doesn't really push up against the historical implications of having had centuries of inequitable practices in museums overall. Equality doesn't engender equity if you do it that way.

I was speaking to a group of advisors at a former institution and being very prideful that we were able to have every school group from that city come to the museum at no cost to them. And for years it was fantastic that we had enough money and resources to support that. Then one of the advisors said to me, *Why are you doing that? Why aren't you requiring those who can pay to pay? Couldn't you invest in even more schools that are in need if your practice was equitable?*

It seems somewhat innocuous to say, *Everyone comes here for free.* But then you start striving toward not just equal acts but equitable practice, and you realize those are different, because the latter requires muscle and attention to details. It requires being uncomfortable having the discussion, being self-reflective (and by self, I mean both individuals and institutions) and asking oneself, *Do we actually have the skills and resources at the institution to be able to do that on a regular basis?* I ask myself and I ask others to ask themselves, *If I'm not in the room or if this other person that shares these values isn't in the room, will X still happen?* So then you realize that we need to create systems and structures where X happens in your absence. Which means that you actually can't be the person getting all the credit and the glory. This is where distributed leadership wrapped in skill and accountability is essential.

NW: I rock with that in a major way. There is this great quote about shared leadership by adrienne maree brown where she states, "If you are in a leadership position, make sure you have a circle of people who can tell you the truth, and to whom you can speak the truth. Bring others into shared leadership with you, and/or collaborate with other formations so you don't get too enamored of your singular vision."[1] From your anecdote above, it sounds like those advisors served as that circle of truth for you.

Let's also discuss the challenges to shared leadership—gatekeepers and ego. Who's monitoring the gatekeepers, and what is the policy and procedure for that? I was in discussion recently with the leader of a prominent arts institution in the region, and they were feigning outrage at the salaries of people of color on their staff. Their solution was, *I cannot knowingly encourage youth of color to enter a career in the arts because they will never make a living wage. It is irresponsible of me to set them up for failure like that* and *You have no idea how hard it is to find qualified candidates of color!*

After a *deep* breath, I was like, "Hold up, wait a minute—in your imagination, you've only put people of color in front of house, security, and maintenance jobs? You make a living wage, right? Why aren't you imagining us at all levels of leadership within your organization, including your own?" The gatekeepers are many, even if they are seemingly unaware that the keys are right there, hanging around their neck.

SJD: Oh, there are plenty! So how do you create an environment where we actually don't have gatekeepers, but instead have custodians? Oftentimes, we have folks in roles, or find ourselves in roles, where we know we don't have the full capacities and skills. However, we also know that we need to rise to the occasion. We need to learn how to pressure test whether people actually have the skills to do the work that they're meant to do, not the thing that they *think* they should be doing. It's not just about recruiting—it's also about creating an environment of belonging and an environment where people don't have to bankrupt themselves of who they are, but can instead be their full professional selves and bring a quality, texture, and diversity of thinking to the table.

So how do we actually catalyze that and, at the same time, help people be realistic? How can we be more transparent about that? That kind of tangible, everyday, specific thinking oftentimes isn't clearly articulated.

Equity is not a program or a project—it's a practice, and until people really see it as a skill set and a competency, we won't arrive at holistic professional practice. Equitable practice for me is in the policies, practices, culture, and procedures. As I said in *A Note for Now*, as we continue to pour the foundation of the Lucas Museum, everywhere I can make the hire or influence the hire, I will. There will be a day that institutions will require basic knowledge of DEAIB [*B* for "belonging"] labor to walk through the door. It'll be a part of basic professional preparedness.

NW: Exactly. So what hiring policy might you create on a local level that could extend to become a necessary and more global museum practice?

SJD: I'm currently hiring for the deputy director of strategy and administration, who will articulate how strategy will flow through the entire organization, just like exhibitions flow through the entire organization. Somehow, when we get to strategy, there's always a full plan that lots of folks informed, but for whatever reason, it gets filed away. So this person will ensure that the strategy, behaviors, practices, norms, actions, and objectives are implemented by the whole museum.

This area will also oversee diversity, equity, inclusion, culture, and people. What would it look like for human resources to fall under that, rather than DEAI falling under HR? At the Lucas, all that we do from a human perspective and from a strategic perspective will be through this lens of diversity, equity, inclusion, accessibility, and belonging—that's what I'm considering as I recruit for this role. Strategy and people are tied up together, not separate. For me, that means that anyone who is hiring has an opportunity to ask, *Have you read the following books? Did you ever take an in-person training around bias awareness?*

As I've read the stream of solidarity statements from museums, I've been struck by how many of them ended with, *We're going to put $3,000 toward this, we're going to put $3 million toward that, and we're working really hard, but we are all learning.* The argument that we're all learning and no one knows enough is just not fair to those on the receiving end. Also . . . it's actually not true that no one knows what they are doing. Many folks do know and have a professional practice. Some institutions should admit to themselves that they specifically don't know. The entire field is not bankrupt of this knowledge.

NW: During this economic recession brought on by COVID-19, you might be the only person I know that's actively hiring, full steam ahead! As you know, many museums are scaling back, cancelling exhibitions, and furloughing staff, often predominantly educators of color. How do you experience the paradox of instead ramping up, hiring staff, and planning for future exhibitions during this time?

SJD: A reporter writing about a few new hires I made asked me, "How did you do this?" My response was, "These are not unicorns." I didn't go to some parallel universe to find these people. I've been following them for quite some time or someone in my network shared their work with me. She asked, "Were you looking for people of color to fill these roles? Were you looking for women, because they're all women?"

Initially I said, "No, I wasn't looking for people of color." As it was coming out of my mouth, I was like, "What am I saying?" After we moved on to the next question, I stopped myself and said, "You know what? I have to go back and say they don't happen to be women. These particular people self-identify as women. And the ones who

---

are people of color don't happen to be people of color, they are people of color. I don't happen to be a Black woman in leadership. I self-identify as a Black woman. It's not by happenstance that I am, it is by chance that people see me."

NW: Well, *damn!* OK, so you are intentionally pulling together this fierce team of, so far, predominantly women of color. What's next in your overall strategy?

SJD: We, not just me, are intentionally pulling together a fierce team of extremely smart and talented people. We are making efforts to implement policies and practices and create behavioral norms so that, when we hire people, they actually understand how they are contributing from an intellectual and a personal level to the growth, development, and implementation of all that we do. I'm always trying to think about these two questions: *What inspires you* and *What frustrates you?*

It takes work to ensure that we are aligning skill sets, aspiration, and vision with the people we are putting in roles. We need to not only get diverse candidates in those roles but we need to make sure that we support them in those roles and not cut their legs from under them.

One of the news articles said, "Lucas Museum goes on a hiring spree"! And so when people ask me, "What do you say about that?" I respond, "There's so much amazing and qualified talent on these streets, I'm thrilled to be able to offer them jobs!" I'm thrilled to be able to put colleagues that I have respected and adored in roles where they can grow and expand and be challenged. While I'm sad that our colleagues at other institutions are being laid off, I don't feel any shame about giving people a job.

NW: As I listen to you, I'm reminded of something artist Kevin Beasley said during a recent panel at the Yale University Art Gallery. He was discussing the frenzy around Black artists and the reckless market consumption of Black art in this moment. He said—and I'm paraphrasing—*We're being asked to work so quickly, and we're being consumed with such haste, that the quality of the work is actually suffering. In trying to keep up with the demand, Black artists suffer because the necessary conversations and critiques around skill and craftsmanship are being eclipsed by a market conversation.* This same consumption of Black excellence can be evidenced in the recent rapid-fire appointments of curators of color by countless majority-white museums. It reminds me how slippery the slope is between diversity and tokenization.

SJD: You're right. I mean, we see it with public speaking too. I've been invited to speak a lot, which is such a blessing, because I feel like people think I can make a contribution. Sometimes people say, *Just speak about whatever you want*, and that's not helpful to me and how I work. I am a service leader. So, I respond with, "I'm honored, I appreciate it, but can you give me some prompts?" And what I've found is that because I would say yes to so many things, I needed to have some guardrails so that I could put my best forward.

Recently I've been thinking more about what it means to say no and offer someone else the opportunity. It can be challenging to say no to opportunities, because you don't know when they are going to come to an end. A lot of artists are like, *I got to get this while I can*, and that comes from a very real and particular place. So we are always in a space of trying to reckon with deficiency, deficit, and survival. But then they're some things I'm always going to say yes to. I'm always going to say yes to young people, to elders, to the most vulnerable, etc. You get me.

NW: I do. And everything you just said is the embodiment of the generosity and authenticity that you bring to your leadership. So where is the Lucas now in terms of shifting some of the field's default behaviors, practices, and policies? And how are you building that into the future institutional memory of the organization?

SJD: We are at the beginning of our journey, so our practices are being formed, informed, shaped, and shifted. I imagine the hard part is to be in the space of staying on top of the evolving practice. We are establishing cultural norms as we speak. The policy is the easy part. Policy and practices have to be stitched together, and we must articulate the ways in which we are all accountable for living and breathing them.

NW: In your opinion, how are those best stitched across the entire institution, especially one of the Lucas's scale? As I ask this, I'm recalling your pioneering work doing precisely this within museums across the country—work that often began within education departments yet seeped into the entire culture and fabric of those institutions. How do you stitch policy and practice, while infusing both with the spirit of collaboration and mutual respect that you uniquely bring to the work?

SJD: There has to be a practice of distributed leadership. It's one of those things where you must be shoulder to shoulder in the huddle with your teams. We have to have both uncomfortable and celebratory conversations. Everyone needs to understand how to negotiate and appreciate conflict resolution, not as a way to compromise but as a way to consider what is the best thing for this particular moment. It may not have been the best thing for yesterday or tomorrow, but it works today. Some of my best work has been identifying the *no* people and turning them into *yes* people.

In the end I think we need to further develop a field that understands institution building as well as institutional critique. I think it's essential for people to understand how to get comfortable with discomfort. It's incredibly helpful to start with what we are trying to solve for, because when you work from that place, your best minds can solve any problem.

NW: Saying *no* is an art that I'm still learning today—you literally just put words to it!

SJD: It's not manipulation, it's more like, *How can we be successful and relevant together?* When I launched Teens Take the MET, the guards were initially like, "This is a headache!" But later, when they saw thousands of young people that looked like them in the museum, they were just like, "Sandra, this is amazing. They belong here too!" The guards then got tied up in me being successful.

NW: I experienced a similar learning curve around the production of Uptown Fridays! at the Studio Museum, a program that you founded and I inherited; what an honor it was to carry that particular torch. Which delivers me to a new thought—can we discuss these lineages and living legacies of museum practice? What does it mean to you to be building a new museum today, in this cultural and sociopolitical moment?

SJD: Growing up in San Francisco, I could have taken a long walk to Golden Gate Park and go to a museum, but that wasn't common for my family because museums weren't social spaces for us.

For me, the fact that the Lucas Museum is bringing 11 acres of green space to South LA—and by that, I mean a majority-Brown, Black, and Asian community where the median income as was last reported to me is $30,000—is important. This is a museum for the people, and I'm just like, "Yeah! Let's think from a place of abundance." I can see aunties and grandmas choosing to do their morning walk around the park. I want folks to grab their morning coffee from our cafe. I can see young people coming in and having their first kiss in the rooftop garden.

The part of LA where the Lucas is situated is amazing—there's USC, there's California African American Museum, there's a science center, there's a soccer stadium where they hold concerts, and there's the Museum of Natural History. Also, the Olympics are coming to LA in 2028, and one of the two transportation hubs is nearby. I know that this institution is going to change the physical landscape of this area, as did all of those other places. So the question becomes, What can we do to ensure that young people and elders in this city see this museum as something that has a magnetic pull to them, and that it's relevant to them? Instead of thinking about, *How do we make the museum relevant?* let's ask, *How do we speak to the relevance of people's lives and their stories?* That's the win, you know. So that's one piece of it.

The second piece is that this is an institution that is dedicated to visual storytelling through art, culture, and the mass image. We believe that the art of storytelling connects us to shape a more just society. So think about that. Through visual storytelling, the Lucas Museum expands the role of art and museums for society. The museum inspires thought-provoking ideas and conversations that are relevant within and beyond geographic boundaries. Our work radiates to catalyze more connected and empathetic spaces.

We will meet people wherever they are (physically, intellectually, emotionally). Our inclusive practice will connect who people are and what people find meaningful to works of art and the work of our organization. We believe that art can move you to feel, think, reflect, and act. We also believe that nimble thinking and working together yields exponential results.

We will approach our work and learning with courage, creativity, curiosity, and a sense of adventure. Those are our values.

NW: What I love about how you answered this question—and *A Note for Now*—is that both begin with your lived experience. What was beautiful about your note was that it felt like the leader of an organization talking through the lens of their *own* story. It wasn't overly theoretical or like, *museums today* or *the world today*. . . . You reminded folks that you are a human being with a story and that your institution is about uplifting stories. To me, that felt like a point of entry for folks—a window into what your leadership and the work of the museum will look and feel like every day!

SJD: I think putting this museum in the context of a long-standing history, personal or otherwise, is important. I've been talking about the Lucas Museum in the context of places we see as iconic now. When MoMA was founded in 1929, modern art wasn't believed to be an important thing. It was around, but the reaction was, *What is this?* So then they decided to cut a path forward and built an iconic institution with depth on every level.

Then you have the thirties and Gertrude Vanderbilt Whitney. Whitney goes over to the MET and tries to submit her collection, and they are like, *No.* Then she was like, *OK, I have money, I'm going to go down the street and I'm going to build a beautiful building and cement this.* Then they cement American art, like 20th-century American art, and it's all about nationhood—it's really about the American visual landscape from a fine-art point of view and saying that Europe is not the only thing to exist.

Then you have the Studio Museum come on the scene in the sixties and they're like, *I know you guys had this Jacob Lawrence exhibition at MoMA, but we don't have enough people collecting and showing our work in depth.* So then the Studio Museum gets founded to go deep, to catalyze experimentation with artists, and not have it just be figurative but also abstract. The Studio Museum wasn't that different from the Whitney or MoMA, as they, too, were tied up in the Studio Museum's success. Then you have ICP [International Center of Photography], a medium-specific institution that spawns a movement and a nationalist approach.

Now we have the Lucas Museum saying the same thing. It just happens to be happening while we're alive, and we're saying that comic art, the people's art, the mass image, can sit alongside Kerry James Marshall, and he wants it to be such. We are also saying there is a slew of artists who have not been accepted, nurtured, and catalyzed by the academy, nor has exploratory practice through technology.

But what we're saying in all those other cases is, *While the thing existed, it wasn't broad or deep enough.* That's what this institution is saying now in this moment around narrative art—that it can have Kara Walker, cave paintings, Jericho, and Time-Life photographs coexist.

So when I'm thinking about the purpose of a place like this, it's to be used; it's not just to be seen. It's to participate and to learn, but it's also for those histories to comingle, and for us to explore things we actually know weren't right before. In this moment, what's been interesting is being focused on building not just a building but an institution with a hundred-year proposition, like the many that came before.

NOTE

1. brown, adrienne maree. *Emergent Strategy: Shaping Change, Changing Worlds.* New York: AK Press, 2017.

CONCLUSION
Cultivating Change

Small is good, small is all. (The large is a reflection of the small). Change is constant. (Be like water.) There is always enough time for the right work. There is a conversation in the room that only these people at this moment can have. Find it. Never a failure, always a lesson. Trust the people. (If you trust the people, they become trustworthy.) Move at the speed of trust. Focus on critical connections more than critical mass—build the resilience by building the relationships. Less prep, more presence. What you pay attention to grows.[1]

—adrienne maree brown

In the process of writing and compiling this book, I often considered the complexities of the systemic change its pages call for. Of primary interest were where arts-led social change is initiated and by whom, how it's organized into movements and at what speed, where movements impact systems and how, and who nurtures and sustains these impacts over time.

A key takeaway from the discussions herein is that systemic change is a dynamic, daily practice fueled by the will of individuals and mobilized by collective imagination, participation, and action. And despite the urgency of the issues change seeks to address, the nature of change itself is slow and steady. While this book documents evidence of social change well under way in various corners of the museum field, it, too, points to the colossal efforts that lie ahead in transforming the entire ecosystem into one that is for, by, and of its people. *So what are some strategies to get us there?*

CHAPTER 15

EMERGENT STRATEGY

Social justice facilitator, healer, and doula adrienne maree brown offers an excellent model for understanding the change of any given moment in relation to its broader change ecosystem. In her book *Emergent Strategy: Shaping Change, Changing Worlds*, she discusses how systemic change is shaped by the seemingly small patterns, behaviors, and interactions that constitute the minutiae of the everyday. Her observations empower us to perceive change with enhanced patience and faith, positioning ourselves—both philosophically and energetically—in relationship to the change we want to see in the world. She emboldens us to imagine change, not as a utopian ideal but as a worldly reality already taking shape around us. And in so doing, she empowers us to imagine ourselves as essential changemakers.

Above, she names a few core principles that guide her *own* application of emergent strategy in working toward justice and liberation. I was particularly struck by *build the resilience by building the relationships*, which, when mapped atop the crisis of relevance that museums face, reminds us that institutions are, in fact, merely containers for human relationships. And that to build relevant and resilient institutions, one must also build and nourish the *critical connections* that they are comprised of. By prioritizing people over possessions, and connectivity over *critical mass*, museums may finally learn to liberate themselves from the burden of accumulation we discussed at the onset and mold themselves into the more vital and nimble forms we imagined throughout.

Later in *Emergent Strategy*, brown discusses the importance of *decentralization*, a concept this book takes up as a core strategy to move museum authority from center to margin and reclaim people power in an acutely hierarchical ecosystem. She investigates decentralization—or the *distribution of functions or powers*—in relation to *interdependence*, the notion that mutualism characterizes the human condition and relationships between *all* things. She states, "The idea of interdependence is that we can meet each other's needs in a variety of ways, that we can truly lean on others and they can lean on us. It means we have to decentralize our idea of where solutions and decisions happen, where ideas come from."[2] Central to this idea is a belief in the capacity of distributed leadership to produce shared accountability and sustainable change, something Sandra Jackson-Dumont touches on in her interview.

This sketch of an arts-and-culture ecosystem where shared solutions and collective decisions emanate from the people is a vision I hold steady in my sights, and I work daily to ensure it remains within our grasp. *So if we are to decenter museum authority and replace it with distributed leadership and mutual accountability, what exists in the wake of dismantled hierarchies? How do we understand and lean into our new roles? And what does cultural citizenship look like as a true democracy?*

SOCIAL CHANGE ECOSYSTEMS

> *In our lives and as part of movements and organizations, many of us play different roles in pursuit of equity, liberation, inclusion, and justice. . . . Some of us are community storytellers and artists, binding the past and the present, channeling the histories and experiences of our ancestors to shed light on what is possible today. . . . Some of us are proud disruptors who speak up and take action—especially when it is uncomfortable and risky. . . . And others of us are builders who are actively developing the ideas, the structures, and the scaffolding for our organizations and movements. Not all of us can (or should) play each of these roles.*[3]

—Deepa Iyer

Equally essential to my exercise of grounding and characterizing change was my research into the work of writer, strategist, lawyer, and racial justice advocate Deepa Iyer (italicized words and phrases for the remainder of this section borrow from the definitions in her framework). Her tool, *Mapping Our Roles in Social Change Ecosystems*—developed in 2019 and most recently updated to version 4.0 in 2020—is revelatory, and I hope that you will find your way to it (and through it) at your own speed. In it, she offers a framework to "help individuals, networks, and organizations align and get in right relationship with social change values, individual roles, and the broader ecosystem."[4] Her framework—which includes a map, description of roles, and reflection guide—empowers people to locate themselves within their respective change ecosystems. It also articulates a broad spectrum of essential roles, from the *visionaries* who boldly envision the future worlds we will inhabit to the *builders* who bravely construct the infrastructure to deliver us there.

While initially drawn to Iyer's framework as a tool for self-discovery and accountability in my independent work, I later came to value it as a call to collective action—to audit my perceived location within my change ecosystem, to broaden my community of practice by cultivating relationships with change agents whose skills and methods differ from my own, and to work together to build the change. Despite Iyer's model not entering my consciousness until well after the inception of this book, it certainly deepened aspects of its evolution upon my discovery of it. I like to imagine that—through some process of brown's *interdependence*—this alignment and convergence had actually been happening all along, despite my inability to perceive it at the time.

In the process of editing this volume, I continued to sit with Iyer's framework and found myself—through my own biased and wild perceptions—mapping her social change roles onto the dynamic community of this book. I share my thoughts on this now, though not to project or essentialize the role of any one contributor—their role is certainly *theirs* alone to define. Rather, I offer this as an experiment in dreaming out loud and naming what *I* perceive to be the breadth of change well underway in the social change ecosystem of which I'm emphatically a part.

In part 1, Jordan, Shaun, Miguel, and Lina share their experiences effecting change as *storytellers*, those who mobilize their unique skills of perception and translation to *craft and share our community stories*. Deborah, Mario, and Maitland offer tools to both dismantle and rebuild the museum space as *experimenters*, who use the language of architecture to *innovate, pioneer, and invent* new sociospatial paradigms. Eric, Maren, Kendal, and Diya serve as both *guides* and *weavers*, building a pedagogy for public art and articulating its ability to manifest *through-lines of connectivity* between artists, communities, and institutions. Jamaica, Kemi, and Shani share their work as *visionaries* and architects of culturally specific space, who *imagine and generate our boldest possibilities*. (Read also: "Be bold, y'all!") Chayanne, David, and Lauren discuss public programs as a form of institutional *caregiving*, and their work building and bridging safe space to *sustain a community of care, joy, and connection*. Ryan, Vashti, Lauren, and Jasmine lay bare the synergies between *healers* and *disruptors* and discuss their work both tending to the *traumas caused by oppressive systems* and taking action to *shake up the status quo, to raise awareness, and to build power*. And at the conclusion of part 1, Shawnda, Ruby, and Melissa ultimately return us to the transformative power of *storytelling*, this time with a focus on building the operational and economic infrastructure to ensure that our institutions work as hard as our artists on behalf of our shared *cultures, experiences, and histories*.

In part 2, the case studies shared by Elia, Tina, Connie, Leslie, Shanta, Jordan, Dawn, Kyle, Nisa, Alexandra, Victoria, Juliana, Michelle, Zoë, Gabriella, and Amber embodied the fierce work of nearly *all* the changemaker roles in Iyer's framework. The Harlem Semester shifted expertise (or *wisdom*) from Barnard College faculty to the local cultural institutions producing the culture of study, empowering the creation of new *guides* and knowledge economies. Find Art Here wove altogether new connections between preexisting partners, inviting the Studio Museum to reimagine *caregiving* outside of the care it shows its permanent collection, and the Horan School and Thurgood Marshall Academy Lower School to *experiment* with new ways of integrating art into both their curricula and their school culture. The Artist Grants Initiative at the Walker Art Center *disrupted* the institution's traditional flow of power, redirecting resources to *build power* among the local BIPOC artist community. And Designing Motherhood offered a radical *vision* for an altogether new politics of *care* and nourishment, within, beyond, and through the museum. And lastly, in part 3, we heard from four *frontline responders*, who—from their respective positions in the social change ecosystem—continue to *address community crises by marshaling and organizing resources, networks, and messages.*[5]

If I were to imagine this work from a bird's-eye view, I would see the necessary activation of cultural spaces within and beyond museums. The flow of the work would follow the flow of the people—resources would pool and community would swell around areas of shared attention and articulated need. The museum would weave in and out of the picture like a shape-shifter, adapting to embody the many vital forms and functions imagined across our various discussions and, at times, receding from the picture altogether. And through its ongoing metamorphosis, the museum would ultimately come to coexist alongside the people as a fellow citizen, not an overlord.

As I grappled with how to conclude this volume, which documents evolving work in a constant state of undoing and becoming everyday, it felt too tidy to end with this utopic vision for decentered museum authority and engaged cultural citizenship. We're so deep in the undoing that any vision for the becoming is merely a mirage! So instead, I commit these final pages to honoring the museum workers and recent museum movements from which this book draws inspiration, strategy, energy, and hope. I offer a brief—and knowingly incomplete—chronology here to name additional changemakers who've impacted the consciousness and moral compass of the museum field, in hopes that you will find your way to their work, support it, and invite it to transform you as it has me.

RECENT MUSEUM MOVEMENTS

In 2012, the Incluseum was founded by Dr. Porchia Moore, Aletheia Wittman, and Rose Paquet to advance "new ways of being a museum through dialogue, community building and collaborative practice related to inclusion in museums." Operating as equal parts space, resource, platform, and project, the Incluseum works through all arms of its work to build inclusive community and mobilize that community to enact change.[6]

In 2013, museum workers and fellow citizens gathered on the steps of the Detroit Institute of Arts to protest the city's plans to sell the museum's collection to pay down its multibillion-dollar debt. The Socialist Equality Party mobilized the campaign "Defend the DIA," a chapter in the ongoing deaccessioning debate that regained attention during the recent recession brought on by COVID-19.

In 2014, following the murder of Michael Brown Jr. by Missouri police, Adrianne Russell and Aleia Brown cofounded #MuseumsRespondToFerguson. The hashtag was used to share information and strategies between monthly meetings where they—alongside a group of fellow museum workers and bloggers—called on museums to respond to mounting injustices and, in so doing, their own legacies of trauma, violence, and racism.[7]

In 2015, #MuseumWorkersSpeak was formed, following the American Alliance of Museums' 2015 annual meeting, to address how museum labor practices perpetuate ongoing social injustices. The group has since grown into a "collective of museum activists pushing for social change at the intersection of labor, access, and inclusion." Their ongoing work includes "organiz[ing] from outside the walls of museums to build solidarity and exert pressure on museum leadership to protect workers."[8]

That same year, Stephanie Johnson-Cunningham and Monica Montgomery founded Museum Hue, "a cultural movement and structural intervention within the creative ecosystem" that "provide[s] authentic participation in various forms of expression as well as disrupts the homogeneity of the mainstream art world."[9] From tours to professional development workshops to mixers, Museum Hue builds community and opportunity for creatives of color in a majority-white field and does so in partnership with its over 150 institutional members.

Between 2015 and 2016, MASS Action—founded by Elisabeth Callihan, of the Minneapolis Museum of Art—transformed an internal working group into a field-sourced tool kit and annual convening that addresses "issues of institutional transformation, creating an inclusive culture, widening interpretation, sharing authority, decolonizing collections and the museum."[10]

In 2016, author and professor Susan E. Cahan published her book *Mounting Frustration: The Art Museum in the Age of Black Power*, which canvasses museums' complicity in the living legacies of institutional racism in America and foregrounds the tools Black artists and museum professionals used to combat it.[11]

In 2017, the advocacy initiative-turned-groundswell #MuseumsAreNot Neutral was launched by coproducers La Tanya S. Autry and Mike Murawski. The movement asserts, "Museums can be agents of social change in our communities" and that, to achieve this, we must first "expose the myth of museum neutrality and demand equity-based transformation across institutions."[12] That same year, then-commissioner of New York City's Department of Cultural Affairs, Tom Finklepearl, announced the city's first-ever cultural plan, one that sought to "serve as a roadmap to a more inclusive, equitable, and resilient cultural ecosystem, in which all residents have a stake."[13] Elsewhere in the city, at the Whitney Museum of American Art, artist Hannah Black launched a campaign demanding the 2017 Whitney Biennial curators remove and destroy Dana Schutz's painting *Open Casket*, 2016, that "transmute[d] Black suffering into profit and fun,"[14] by depicting a white painter's abstract interpretation of a slain Emmett Till. Artist Parker Bright also mobilized a group of people to stand in front of Schutz's painting in protest, obscuring it from public view.

In 2018, author Aruna D'Souza published her book *Whitewalling: Art, Race & Protest in 3 Acts*. This seminal text—which, like Cahan's, uses the case-study method to expose a long history of institutional racism perpetuated by museums, including the aforementioned 2017 Whitney Biennial—also celebrates the enduring power of organizing and collective action.

In 2019, POWarts published a salary survey that, in addition to exposing vast inequities in pay across the nonprofit and commercial arts sectors alike, delivered "actionable compensation data to inform and assist career progression and compensation negotiations."[15] At the 2019 American Alliance of Museums Annual conference, writer, curator, and activist Kimberly Drew delivered a keynote address in which she named the salary inequity she'd experienced at the MET and her strategies to build equity in museums more broadly. That same year, Art + Museum Transparency was founded by "a non-hierarchical group of arts and museum workers" who created an editable Google Doc containing their salaries, past and present, and invited others to contribute.[16] They followed this spreadsheet with another in which they crowdsourced "data on internships in arts and museum organizations, pointing to one of the largest sources of inequities in our system: unpaid internships."[17] Elsewhere, the Whitney was once again home to controversy and protest—this time in opposition to vice chair Warren Kanders's connections to weapons manufacturing—and museum workers from New York to California launched public unionization campaigns and went on strike.

In 2020, countless hashtags, petitions, web platforms, social media accounts, and museum movements were formed to challenge museum complacency in addressing institutional racism as magnified by the Black Lives Matter movement and the COVID-19 public health crisis. Death to Museums—"an unconference created by emerging professionals who graduated from a museum studies master's program amidst a global pandemic"—mobilized a community of practice to "question the efficacy of changing museums from within when inequity is built into their core identity." [18] Indebted Cultural Workers, a group of NYU graduate students and cultural workers, also formed, circulating a salary spreadsheet designed as a tool to "help workers to compare their salaries to those of their top managers or calculate what fraction of the institution's endowment they constitute." [19] #DismantleNOMA, a group of former New Orleans Museum of Art employees who resigned due to a "toxic work environment and institutional racism," issued an open letter to the NOMA in which organizers called out a "recently installed plantation exhibition on display at the museum" and the "plantation-like culture behind its façade," among other issues. [20] DIA Staff Action circulated a petition to address "unethical, abusive, and narcissistic workplace behaviors" at the Detroit Institute of Arts, calling for an immediate transition of leadership and workplace culture investigation. [21] A Better Guggenheim was formed to hold the museum accountable for "systemic racism and a toxic work environment" and penned a letter to the board of trustees calling out leadership's inability to "demonstrate a sincere commitment to addressing an internal white dominant culture that has long created hostility for Black staff members and staff members of color." [22]

@changethemuseum Instagram account was founded by a group of artists, curators, and other museum-adjacent people to "pressure US museums to move beyond lip service proclamations by amplifying tales of unchecked racism." [23] The Instagram account shares anonymous first-hand accounts of museum workers encountering the full spectrum of overt and covert racism in their workplaces.

Which delivers us to the present moment: 2021 and its continued solidarity statements issued by museums in support of social justice movements they are only beginning to acknowledge, let alone understand. In a *Museum Magazine* article earlier this year, Melanie Adams, PhD, and Kayleigh Bryant-Greenwell of the Smithsonian's Anacostia Community Museum discussed what museums might learn from Black Lives Matter as a theory of change. In it, they discuss the need for museums to first address internal work before "developing external products because they will be viewed as inauthentic and performative," a sentiment echoed throughout this book. They move on to state, "BLM is more than a moment; it is a movement. Museums need to recognize that the fight for equality that is taking place on our streets continues a historical movement centuries in the making. Instead of looking for quick solutions to solve deeply systemic problems, museums should take the time to live within and work through their discomfort and not search for shortcuts around it."[24] Because the only way around it is through it.

Of *course* this chronology is incomplete—the intellectual, emotional, and physical labor it chronicles exist on a broad spectrum of visibility, and I have my own blind spots and biases in documenting it. But its evidence is irrefutable—there is a crisis within our nation's public institutions, and the public is calling them out. From the proliferation of racist and inequitable workplace cultures to practices of cultural tokenization and exclusion to the denial of the living legacies of colonialism and white supremacy in museums, the crisis is as wide as it is deep. However, much like evidence of the crisis exists, so, too, does evidence of another way; because the communities most affected by this violence have already built it, just simply beyond the boundaries of what the museum field is currently able to perceive.

As museums continue to mobilize their resources in rapid response to what this book has termed *slow work*, I—like Adams and Bryant-Greenwell—would encourage them to resist this impulse and first attend to the important work of self-reflection while considering the following questions: What harm has your institution inflicted over the years and against whom? How do you plan to redress it? What changes must transpire within your walls before you can support ongoing and necessary change beyond them? How will you support social justice movements without capturing, colonizing, commodifying, or deradicalizing them? How will you invest not only in the valuable change these movements produce but also in their organizers upon whose shoulders this work is carried? And how will you leverage every resource at your disposal to not only sustain the change in the present but also nourish it well into the future?

LONGING TOGETHER

> *There are times when personal experience keeps us from reaching the mountain top and so we let it go because the weight of it is too heavy. And sometimes the mountain top is difficult to reach with all our resources, factual and confessional, so we are just there, collectively grasping, feeling the limitations of knowledge, longing together, yearning for a way to reach that highest point. Even this yearning is a way to know.*
>
> —bell hooks[25]

In the face of more questions than answers, and more longing than knowing, I would encourage us to savor the full richness of this slow work in which we are each uniquely engaged. Yes, it is tedious, exhausting, unsexy, isolating, uncomfortable, and at times downright dangerous. It pushes our spiritual limits, tries our emotional capacity, and tests our physical and psychological endurance. It often leaves us yearning together in the dark with no clear mountaintop in sight. Yet and still, it is necessary work. It is collaborative work. And—thanks to the unwavering efforts of generations of changemakers, only a handful of whom are documented or discussed in this volume—it is *doable* work, many of the tools for which are already at our collective disposal.

As you work to locate yourself within your social change ecosystem, I would encourage you to build respect for those who work at a different pace or through a different mode than you—as brown suggests, you will likely need them just as much as they will need you. And if you, as I have, find yourself lost in your desire to see and effect change with each waking breath, then sit back, close your eyes, and engage a long view of time. Because transformation doesn't happen overnight, nor will it happen without you.

NOTES

1. brown, adrienne maree. *Emergent Strategy: Shaping Change, Changing Worlds.* New York: AK Press, 2017, 41–42.
2. Ibid., 87.
3. Iyer, Deepa. "My Role in a Social Change Ecosystem: A Mid-Year Check-In." Medium, May 13, 2019, https://dviyer.medium.com/my-role-in-a-social-change-eco system-a-mid-year-check-in-1d852589cdb1.
4. Iyer, Deepa. "The Map: Social Change Ecosystem." Deepa Iyer, 2020, http://deepaiyer.com/the%20map-social-change-ecosystem.
5. Exercise inspired by roles from Iyer, "The Map."
6. "About." The Incluseum, March 5, 2021, https://incluseum.com/about.
7. Fletcher, Kami. "#MuseumsRespondtoFerguson: An Interview with Aleia Brown and Adrianne Russell." AAIHS, September 27, 2016, https://www.aaihs.org/museumsrespondtoferguson-an-interview-with-aleia-brown-and-adrianne-russell.
8. "About Museum Workers Speak." Museum Workers Speak, https://sites.google.com/view/museumworkersspeak/about-museum-workers-speak?authuser=0.
9. "About Us." Museum Hue, https://www.museumhue.com/about-hue.
10. "MASS Action Toolkit." MASS Action, https://www.museumaction.org/resources.

11. Cahan, Susan E. "Introduction." In *Mounting Frustration: The Art Museum in the Age of Black Power*. Durham, NC: Duke University Press, 2018.

12. "Join the Movement." Museums Are Not Neutral, https://www.museumsarenot neutral.com.

13. "Executive Summary." CreateNYC, https://createnyc.cityofnewyork.us/the -cultural-plan/executive%20summary.

14. "Open Letter to the New Orleans Museum of Art." #DismantleNOMA, June 24, 2020, https://sites.google.com/view/dismantlenoma/collective-statement.

15. "POWarts Salary Survey 2019." POWarts, https://www.powarts.org/surveys.

16. "Tweets." Art + Museum Transparency, https://www.artandmuseumtranspar ency.org.

17. "Art + Museum Transparency End Unpaid Internships Spreadsheet." Google, https://docs.google.com/spreadsheets/d/1VY3GzxL59xJ6Iv67m2Qlg0xZdqFBiKJapC U6INqrMY/edit#gid=654169754 (site discontinued).

18. Death to Museums, deathtomuseums.com.

19. Bishara, Hakim. "Spreadsheet Highlights Major Income Disparities at Cultural Institutions." Hyperallergic, April 29, 2020, https://hyperallergic.com/560132/spread sheet-highlights-major-income-disparities-at-cultural-institutions.

20. "Open Letter to the New Orleans Museum of Art."

21. "Petition to the DIA's Leadership and the Board of Directors for Immediate Action." Change.org, https://www.change.org/p/detroit-institute-of-arts-petition-to-the -detroit-institute-of-arts-leadership-and-the-board-of-directors-for-immediate-action.

22. "Letter to the Board." A Better Guggenheim, January 17, 2021, https://abetter guggenheim.com/letter-to-board.

23. Cited from @changethemuseum Instagram account tagline on May 1, 2021.

24. Adams, Melanie, and Kayleigh Bryant-Greenwell. "Point of View: Movements, Moments, and Museums." American Alliance of Museums, March 1, 2021, https://www .aam-us.org/2021/01/01/point-of-view-movements-moments-and-museums.

25. hooks, bell. *Teaching to Transgress: Education as the Practice of Freedom*. New York: Routledge, 1994.

INDEX

ABOUT THE AUTHOR

nico wheadon is an independent arts consultant, curator, educator, and writer. Through her consultancy, she delivers cultural strategy and curatorial guidance to artist-entrepreneurs, cultural institutions, government agencies, and philanthropic foundations. She's supported museums in developing strategic plans and mounting landmark exhibitions and programs; foundations and funders on deepening their support of individual artists and culturally specific nonprofits; and artist-entrepreneurs on strategic planning, business development, and start-up operations.

Her approach is informed by her unique perspective as a practitioner working across both the nonprofit and commercial sectors. She, alongside her partner Malik D. Lewis, is founder and principal of bldg fund, LLC, an innovation platform for BIPOC artists, entrepreneurs, and neighbors. An advocate for BIPOC and womxn artists in all endeavors, she uses her myriad platforms to expand the canon of contemporary art while cultivating an engaged community of professional practice.

nico is an adjunct professor at Barnard College, Brown University, and Hartford Art School, where she teaches at the intersections of art history, cultural entrepreneurship, and museum studies. Her scholarship centers artist- and community-led innovation, and manifests art history's contemporary relevance in our evolving cultural ecosystem. Beyond the classroom, nico has lectured internationally on topics including the future of museums, art and entrepreneurship, navigating risk in the nonprofit industrial complex, and aligning individual values with institutional practice.

A thought leader in the field, nico currently serves as a board governor at the National Academy of Design, a board director at the Arts Council of Greater New Haven, an advisory board member for Lubin School of Business's Transformative Leadership Program, a guide at the Institute of Possibility, and a cohort member of Arizona State University's Readying the Museum initiative. In recent posts, nico served as inaugural executive director of NXTHVN (2019–2020); inaugural director of Public Programs & Community Engagement at the Studio Museum in Harlem (2014–2019); curatorial director of Rush Arts Gallery (2007–2010); and curatorial assistant at the Studio Museum in Harlem (2006–2007). nico holds an MA in creative and cultural entrepreneurship from Goldsmiths, University of London (2011), and a BA in art-semiotics from Brown University (2006).